HIGH PERFORMANCE DISABILITY SPORT COACHING

As the profile of disability sport has risen, so has the emphasis grown beyond participation to include the development of a high performance environment. This book is the first to take an in-depth look at the role of coaches and coaching in facilitating the professionalisation of disability sport, in raising performance standards, and as an important vector for the implementation of significant political, socio-cultural and technological change.

Using in-depth case studies of elite disability sport coaches from around the world, the book offers a framework for critical reflection on coaching practice as well as the reader's own experiences of disability sport. The book also evaluates the vital role of the coach in raising the bar of performance in a variety of elite level disability sports, including athletics, basketball, boccia, equestrian sport, rowing, soccer, skiing, swimming and volleyball.

Providing a valuable evidence-based learning resource to support coaches and students in developing their own practice, *High Performance Disability Sport Coaching* is essential reading for all those interested in disability sport, coaching practice, elite sport development and the Paralympic Games.

Geoffery Z. Kohe is a Senior Lecturer in Sociology and Sport Studies at the University of Worcester, UK. His research, which sits within the Sport, Exercise and the Body Research Interest Group, is in the areas of sport organisational politics, young people's experiences of Physical Education and the Olympic movement, and the socio-historical aspects of sport and physical cultures. He has recently published work in the *International Journal of the History of Sport*, *International Review for the Sociology of Sport, Sport, Education and Society*, and the *Journal of Sport & Social Issues* examining Olympic legacies, sport and Physical Education policy.

Derek M. Peters is Professor of Sport, Health and Exercise Science at the University of Worcester, UK; Professor II in the Faculty of Health and Sport Sciences at the University of Agder, Norway; a Fellow of the European College of Sport Science; and a Level 5 Academic Expert Sport Performance Analyst. His interdisciplinary research expertise traverses a number of fields within and across sport, exercise, health and wellbeing. His recent projects have included work on elite sport training and performance, physical activity and health measurement, psychological and social behaviours, occupational health, and sport performance analysis.

HIGH PERFORMANCE DISABILITY SPORT COACHING

Edited by Geoffery Z. Kohe and Derek M. Peters

Routledge
Taylor & Francis Group

LONDON AND NEW YORK

First published 2017
by Routledge
2 Park Square, Milton Park, Abingdon, Oxon OX14 4RN

and by Routledge
711 Third Avenue, New York, NY 10017

Routledge is an imprint of the Taylor & Francis Group, an informa business

© 2017 Geoffery Z. Kohe and Derek M. Peters

British Library Cataloguing-in-Publication Data
A catalogue record for this book is available from the British Library

Library of Congress Cataloging in Publication Data
Names: Kohe, Geoffery Z., 1983- editor. | Peters, Derek M., editor.
Title: High performance disability sport coaching / edited by Geoffery Z. Kohe and Derek M. Peters.
Description: Abingdon, Oxon ; New York, NY : Routledge, 2016. | Includes bibliographical references and index.
Identifiers: LCCN 2016013507 | ISBN 9781138860360 (hardback) | ISBN 9781138860377 (pbk.) | ISBN 9781315716497 (ebook)
Subjects: LCSH: Sports for people with disabilities--Coaching. | Athletes with disabilities--Health and hygiene.
Classification: LCC GV709.4 .H54 2016 | DDC 796.04/56--dc23
LC record available at https://lccn.loc.gov/2016013507

ISBN: 978-1-138-86036-0 (hbk)
ISBN: 978-1-138-86037-7 (pbk)
ISBN: 978-1-315-71649-7 (ebk)

Typeset in Bembo
by Saxon Graphics Ltd, Derby

CONTENTS

Notes on contributors   *vii*

Introduction to high performance disability sport coaching   1
Derek M. Peters and Geoffery Z. Kohe

1 Going the distance: a tale of energy, commitment and
   collaboration: Drew Ferguson, Head Coach of Canada's
   Para Soccer Team   7
   Laura G. Purdy, Jennifer Purdy and Paul Potrac

2 Creating a high performance Para-rowing programme
   in the USA: from the geography of the land to the
   generosity of the spirit (and everything in between)   24
   Natalie J. Campbell

3 Coaching across the species barrier: para-equestrian dressage   45
   Georgina Holmes

4 'Just doing it': a strength-based approach to coaching athletes 60
   Tania Cassidy, Lisette Burrows, Raylene Bates and Joan Merrilees

5 On the way to Rio 2016: coaching Paralympic volleyball
   in Brazil   77
   Carla Filomena Silva

6 Coaching wheelchair basketball players: from the beginning to the top 98
Hana Válková, Jakub Válek and Štěpán Válek

7 Coaching in the flagship Paralympic sport: a tale from trackside 113
P. David Howe

8 Ozzie Sawicki – coaching Alpine skiing: the curiosity to be the best 127
David F. H. Legg and Bradley M. J. McClure

9 Glynn Tromans: in search of 'fearless' boccia and the 'big hairy audacious goal' 145
Ian Brittain

10 From Melksham to Rio: a coach's 20-year journey in para-swimming 163
Anthony J. Bush

11 Beyond high performance disability sport coaching? 186
Geoffery Z. Kohe and Derek M. Peters

Index 208

CONTRIBUTORS

Raylene Bates is Athletics New Zealand High Performance Para Athlete Manager/ Head Coach and a coach facilitator for the International Paralympic Committee. She has been a team Leader/Head Coach at two Olympic Games, two Paralympic Games, two Commonwealth Games, numerous IAAF World Champs and IPC World Champs, World University Games, World Junior Athletics Champs, Oceania Champs. She has a Bachelor of Applied Management.

Ian Brittain is a Research Fellow in the Centre for Business in Society at Coventry University in the UK. He is also the Heritage Advisor to the International Wheelchair and Amputee Sports Federation (IWAS) and has attended the last four summer Paralympic Games in Sydney, Athens, Beijing and London. His main areas of research interest are sociological, historical and sports management aspects of disability and Paralympic sport. He is author of *The Paralympic Games explained* (2nd Edition) to be published in 2016 by Routledge, and lead editor on *The Palgrave handbook of Paralympic studies* to be published by Palgrave MacMillan in 2017. His work currently focuses on the area of legacy and the Paralympic Games. In connection with this he is currently working with the Invictus Games Foundation to investigate the impact of sport, and in particular participation in the Invictus Games, upon the lives of the participants, who are all current or former military personnel on the Wounded, Injured or Sick (WIS) register, and their friends and families.

Lisette Burrows is a Professor of Physical Education Pedagogy at the University of Otago. She has a doctorate in Education and has published widely in the fields of physical education pedagogy, health sociology and critical health education perspectives. Her interest in how subjectivities are shaped and made informs her contribution to the chapter.

Anthony J. Bush is a Lecturer in Sports Studies, Education, and Coaching at the University of Bath in the Department for Health. Dr Bush is a former professional badminton player and has over 20 years of coaching experience. Dr Bush is an interdisciplinary scholar specialising on issues concerning the physically active body in a myriad of spaces and sites including, but not limited to, the elite sporting context. His work pushes at the ontological, epistemological and methodological boundaries of that which counts as the critical, social-science-oriented study of sport, physical activity and coaching.

Natalie J. Campbell is a Senior Lecturer at St Mary's University London, and a consultant for the English Institute of Sport. Developing an interest in sport for students with disabilities, Natalie completed her PhD with the University of East London whilst continuing to compete as a senior level rower and coaching basketball for adults with learning disabilities. In 2011 Natalie was invited by US Rowing to support the initiation of their Adapted Rowing and Paralympic Pathway Talent ID programme. The programme supported the development of para-rowing athletes up to the London 2012 Paralympic Games and continues to be used today as part of their screening, training and development process. Over the past decade, Natalie has worked with Team GB and Team USA athletes in both athlete support and team management roles and continues to provide bespoke support to para-athletes and able-bodied athletes. She is currently completing a part-time post-graduate degree in Coaching and Mentoring from the Institute of Leadership and Management.

Tania Cassidy is an Associate Professor in Sport Pedagogy at the University of Otago. She is the lead author of *Understanding sports coaching. The pedagogical, social and cultural foundations of coaching practice* (3rd ed) (Cassidy, Jones & Potrac, 2016). Tania also adopts playing, administrating and governing roles across various sporting codes within local and national sporting communities. A consequence of Tania working across, and within, various communities enabled her to bring together the team of authors to write their chapter.

Carla Filomena Silva undertook her PhD at Loughborough University in the sociology of sport, developing an ethnographic study of the sitting volleyball sub-culture, during the years that preceded the Paralympic Games. After sporting and professional experience as a volleyball player, a coach and a PE teacher, Carla is presently lecturing in the sociology of sport at Nottingham Trent University. It is Carla's research aim to give a voice to the marginalised populations in a variety of sporting contexts.

Georgina Holmes BSc (Hons) MA Academic MCIPD is Senior Lecturer and Programme Leader, Sport Management at University Centre Shrewsbury, part of the University of Chester. With a background in Economics and Human Resource Management, Georgina brings a strategic eye to the management of sport. Her research interests cover people in sport, volunteer management and governance issues in sport. She has a particular interest in all things equestrian, being a long-term volunteer with Riding for the Disabled as well as being actively involved in Dressage in the UK.

P. David Howe trained as a medical anthropologist and is a senior lecturer in the social anthropology of sport in the School of Sport, Exercise and Health Sciences at Loughborough University. David is a leading figure in socio-cultural analysis of Paralympic sport and holds a visiting professorship at Katholieke Universiteit Leuven, Belgium and an adjunct Professorship at Queen's University, Canada. David is the current Vice President of the International Federation of Adapted Physical Activity.

David F. H. Legg is Professor at Mount Royal University in Calgary, Canada. He has published extensively within the realm of Paralympic sport and sport policy. He is co-editor of the book *Paralympic legacies* and was the Canadian researcher for both Sport Policies Leading to International Sporting Success (SPLISS) research studies. David is Past President of the Canadian Paralympic Committee, current member of the International Paralympic Committee Sport Science Committee and past Board Member for the 2015 Toronto Parapan American Games.

Bradley M. J. McClure, who is currently a Ph.D. Candidate in Sociocultural Studies at Western University, holds an M.A. in Kinesiology with a Coaching Specialization (Indoor Volleyball) from Western University and a B.Sc. in Honours Kinesiology from the University of Waterloo. At Western, he is currently focusing his studies primarily on sports philosophy and has research interests in coaching pedagogy, athlete development. the coach–athlete relationship and ethical conduct. He is currently a beach development coach for the Ontario Volleyball Association, working with athletes at both the grassroots and high performance levels. Additionally, he has held coaching positions in indoor volleyball at the club (travel) and post-secondary levels.

Joan Merrilees has been coaching for over 25 years, working primarily with performance oriented young athletes, specialising in jumps (horizontal & vertical) and speed development. She is currently the National Technical Official, which sees her regularly officiating at national and international meets. The interview data used in Chapter 4 came from Joan's Master's thesis.

Paul Potrac is a Professor in the Department of Sport and Physical Activity at Edge Hill University, UK. His research interests lie in the interplay between emotion, micro-politics, and practice in coaching and coach education.

Jennifer Purdy is an independent researcher.

Laura G. Purdy's research focuses on high performance sporting cultures and the everyday realities of coaches and athletes who operate in these contexts. She works in the Department of Sport and Physical Activity at Edge Hill University, UK.

Jakub Válek is an external lecturer of sports management in the area of adapted physical activity (APA), Faculty of Sport Sciences, Masaryk University in Brno, Czech Republic. His scientific and exploration activities are oriented on the field of Kinanthropology with orientation to history of physical culture, particularly on history of Czech and Slovak sport emigration 1948–1989, history of APA, and wheelchair basketball. Jakub is also a long-term referee of walking and wheelchair basketball.

Štěpán Válek is a doctoral student of Kinanthropology, Faculty of Sport Sciences, Masaryk University in Brno, Czech Republic. He graduated from the Faculty of Education as a teacher of PE and English. His research covers topics of active engagement and discontinuation in children's and youth sport. He is also a long-term coach of basketball on various levels and an international lecturer at basketball clinics.

Hana Válková is Professor of Sport Psychology and Adapted Physical Activity (APA), Faculty of Sport Sciences, Masaryk University in Brno, Czech Republic, and recent President of the Czech Special Olympics. She is the founder of APA in the Czech Republic with a significant influence in Central and Eastern Europe. She is a long-term consortium member of Erasmus-Mundus APA and her strong research interest is in psychosocial aspects of physical activities and sports of wheelchair users and Special Olympians.

INTRODUCTION TO HIGH PERFORMANCE DISABILITY SPORT COACHING

Derek M. Peters and Geoffery Z. Kohe

The genesis of this book lay in our desire to explore the relatively unknown world of 'coaching' at high performance levels in disability sport. When researching the potential marketplace for this book, it was clear that there were texts available that address in great depth the history of disability sport, its politico-social influences and ethics (Jesperson & McNamee, 2012; Thomas & Smith, 2008), disability sport *per se* (DePauw & Gavron, 2005) or specifically in relation to the Paralympic Games (Brittain, 2009), but there was no book devoted solely to examining coaching in disability sport.

Our idea was to fill this void in understanding by providing a readable academic book underpinned by high-quality research evidence gleaned by world leading academics speaking with world leading disability sport coaches. Essentially, our intention was to better understand the breadth and depth of coaches' experiences across a broad spectrum of disability sports at the highest international levels with the greatest degree of global representation possible. To achieve this, we adopted a case-study approach whereby leading academics were identified who were able to work with internationally recognised coaches that could provide material for chapters that would bring to light the diversity of issues shaping high performance disability sport coaching. From the outset, we sought expressions of interest from leading academics in sports coaching, sports pedagogy, sport development and management, and the psychology and sociology of sport who were able to offer a suitable high performance disability sports coach as their case study. Our objective then was to use these case studies to build upon the existing literature and debates within disability sport coaching, and draw out prevalent, distinct and/or unique themes for further consideration across and within the chapters via critical discourse analysis. A consequence of such an analysis, we hoped, would be to engage a variety of readers (e.g. academics, students, coaches, athletes, sport governing bodies) with the coaches' stories and consider their relevance within the context of their lives and professional practice; effectively to *learn from the best* and be able to make recommendations to further enhance the coaching of disabled athletes at all levels. The niche for the book was there; the willingness of leading academics with access to high performance disability sport coaches was there, we just needed an appropriate title.

High Performance (dis)Ability Sport Coaching was our first attempt and we sought comment on this from Sir Philip Craven, President of the International Paralympic Committee (and recipient of an Honorary Doctorate from the University of Worcester). His response was enlightening and ultimately inspirational! He was very supportive of the book proposed but raised issue with the word 'Disability' in the title and throughout the book rationale, and suggested 'Para' sports instead. However, our first conundrum was that our case studies were not all intended to be solely Paralympic sports; so, that presented an issue. The word 'adapted' was also a concern as there is limited use of that term in the disability context in the UK. Nor, for that matter, is it immediately associated with 'high performance'. The two undergraduate degree programmes currently in the UK that had this specific focus were both 'disability sport' programmes. Furthermore, the University of Worcester Strategic Plan and the Institute of Sport & Exercise Science literature regarding developments in this area all used the term 'disability' sport. Moreover, since the conception of the book, the conception and use of the term disability has been subsumed at the university within the domain of, and discussions around, 'Inclusive sport/Inclusion'. Also, the key national, and to some degree international bodies that oversee these areas of sport provision mostly use the term 'disability sport', and in many cases were named 'disability sport' organisations. We reflected and replied.

Sir Philip again responded to our email including the sentence 'the key is to drop the "d" word, not to replace it and that takes time'. To do this per se of course will take time, but to do this in the title of our book was immediate. The title was changed to *High Performance Sport Coaching* – it would just transpire to be about coaches working in high performance sports with athletes with disabilities … why was it necessary to put the word 'disability' or even '(dis)ability' in the title at all … they were all high performance sports coaches … Eureka!

Routledge, however, were less convinced by this revolutionary title change or the possibility for the book to be a cornerstone, landmark publication that would go down in history as the first, and set the bar for all future publications in the field just from reading the title and realising that the word 'disability' was not deemed necessary! It was appreciated as an interesting conversation and the point of what we were trying to do by removing the "d" word was very much understood, but there was a very pragmatic decision to make: if we (us and the publishers) wanted people to read the book we needed to help the target audience (i.e. people with an established interest in disability sport) find the book in the first place, and they would be looking (rightly or wrongly) for books with the word 'disability' in the title. There was no point including ground-breaking, unconventional material in a book that nobody would ever find or read! As a compromise, in the peer-reviews solicited for the book proposal, Routledge kindly added the following title specific questions:

What do you think is the most appropriate term to use in the title of this book: 'disability sport', '(dis)ability sport', or another? Do you think it would be appropriate simply to call the book '*High Performance Sport Coaching*', even if all the content was focused on disability sport?

The responses (abridged) were as follows, and we are very grateful to the reviewers for these and their other exceptionally helpful comments regarding the original book proposed:

> The title of the book is both appealing and warranted.
>
> If the authors choose to remain with the current title, I would encourage the authors to remove the parentheses around '(dis)Ability' as it seems to interrupt the smooth flow of reading the title, and typical language is 'disability sport'. In my opinion, the authors would not wish to use 'High Performance Sport Coaching' because it leaves out the targeted focus ... We would want the title to attract the targeted audience.
>
> I think as the USP of this text is on coaching elite [high performance] athletes with a disability, then this needs to be in the title. However, many of the case studies will reveal that coaches treat the athletes as high performance athletes (regardless of the disability) ... so I think that the title in the proposal is the most appropriate (High Performance (dis)Ability Sport Coaching).
>
> I think it's appropriate to define it as either disability or adapted sport. I like adapted better because it focuses more on the sport and less on disability. I think, too, that defining it for the audience is really helpful. If we don't know it's about adapted sport how can we use it in our courses?
>
> Although there remains a stigma attached to the term Disability Sport in some regions, it remains reflective of the discipline. In other words, High Performance Sport Coaching does not reflect the proposed content.
>
> The use of the '(dis)ability' device seems to both challenge the need for linguistic difference and at the same time draw attention to it. Personally, almost four decades of full-time involvement in this area has revealed an ever-changing obsession with terminology around disability and impairment. '(Dis)ability' is sadly reminiscent of cosmetic terms such as 'differently abled', 'physically challenged' or the ludicrous 'handi-capable'. Disability jargon of this nature emerges cyclically and disappears without trace as usage evaporates ... To answer the question posed in the guidance notes, my suggestion would be 'Coaching High Performance Disabled Athletes'

These responses reflected great diversity of opinion, but there appeared to be acceptance that the word 'disability' or 'disabled' needed inclusion and supported Routledge's pragmatic approach that to get the book to the right audience, who would benefit most from exposure to just this sort of discussion of terminology and identity, we had to use a term that was most globally known. Neither reviewers, nor publisher were therefore supportive of removing the term 'disability' from the title ... but maybe including this discussion in our introduction might change a few minds in future publications in this area?

Martin & Whalen's (2014) article, 'Effective practices of coaching disability sport', provided a review of the available research relating to coaching disabled athletes in order to make recommendations for effective practices in coaching disability sport. Many of the findings from this review informed the thematic content analysis and discussion in our book, for example: the absence and/or lack of quality in coach education programmes in disability sport; the lack of disability-sport-specific coaching materials; tensions between coaching the sport and coaching the athlete; coaches learning disability-sport-specific skills on the job; limited provision of additional sport science knowledge and support; the importance of the coach–athlete relationship; the heightened impact of the environment and travel; and the ethical issues associated with classification, most of which have emerged from research with coaches and/or athletes at sub-elite levels.

Through the qualitative case-study approach and the involvement of leading academics and world-class coaches, each researching the issues independently, however, our book provides a far greater level and depth of knowledge and understanding regarding coaching disability sport, especially at the elite level, than has been previously available. Indeed, we have responded to Martin & Whalen's (2014) identification of the importance of future qualitative research 'which has the potential for revealing unique considerations in disability sport' (p.20) and in so doing, have produced a significant advancement of knowledge in the field.

So what is our book about? The underpinning rationale for the book was to provide a key text that explores the intersections between the developing yet dynamic area of high performance disability sport and elite coaching contexts. The demand for such an investigation has been precipitated to a large extent by significant socio-cultural, economic, political and technological changes in and beyond sport that have contoured the relationships, lives and experiences of athletes with disabilities and their coaches/training teams. Constant political restructuring and economic uncertainties, for instance, continue to plague the progression of disabled athletes to the podium. Concomitantly, although the exposure and popularisation of athletes with disabilities may have improved, prevailing public perceptions surrounding notions of disability and performance have been slow to change. Notwithstanding such challenges, landscapes of the disability sport profession have been altered; not least of all as a result of radical advancements in the avenues of high performance sport (e.g., physiological, mechanical, biological, and performative) that are now more readily and widely effecting elite-level disabled athletes and their coaches.

Our book therefore seeks to:

- contribute to the enhancement of the international profile of disability sport;
- respond to the rapid change in disability sport from participatory to high performance – a change that has seen shifts in both principles and practices, congruent with those seen in other sports as a result of 'professionalisation';

- improve and enhance the recognition of coaches working in the upper echelons of disability sport;
- evaluate the place of the coach in raising the bar of performance for elite level disability sport;
- fill a niche for a specific, tailored text that will provide readers with a critical framework for developing their knowledge and application in disability sport settings;
- provide a resource for coaches to read to question their own practice; and,
- provide an evidence- and research-based learning and teaching resource to support emerging academic curricula in disability sport world-wide.

As such, our book responds to the student and teacher need for a specific core text for coach learning and disability sport that will have enormous application to other generic sports coaching modules. It is the first publication to exclusively focus on the learning experiences that can be drawn from high performance coaches in a range of disability sports from around the world. As such, it is also a must-read handbook for practitioners coaching at all levels in disability sport.

We hope our book will broaden your perception and understanding of athletic/ sporting ability, and challenge you to reconsider the ways in which you approach the study of, and employment within and across, high performance disability sport contexts.

The book will appeal to diverse groups interested in disability sport including students, researchers, coaches, physical educators, adapted physical activity specialists, coach educators, and athletes with disabilities as it advances the limited existing knowledge on disability sport coaching at the elite level and highlights prevailing themes and issues pertaining to a unique and developing sport setting and career pathway.

High Performance Disability Sport Coaching is a must read for everyone studying, researching or coaching disability sports.

How the book is organised

Following this Introduction our book contains ten case-study chapters written by leading academics focussing on world-leading coaches working at high performance levels in a range of disability sports with global representation. The case-study authors were provided with the following guidance regarding the skeleton structure of their data collection and subsequent chapter:

- Historical context of the sport.
- Curriculum Vitae of the case-study coach.
- The contributing author's case study of the coach to provide a critical examination of their chosen coach–athlete and sport context. Drawing on the previous historical contextual details and the coach's experiences, the authors were encouraged to explore, variously, the genesis of the coach's interest and engagement, significant developmental milestones in the sport that influenced

their coaching, their entrance into elite environments, their coaching philosophy, coaching pedagogy and, the prevailing concerns within their specific industry. Authors were asked to provide a cogent examination that situated their case study within current debates and contemporary literature from coaching, elite sport, and disability sport domains. The authors were also encouraged to variously consider how these prevailing issues may/may not contour the future of the sport, the roles and responsibilities of their examined coaches, and, the generalities and idiosyncrasies of the coach–athlete/team/sport relationship.

- Recommendations for coaching, education and practice, drawing on the issues raised in the case study. These sections emphasise the possible implications and influences on coaching practices. The authors were also asked to consider strategies or suggestions that might affect broader social changes in the ways in which coaches and athletes go about their collaborative work.

- Editors' summary reflections: for each case-study chapter we have provided our short reflections on the content of the case study, and, any significant issues covered therein. We have also, when and where appropriate, provided tentative commentary on any broader questions raised by the respective authors within the chapters.

- Additional resources and supplementary material for further information for the interested reader.

Other than this skeleton guidance, the authors were at liberty to explore the issue or range of issues that they and their case-study coach felt most worthy of representation. Each author sought the ethical approval appropriate to them in their institution and each identified coach gave written permission to be identified in the book. Apart from this basic editorial guidance and ethical requirement, the case-study authors worked independently with their coach and in isolation from the other chapter authors.

To attempt to learn from the ten chapters as a whole, we then used their rich source of information as the data for our thematic content analysis to underpin Chapter 11, 'Beyond high performance disability sport coaching?', in which we have sought to provide critical discussion of the key overarching themes that have emerged and evidence- and research-based recommendations for the further enhancement of the standing and appeal of coaching in disability sports at all levels.

We hope that you enjoy our book and that reading it inspires you to consider how **you** can contribute to the further development of disability sport at all levels.

References

Brittain, I. (2009). *The Paralympic Games explained*. London: Routledge.

DePauw, K.P. & Gavron, S.J. (2005). *Disability sport* (2nd Ed.). Champaign, IL: Human Kinetics.

Jesperson, E. & McNamee, M.J. (2012). *Ethics, disability and sport*. London: Routledge.

Martin, J.J., & Whalen, L. (2015). Effective practices of coaching disability sport. *European Journal of Adapted Physical Activity*, 7(2), 13–23.

Thomas, N. & Smith, A. (2008). *Disability, Sport & Society: An introduction*. London: Routledge.

1

GOING THE DISTANCE

A tale of energy, commitment and collaboration:
Drew Ferguson, Head Coach of Canada's
Para Soccer Team

Laura G. Purdy, Jennifer Purdy and Paul Potrac

Introduction

In this chapter, we examine the career and practice of Drew Ferguson, the Head Coach of Canada's Para Soccer Team. The chapter begins with a brief introduction to Para soccer, which is also known as cerebral palsy (CP) football or 7-a-side football. Following this background information, an overview of Drew's playing experiences and entry into coaching are provided. The focus of the chapter then shifts to illuminating the various everyday challenges that Drew has to contend with in his work as a Para soccer coach. In the programme's early days these related to player recruitment and programme awareness, while current issues relate to the decentralised nature of the programme and the classification of players. In the final section, Drew provides recommendations and suggestions for coaches who aspire to work in Para soccer.

Historical context of Paralympic soccer

Paralympic soccer is also known as CP (cerebral palsy) football or 7-a-side football. In this chapter, the term Para soccer is used. The sport was developed in the late 1960s in response to the limited sporting opportunities for people with cerebral palsy. It was introduced to an international competition in 1978 at the Cerebral Palsy International Sport and Recreation Association (CPISRA) Games in Edinburgh, Scotland. The first World Championships were held in 1982, followed by its Paralympic debut in 1984 (Moore, 2014). In its early years, the tournaments were dominated by the teams from the Netherlands. However, since 2000, Russia, Ukraine, Brazil and Iran have, consistently, been the top ranked countries. The sport has focused on increasing participation around the world and in 2014, 39 teams were featured on the world ranking list.

Until January, 2015, the sport was governed by the CPISRA, an organisation comprised of 59 nations and three associations (cpisra.org). The CPISRA was formed in 1972 with the vision to 'promote and develop the means by which people throughout the world can have access to opportunities for participation in sport and recreational activities' (cpisra.org). From January 2015, the newly developed International Federation of CP Football took responsibility for the governing of the sport.

Para soccer is open to male players with mild cerebral palsy, acquired head injuries or those recovering from stroke. To be eligible to participate, players must be 15 years of age or older and receive a classification between 5 and 8.[1] The classifications are:

- Class 5: Players with cerebral palsy who have difficulties walking/running, but not standing or when kicking the ball.
- Class 6: Players with moderate to severe athetosis (an explanation of terms is provided at the end of the chapter), ataxia or a combination of spasticity and athetosis involving all four limbs.
- Class 7: Players with hemiplegia.
- Class 8: Players with mild hemiplegia, diplegia or athetosis or monoplegia.

(International Federation of CP Football, 2015)

In contrast to the 11-a-side version, the 7-a-side sport has a smaller playing field and goalposts. Teams consist of 12 players, of which at least one player classified as a C5 or C6 must be on the field throughout the match. In addition, one further player must be classified as C8. If this is not possible, the team is required to compete with six players instead of seven. Each half is 30 minutes in duration with a 15-minute halftime break. In terms of rules, there is no off-side regulation, three substitutions are allowed and players are permitted to use one-handed throw-ins.

In Canada, Para soccer was originally under the remit of the Canadian Cerebral Palsy Sports Association. However, in 2005, the Canadian Soccer Association took control of the programme (this will be explained later in the chapter). The programme also receives support from Sport Canada and Own the Podium.[2] Sport Canada, through its athlete assistance programme, currently supports 18 of the Para soccer players through a living and training allowance, and, when relevant, tuition and special needs assistance. Through the Bell Athletes Connect programme, Bell Canada (a telecommunications and media company) also provides players with free cell phones with free minutes.

Historical context of Drew Ferguson

Although the last two decades have witnessed an increase in the scholarly attention given to the lives and practices of high performance coaches (e.g. Jones et al., 2004; Shaw & Allen, 2009; Rynne & Mallett, 2012; Purdy & Potrac, 2014), there is a dearth of information on the experiences of coaches working within

Paralympic sport. Therefore, the purpose of the following sections is to draw attention to the career and practice of Drew Ferguson, the Head Coach of Canada's Para Soccer Team. Our coverage here also includes Drew's recommendations to people interested in getting involved in soccer programmes for people with disabilities.

Drew Ferguson was born and raised in Powell River, British Columbia, Canada. An avid footballer, at 15 years of age, he was identified as a talented player by Jackie Charlton (an English football manager and former player who was part of the 1966 World Cup winning team) and asked to move to the United Kingdom to train with Leeds United. Following his experience in the United Kingdom, he signed his first professional contract with the Vancouver Whitecaps. Over the next 11 years, Drew played in Canada, the United States of America and the United Kingdom. His former teams include: the Edmonton Drillers, Burton Albion, Buffalo Stallions, Cleveland Force, New York Cosmos, Chicago Sting, Hamilton Steelers and Cleveland Crunch. In addition to representing his province, from 1985 to 1991, Drew was also a member of the Canadian national team. One of his most notable achievements is that he is the only premier league player in Canadian history to be awarded the MVP in three different decades.

Drew's coaching career started during his time as a player when, in the 1990–1991 season, he undertook the role of player/coach/general manager with the Kitchener Spirit. He continued as a player/coach for Powell River Villa until his retirement as a player upon which he moved into a full-time coaching role. In addition to coaching, Drew has delivered coach education courses, was a selector for a provincial representative team, the general manager and head coach of the soccer academy in Powell River, as well as the technical director of the Powell River Youth Soccer Association. In terms of coaching qualifications, Drew has achieved the Provincial B, National B and National A (part 1). He is a member of the National Coaching Certification Program (NCCP) and was a contributing member to the development of the LTPD (long-term player development model) for athletes with disabilities in Canada. He is based in Powell River, British Columbia.

During his time with Canada's Para soccer programme, Drew has seen the team rise through the rankings to their current world position of tenth, which is the highest world ranking of all of the Canadian Soccer Association's programmes. The programme's progression through the world rankings is as follows:

- 2007: CPISRA World Championship: 15th place.
- 2007: ParaPan American Games: 3rd place.
- 2009: CPISRA International Championships: 14th place.
- 2011: CPISRA World Championship: 12th place.
- 2011: Porto, Portugal invitational: 2nd place.
- 2012: 7-a-side Futbol Tournament in Barcelona, Spain: 1st place.
- 2013: Intercontinental Cup: top 8; World Ranking: 11th place.
- 2013: Defi Sportif, Montreal: 3rd place.

- 2014: America Cup: 4th place.
- 2015: CPISRA World Championship: 10th place; ParaPan American Games: 4th Place.

The following section focuses on Drew's introduction to Para soccer, his role and the everyday challenges he faces in his work as the Head Coach of the programme. In the programme's early stages, these challenges related to player recruitment and awareness, while more present-day challenges relate to the decentralised nature of the programme and the classification of players.

The case study of Drew Ferguson

In 2005, Drew was running a private soccer academy and conducting coaching courses when he was approached about the Para soccer programme. He recalled his introduction to Para soccer.

> At the time, it was actually run by the Canadian Cerebral Palsy Sports Association ... and they made a little group to try to find a coach ... I used to run an academy when I first retired from playing ... one of the Board of Directors just kind of approached me. I guess he did a bit of homework on me, and approached me to see if I'd be interested ... I went to have a look at it, just one day, well one weekend actually, and at the time the players were not soccer players and they were definitely not at a very high level, but their attitudes and willingness to work was so much better than the professional soccer players ... It was fun, it was enjoyable, their attitudes were tremendous ... So I agreed at that time to oversee the programme for them, kind of as a part-time role.

At that time, the Canadian Cerebral Palsy Sports Association was also supporting boccia, so Drew was aware that the Canadian Cerebral Palsy Sports Association would be 'stretched thin' in terms of providing the resources to support two high performance programmes. In seeking to assist the CCPSA efforts to develop a soccer programme, Drew used the networks he had developed as a player and a coach to help grow the programme. Such networking was crucial in securing the Canadian Soccer Association's support.

> [With the Canadian Cerebral Palsy Sports Association] there wouldn't have been enough money to pay a salary or even for two or three training camps and a competition, so I set up meetings with [Canada Soccer] ... and they came to a few training camps and to the first competition ... and then we decided to shake hands, create a partnership and on we went.

In addition to having the support of the Canadian Soccer Association, Drew mentioned that the team's early success was a large contributor to its development.

A bronze medal at the ParaPan American Games in 2007 'helped [Canada Soccer] believe in the programme. And Canada in general, because once you start medalling or are on the edge of medalling, [Own the Podium] gets involved and things grow from there. So that was a big year'. In addition to the support of Canada Soccer, Sport Canada, and Own the Podium, the Para soccer team receives support from the wider soccer community. This support ranges from reduced prices on the facilities for training camps to free advertising or promotion of the team. Drew commented: 'We get some great support from the professional clubs and the provincial/territorial soccer associations … And I use my contacts through ex-players I played with.'

As mentioned previously, it was the players' positive attitudes and hard work that initially attracted him to the programme, however, upon taking the post of Head Coach, Drew's first task in the programme was to recruit additional players. As Para soccer was a relatively new sport, recruitment consisted of athletes who had transferred from other sports with few having a strong knowledge of soccer. Therefore, not only did Drew face the challenge of recruiting players to the programme, but he also had to try to help them develop a good knowledge of the sport quickly.

> In 2005 there were eight or nine kids that said they were soccer players or wanted to be soccer players … There were maybe one or two of them who knew a little bit about the game, but most of them were athletes coming from athletics or sledge hockey … we spent a lot of time teaching them the basics of the game, the technical side of the game, that mental side of the game, and that was very difficult to do.

Drew's experience is similar to that of coaches within other Paralympic sports who have witnessed a 'coming of age' as sport for people with disabilities has matured. In its early days it was not uncommon for a competitor to compete in a variety of sports at the same games, however, the Paralympics has become a serious sporting endeavour (Buckley, 2008) in which athletes must specialise in their chosen event. Parallel to this, Drew acknowledged the transformation he has seen in the players who are now in the 'talent pool':

> We're finding 11-, 12-, 13-, 14-, 15-year olds that are playing daily in the able-bodied world and then graduating to our programme, so they're ready to step in technically and mentally … Our young players now want to play for Canada in the able bodied world … That's the mentality of our newer players versus the mentality of maybe a player ten or 15 years ago. So … now we have soccer players with a disability whereas before we had athletes with a disability who we were trying to turn into soccer players.

Drew has been and continues to be the only full-time member of staff for the Para soccer programme: 'Once we leave the field, I'm the only person working for this programme, except for some Canada Soccer staff sometimes for the paperwork and that, but as far as the soccer side of the role, I'm the only one that does it'. As such, in addition to overseeing the programme and its daily management, Drew can also be found organising the team's kit or doing the team's laundry on training camps! In spite of the administrative workload, Drew has not taken a step back from the daily coaching responsibilities. He admits he still gets enjoyment out of watching the players develop inside and outside of the sport.

> I still do most of the coaching because it is the teaching part of the game I love and always have loved that … So I think that's one of the reasons I like this role … I'm managing and I'm coaching and I do it all. It's fun to watch kids that are 15, 16, 17, or even if they're 22/23 … It is great to watch these players grow on and off the field.

It is this passion for the game and the players' development that has been a key driving force for the programme. Such enthusiasm has resulted in successful team performances which have secured the support of others for training camps and competitions.

> We have a sport psychologist, we have a goalkeeper coach and we have an assistant coach and a speed coach, etc. but we'll only see and talk in general when we get to our camps or competitions. Once we get to the event, we sit down the night before and go over the next four or five days or if it's a competition, the next three weeks and explain their roles and what we're looking at … They're all very experienced in what they do so it would just be like any other professional team – for a training session, the keepers are at one end of the field with the goalkeeper coach and we work somewhere else with the defenders or forwards, etc.

A decentralised programme

Although there has been a trend for elite sports to centralise their training, there are exceptions, with some programmes preferring to adopt a decentralised approach. This entails players training within their home clubs as opposed to full time as a national team (de Bosscher et al., 2009; Petry et al., 2008). Canada's Para soccer programme has adopted a decentralised approach, opting to bring the team together at various times throughout the year. However, the country's size, at 9.98 million square kilometres (including six time zones), makes it difficult and expensive to bring the players together for a weekend of training. As Drew commented, 'it's a nine-hour flight [from one end of the country to the other], so if we have a training camp in Canada … to bring all the players and put them in hotels and pay their per diem, pay the coaching staff, it's $30,000, $35,000 for one camp for three days'. Therefore, the variable annual budget has a significant impact upon the number of times the players can train together as a team. Drew noted that this was one of the biggest differences for his programme versus the team's international competitors.

A lot of the other teams train every weekend throughout the year or Wednesdays through Saturdays throughout the year. And that gives them obviously a better chance to blend their team and tactically put how they're going to play together. So we have to rely on when we have these little three-day camps every couple of months, [we have to be] really intent on how are we going to play and work out how we play. So we don't have a lot of time to work on their individual technical skills 'cause there's not that many hours in a day during that time period. So one of the biggest, hardest parts for us is getting the guys together to prepare for a big competition.

As a result of the limited time that Drew and the team can spend together in training camps, most of the time together is focussed on 'blending the team' as opposed to concentrating on individual skills. Consequently, Drew relies upon the players to work on their individual skills at their home clubs. Additionally, bi-weekly sessions are organised for players who are in close proximity on the east and west coasts. Outside of the training camps Drew ensures that the players are on task by flying from coast to coast to see them: 'I'm flying back and forth and seeing them, so in general I'll see the players at least once a month or once every five weeks'. In addition to making frequent visits to see the players, he also uses technology to help him keep in touch with the players and part-time members of staff.

Technology is big for us as we don't have a lot of time together ... Phone, emails and a website. We do a lot of that ... If we are in a training camp, and we're normally there for three days or something, and the goalkeeper coach is doing video work with the keepers and by the time you do these, and dinners, you don't get time to review it all so we've got a site where we put everything on our site where the goalkeeper coach can go on with the players and review the videos and do this and do that ... So the good thing about the website is the players can chat amongst each other as well. ... So it's a good way for players to keep in touch with each other.

In addition to visiting the players, Drew asks that the players submit weekly training reports to him: 'Every week they have to send their training reports ... we've got a programme built of what they're supposed to be doing in the gym, on the field, etc. So they send those to me every week we review them and then we test them at each camp'.

As the programme is structured to enable athletes to train in their preferred clubs, one of Drew's responsibilities is to coordinate with the club coaches in relation to players' training and progression. He recognised that, for a club coach, this was not the easiest position. Drew stated: 'It's very demanding because the club coach will be running the practices not for the Para players and then he's got this cranky old Para coach phoning him all the time!'.

While Drew has managed the geographical issues by relying upon training camps and technology, the team has yet to qualify for the Paralympics. Drew believes that game experience and the team's ability to train together would make the biggest differences in terms of qualifying for major international tournaments.

> We need more game experience – game experience and game experience and that will come. But saying that, we're stronger now than we were yesterday and we're stronger than we were a few days before that. So the future's great, we're not that far away, we're banging on the door, but we don't have the advantages of some of the other countries as much as playing and getting together.

Creating awareness

In addition to focusing on the current players and staff who are involved in the programme and trying to improve its world ranking, Drew also needs to consider the recruitment and development of future players. Here, the public's increasing awareness of the programme has aided his work.

> Soccer in Canada in general is growing, you know, in leaps and bounds and the women's programme has got very popular in Canada, there's the Para programme with more people being aware of the programme now. So maybe in 2005, 06, 07, 08, 09, you know, 99 per cent of Canada probably didn't know there was a programme, so to find a player was very difficult. But now with the bit of success we've had and the Canadian Soccer Association work at it, most provinces/territories and staff coaches know about the programmes, so they help with their recruiting now and if they see a player that looks like, you know, they have a physical disability, that maybe meets our criteria then they get hold of me versus the old days me running around cross country by myself looking for athletes.

Although there is increasing recognition of disability sport, it is not attracting the same coverage received by able-bodied events (Brittain, 2004). In addition, funding issues have often impacted upon sporting organisations to effectively promote the programmes. As such, there is still a lack of awareness of the sporting opportunities that are available for people with disabilities. For example, Drew recalled an incident during an international Para soccer tournament in Toronto that led to the serendipitous recruitment of a new player. In his words:

> Just last year we hosted the America Cup, so Brazil, Argentina, Venezuela, Mexico were at the University of Toronto. It's a huge place, a big stadium, lights on, games going on, music … We finished the game and myself and the assistant coach were leaving the stadium … We were walking and it was only 500 yards from the stadium and this person with CP was walking right in front of us … So we just went up and introduced ourselves, and he had mild CP and he'd played a bit of soccer. So now he's in our programme. It was a

perfect example! [A guy] who was 500 yards away from a huge championship and didn't know about it, so that is the awareness we need also ... If somebody's walking around and looking at things and they should be seeing buses and all that going on, yet he didn't even know there was a tournament on or a programme, so that's the biggest challenge in recruiting players.

'Adapting' his coaching

Consistent with previous work (Cregan et al., 2007; DePauw & Gavron, 2005; Jones et al., 2004), Drew places emphasis on coaching people, not on their disability. As such, Drew notes that there are minimal differences in his approach to the Para soccer team as opposed to an able-bodied soccer team.

> I don't see too much difference between the able-bodied world and the programme that we're running ... I run our training sessions and our game plans and our philosophy, curfews, travel days and dress codes. I run that whole programme as if I was coaching able-bodied professional athletes.

Drew believes that the professional approach of the team is one of the components in development of a positive working environment. Such an environment is important to Drew: 'We want an environment that everyone gets along and enjoys working hard for each other, players and staff. If they don't buy into that, then they won't stick around very long, in fact we have let stronger players go, just for that reason'. According to Drew, one of the key features of creating this environment is the consistency of staff. As previously stated, Drew is the only full-time member of staff; however he has an assistant coach and a team of staff for training camps or tournaments (i.e. a goalkeeper coach, a sports psychologist and a physiotherapist). He relies upon the same staff as he believes the continuity of this staff is of importance to the players. Here, he recognised that 'The players need to feel comfortable with the staff and, you know, if I'm grumpy or don't want to see their face for a day or two they know they can go and see the other coaches, or there's some other person to talk to. We have to be able to be comfortable with each other as well'.

In terms of the actual game, Drew commented: 'the only thing that would be different would be your philosophy, when you're elite level soccer you're building your team game plan on coaching 11 players ... and now you're coaching seven players ... but if you had your coaching badges for 11-a-side you should be able to adjust to that'. In addition to adjusting to the number of players, Drew clarified that the content of the sessions differ slightly to that of an 11-a-side training session. For example:

> We have to spend a lot of time on teaching some of the athletes the technical side of the game which takes away your time of building your team aspect, how you're playing and going into the competition. Most of them can only

play with the one foot and the other one can trap the ball, pass a bit with it, it's just a fact of life. If you're coaching a 20-year-old able-bodied person, you wouldn't have to spend time, you know, trying to drill in their brain how to get set up and how to get the ball here and get it up here, you know, that wouldn't have to be done, but it's done at the Para programme.

In addition to the need to consider para-athletes' technical adaptations within this coaching environment, Drew draws attention to the additional challenges of Paralympic sport, in particular, the classification of players. The classification of athletes or players has been an area of considerable discussion within Paralympic sport (see Tweedy, 2003; Buckley, 2008; Beckman & Tweedy, 2009; Vanlandewijck et al., 2010). In Para soccer, the main controversy centres on the classification of C8 players. As mentioned previously, C8 players are minimally impacted by their condition and therefore, very difficult to classify. These players might experience tremors or small joint movements, be unable to place their heel completely on the ground, may not be able to turn on the affected side in the same way as the non-affected side, a possible impulse impairment may create a slight hesitation when attacking the ball (British Paralympic Association, date unknown). According to Drew: 'The C8s are usually former professional soccer players or high-end soccer players who've had an accident so they're going to be your most dominant players'. As the C8 players are very difficult to classify, most teams bring several players to the tournaments. Drew commented: 'We take five or six CP8s to every competition, hoping that they'd get in, but in general they don't always get classified. We just had a player classified out [at a tournament] just last year'. To clarify, a player can be classified as a C8 in one tournament and not in another. This variation in classifications can be protested, however the nature of the C8 category makes it particularly difficult to class. For Drew, helping a player cope with declassification is one of the hardest parts of the job. In his words:

> I say it all the time to able-bodied coaches that I talk with all of the time, they have to cut players, even the pros, you have to cut players. And that's never fun. But try telling a C8 player who's been training for a year and is trying to make it to the World Championships ... knowing he has had a concussion but only to find out they're saying it's not enough of a concussion ... it's brutally hard on the player. The one that just happened to us [at a tournament] last year, he was just destroyed ... [The player's] first reaction was 'I'm going to go get another concussion or something'. We're like, 'no, no, no, no', we don't want players running around trying to get concussions for the programme. So that's how disappointed he was ... So yeah, I mean so that's a hard thing. It's the reality of the rules and the laws of the game and we as coaches have to prepare ourselves for that and we have to prepare the players for the satisfaction and enjoyment or dissatisfaction and let down.

While the classification process can be very stressful for the players, their classification also impacts upon the coaching team's decisions on the selection of players for important tournaments. Drew explained:

> We'll take three 8s to [our next tournament], one has already been classified and is a strong, strong player. And then we'll take two other ones hoping that they'll get in. If they don't get in, we'll obviously be relying on the one to be dominant and hope that he doesn't get an injury or run down or get beaten up … If all three got classified out, then we are in trouble.

In addition to the possibility that a player might not be classified in the C8 category, Drew also has to consider how the classification process impacts upon player's preparation for a match. In his words,

> When these players get classified they have to play for at least 30 minutes on the field after the doctors look at them, but you might have to win the next two games [to qualify for the Paralympics]. When you put that person on you are taking a chance that he's going to help the team or hurt the team after he's played under pressure [for the classifiers], so that's the decision the coaches have to make. Do you wait and do it at a lesser tournament – not such an important tournament or you take a chance that he's going to be able to help you?

Similar to other sports that rely upon the classification of athletes/players, Drew recognises that it might not be possible to make the classification process an 'exact science'. The variability in classification, according to Drew, is the result of the complicated nature of the C8 class.

> In the soccer world we're working very, very hard at training, the team of doctors and the classifiers, making sure that we're all on the same page. And in that world I don't believe ever in the history, and that's 100 years, we'll always be on the same page, because I just don't see it. In testing C5 and C6 and C7, I see that, but in that C8 world, well I think it's very difficult.

Classification systems are continuously being monitored and modified, however, as Drew has suggested, the uniqueness of the C8 class and its classification will continue to be a challenge for the International Paralympic Committee, the International Federation of CP Football and, subsequently, for Para soccer players and coaches.

Recommendations for Paralympic soccer coaching, education and practice

The preparation, education and development of coaches has been a popular area of investigation. Although coach education programmes have been criticised for being 'divorced from the knotty reality of practice and of not developing new, progressive knowledge' (Jones et al., 2012, p. 313), formal coach education programmes play a role in the wider process of coach development (Gilbert et al., 2006). As such, for coaches who are interested in getting involved in the sport, Drew places high value on coaching badges and licences: 'The first thing you have to do is get all your coaching badges or your licences … [these will help you learn] to deal with everything, from putting players on and off the field, [deal with] fights and going to meetings and talking with the referee'. Although the information covered on the badges and licences does not focus exclusively on Para soccer, Drew notes that it is easily transferrable: 'I think any good quality soccer coach who has worked with their associations and gained valuable experience, would be able to handle a role of coaching in the Para soccer world'.

In Canada, there have been increasing opportunities for coaches to learn about Para soccer via provincial/territorial coach education courses. However, Para soccer is the only Paralympic programme overseen by the Canadian Soccer Association. As such, it is the only programme for people with disabilities that is discussed on the coach education courses. There is, however, room for further development. As such, Drew recommends 'In England … In England … those courses are for all, so they do blind soccer, deaf soccer, Para soccer they do it all. So I think when they do their coaching for that, it involves all sports for disabilities'. Such exposure would make people more aware of the opportunities within the sport and possibly help recruit new coaches (McMaster et al., 2012).

In addition to completing the required coaching badges and licences, Drew recommended that people interested in working in Para soccer get involved by coaching a session.

> I would encourage them to get involved at the youth side of it … and then… come to our training camps. So if you're in Toronto, you know, contact us, come on out and we'll get you involved and run a session if you want with me … And if you liked it, you may be like myself who has got into it and doesn't want to get out of it.

It is this passion for the programme and its players that has kept Drew involved for ten years: 'I love it, I look forward to it every day. There's times when I'm down for a month or two without doing things besides working on a computer, budget, planning and organising the season, I get really rambunctious and want to get back at it!'. Indeed, he commented, 'I'd have a hard time leaving this programme to take an able-bodied coaching job or even a professional job … It's an easy programme to fall in love with because people are good, the programme's great, the players are spectacular, on and off the field. So it's a feel-good programme and we just hope it keeps running'.

Conclusion

At the tail end of his playing career, Drew began coaching; firstly as a player/coach and then, upon retirement as a football player, to full-time coaching in his own academy in Powell River, British Columbia, Canada. In 2005, he was introduced to the Para soccer programme and has 'not looked back'. Although he has been the Head Coach of Canada's Para soccer programme for ten years and the programme's only full-time member of staff, Drew has not succumbed to the administrative aspects of the job, rather, he is as hands-on in his coaching today as he was a decade ago. He attributes his motivation and passion for the programme to the players' positive attitudes, willingness to work and their development in the sport. During his time with the programme, Drew has seen it rise from participating in its first World Championship to its current world ranking of 10. Throughout this trajectory, Drew, and the programme faced many challenges, from the early days of trying to recruit players and build an awareness of the programme to more contemporary issues which relate to the decentralised nature of the programme and the classification of players. Here, Drew's passion for the sport and ability to be creative with resources has been and will continue to be key to the programme's evolution.

Drew's story not only describes the everyday challenges that he has to contend with in his work in Para soccer, but lessons can also be learned regarding the passion, energy, commitment and resilience that has been and continues to be required by the Head Coach. With regard to the latter, our time with Drew has inspired us to want to consider the issues of role immersion, identity commitment, and role embracement in our research into coaches' lives (Goffman, 1961; Scott, 2015; Stryker, 1968). Such work could, from our perspective at least, help us to understand how and why coaches, like Drew, demonstrate high levels of commitment and dedication to their coaching role. Finally, Drew's Para soccer story adds to an emerging appreciation of the working contexts in which professional coaches operate by challenging the rhetorical and often trouble-free representation of coaches' careers that have often been portrayed by the media. While the issues of self-presentation and the micro-political demands of coaching are receiving increased attention in the coaching literature, Drew's comments on his working relationships with his coaching and support staff has stimulated us to want to explore how head coaches and their support staff may act, in Goffman's terms, as a 'performance team' (Goffman, 1959). We believe that such work could usefully advance our thinking beyond individual self-presentation in coaching by considering how coaching performances may, at times, be co-operatively planned, enacted, and evaluated in order to achieve desired outcomes (Goffman, 1959). Indeed, such inquiry may help us gain rich insights into the nature of trust, collaboration, and solidarity in coaching work; topics that have, to date, received scant attention in coaching research.

Additional resources and supplementary material

Information about CP soccer can be found on International Federation of CP Football's website: http://www.ifcpf.com and on the Official website of the Paralympic movement: http://www.paralympic.org/football-7-side.

The Cerebral Palsy International Sport and Recreation Association's (CPISRA) webpage is: http://cpisra.org/dir/

If you are interested in getting involved in CP soccer, contact your regional/ national soccer federation.

Information about Canada's CP soccer team can be accessed by joining their Facebook page (https://www.facebook.com/CanadaParaSoccer/).

Details about coaching and coach education in Canada can be accessed via: http://coach.ca/.

Information regarding soccer-specific coach education can be retrieved on: http://www.canadasoccer.com/training-certifications-s14688.

Terms

Ataxia: a term used to describe a group of disorders that affect co-ordination, balance and speech.
Athetosis: abnormal muscle contraction causing involuntary writhing movements.
Diplegia: paralysis of like parts on both sides of the body (i.e. both legs or both arms).
Hemiplegia: a condition in which one side of the body is paralysed.
Monoplegia: paralysis of one limb.
Spasticity: a term to describe muscles that become rigid or spasm.

(International Federation of CP Football, 2015)

Notes

1   In contrast to most Paralympic sports, the International Paralympic Committee (IPC) does not oversee Para soccer. Rather, it is governed by The Cerebral Palsy International Sport and Recreation Association (CPISRA) which is a member of the IPC, but is structurally and administratively independent (Tweedy et al., 2014). This independence extends to the classification system (Tweedy et al., 2014).
2   Own the Podium is a Canadian not-for-profit organisation responsible for prioritising and determining investment strategies for national sport organisations with the aim of generating more Olympic and Paralympic medals (Own the Podium, 2015).

References

Beckman E. M., & Tweedy, S. M. (2009). Towards evidence-based classification in Paralympic Athletics: Evaluating the validity of activity limitation tests for use in classification of Paralympic running events. *British Journal of Sports Medicine, 43*, 1067–1102.

British Paralympic Association (date unknown). *Football 7-a-side.* (http://paralympics.org.uk/paralympicsports/football-7-a-side) [accessed 21.09.2015].

Brittain, I. (2004). Perceptions of disability and their impact upon involvement in sport for people with disabilities at all levels. *Journal of Sport and Social Issues, 28*(4), 429–452.

Buckley, J. (2008). Classification and the Games. In K. Gilbert & O.J. Schantz (eds) *The Paralympic Games: Empowerment or side show?* (pp. 90–101). Maidenhead: Meyer & Meyer (UK) Ltd.

Cerebral Palsy International Sports and Recreation Association (www.cpisra.org) [accessed 5 June, 2015].

Cregan, K., Bloom, G.A., & Reid, G. (2007). Career evolution and knowledge of elite coaches of swimmers with a physical disability. *Research Quarterly for Exercise and Sport, 78*(4), 339–350.

de Bosscher, V., de Knop, P. & van Bottenburg, M. (2009). An analysis of homogeneity and heterogeneity of elite sport systems in six nations. *International Journal of Sports Marketing & Sponsorship, 10*(2), 111–131.

DePauw, K.P. & Gavron, S.J. (2005). Coaches of athletes with disabilities. *The Physical Educator, 48*, 33–40.

Gilbert, W.D., Côté, J., & Mallett, C. (2006). Developmental paths and activities of successful sport coaches. *International Journal of Sports Sciences & Coaching, 1*(1), 69–76.

Goffman, E. (1959). *The presentation of the self in everyday life.* Harmondsworth: Penguin.

Goffman, E. (1961). *Encounters: Two studies in the sociology of interaction.* Indianapolis: Bobbs-Merrill.

International Federation of CP Football (2015). *Classification rulebook* (Version January 2015). Retrieved from http://www.ifcpf.com/library [accessed 3 September, 2015].

Jones, R., Armour, K. & Potrac, P. (2004). *Sports coaching cultures: From theory to practice.* London: Routledge.

Jones, R.L., Morgan, K., & Harris, K. (2012). Developing coaching pedagogy: Seeking a better integration of theory and practice. *Sport, Education and Society, 17*(3), 313–329.

McMaster, S., Culver, D. & Werthner, P. (2012). Coaches of athletes with a physical disability: A look at their learning experiences. *Qualitative Research in Sport, Exercise and Health, 4*, 226–243.

Moore, K. (2014). Football and the Olympics and Paralympics. *Sport in society: Cultures, commerce, media, politics, 17*(5), 640–655.

Own the Podium (2015). *About OTP.* Retrieved from www.ownthepodium.org [accessed 9 July, 2015].

Petry, K.M., Steinbach, D.E. & Burk, V. (2007). Elite sport development in Germany: Systems, structures and public policy. In B. Houlihan, & M. Green (eds), *Comparative elite sports development* (pp. 114–146). London: Butterworth-Heinemann.

Purdy, L. & Potrac, P. (2014). Am i just not good enough? The creation, development and questioning of a high performance coaching identity. *Sport, Education and Society.* DOI: 10.1080/13573322.2014.941795.

Rynne, S. & Mallett, C. (2012). Understanding the work and learning of high performance coaches. *Physical Education and Sport Pedagogy, 17*(5), 507–523.

Scott, S. (2015). *Negotiating identity: Approaches to social identity.* Cambridge: Polity Press.

Shaw, S. & Allen, J. (2009). The experiences of high performance women coaches: A case study of two regional sport organisations. *Sport Management Review, 12*(4), 217–228.

Stryker, S. (1968). Identity salience and role performance. *Journal of Marriage and the Family, 4*, 558–564.

Tweedy, S. (2003). Biomechanical consequences of impairment: A taxonomically valid basis for classification in a unified disability athletics system. *Research Quarterly for Exercise and Sport, 74*(1), 9–16.

Tweedy, S.M., Beckman, E.M. & Connick, M.J. (2014). Paralympic classification: Conceptual basis, current methods, and research update. *PM and R: Paralympic Sports Medicine and Science, 6*(8) (Supplement), S11–S17.

Vanlandewijck, Y.C., Verellen. J. & Tweedy, S.M. (2010). Towards evidence-based classification – the impact of impaired trunk strength on wheelchair propulsion. *Advances in Rehabilitation, 3*(3), 1–5.

Editors' summary reflections

High performance disability sport appears to offer coaches like Ferguson, and many of his contemporaries examined in this book, a challenging, dynamic and highly rewarding space in which to work. As seen in all of the other coach case studies, over his career Ferguson has endeavoured to do good work for the sport and its constituents, yet his role as coach has not been particularly easy. As Purdy et al. reveal, changes in the organisational structure and support for cerebral palsy sports (in particular, Para soccer) in Canada in general, the increased emphasis on high performance imperatives, persistent classification concerns, geographic constraints, administrative and financial resourcing issues, and the sustainability of player recruitment and development have all shaped Ferguson's working environment. Similar to Bates, Darling, Tromans and Pohlman, Ferguson's ability to draw upon his pre-existing connections with ex-players from his earlier career in professional soccer as well as other coaches, businesses and community networks were, for example, advantageous in growing support for the team and augmenting the financial assistance offered via national governing bodies and their high performance development programmes. Similar to Bates, Pohlman, Darling and Fivash, Ferguson's efforts (along with those who work with him) have not only raised the profile of the sport, the team and its athletes, but, concomitantly helped establish a clearer development pathway for aspiring athletes to reach the pinnacle of Para soccer.

Para soccer in Canada may be on an upward trajectory; however, high performance maxims invariably place coaches under increasing pressure to deliver successful programmes. In Ferguson's case, as the sole full-time employee, this might be considered a significant burden; especially when, similar to other disability sport coaches, he assumes additional responsibilities and duties to his players that may go beyond his professional remit. Yet in this regard, and reflecting what we might start to consider as an *ethos* of disability sport coaching, Ferguson's approach (and general ability to negotiate the daily pragmatics of the job) is ultimately driven by his underlying interest in coaching pedagogy, genuine enthusiasm for Para soccer, and enjoyment in witnessing players' athletic *and* personal development. Such characteristics might, we note, also be shared among other coaches. Like many of his coaching contemporaries, Ferguson has been supported by the national organisation and peers in the industry, but his personal demeanour, leadership and agency has, we can see, evidently helped him to routinely 'get the job done'.

Coaches like Ferguson, for example, may envision a long future with their role. Invariably, however, coaches move on and others take their place (often with new ideas, visions, and performance plans). This may not be an issue for some sports, but when the coach is the sole full-time employee, has established vital rapport and trust among players and staff and is thus central to the continuity of specific high performance strategies, the management of coach change is important (Balduck et al., 2010; Raedeke et al., 2002; Rynne & Mallett, 2014). Consequently, in addition to addressing coach change and securing the sustainability of coaching development programmes within Para soccer, and comparably to Sawicki's assertions further on in this book, Ferguson's experiences also usefully demonstrate that coaches need to be well attuned and able to adapt to the wider working conditions in which they operate. For Ferguson, this has meant being cogniscent of the overarching political/ organisational climate, procuring the resources needed to support Para-sport development, negotiating the decentralisation of coaching programmes, and responding to the technical specialism surrounding disability classification. Although Ferguson points to the increased, and increasingly specialised, opportunities for aspiring Para soccer coaches within Canada, and the general vibrancy of the Para sport and disability sport participation, the aforementioned conditions demonstrate that coaching in this context – though not without reward – is a serious undertaking. Ferguson stands out as a good example of a High Performance disability coach and, as Purdy et al. draw our attention to, his story also raises points for coaches operating, or wanting to operate, at this level to consider.

References

Balduck, A-L., Prinzie, A. & Buelens, M. (2010.). The effectiveness of coach turnover and the effect on home team advantage, team quality and team ranking. *Journal of Applied Statistics*, *37*(4), 679–689.

Raedeke, T.D., Warren, A.H. & Granzyk, T.L. (2002). Coaching commitment and turnover: A comparison of current and former coaches. *Research Quarterly for Exercise and Sport*, *73*(1), 73–86.

Rynne, S.B. & Mallett, C.J. (2014). Coaches' learning and sustainability in high performance sport. *Reflective Practice*, *15*(1), 12–26.

2

CREATING A HIGH PERFORMANCE PARA-ROWING PROGRAMME IN THE USA

From the geography of the land to the generosity of the spirit (and everything in between)

Natalie J. Campbell

Introduction

This chapter explores the past, present and projected considerations of the sport of adaptive rowing in the United States of America. Guided by reflections from Thomas Darling, High Performance Director for US Para-rowing, the sport is considered historically, culturally, politically and socially in regards to the specific accompanying opportunities and challenges identified. With the sport being showcased at the 2008 Paralympic Games, the development of Para-rowing within the USA is in its embryonic stages. The chapter highlights the difficulties faced when developing an elite Paralympic sports programme in a country of such vast geographical space with limited existing coach education and sparse avenues for financial investment. Acknowledging that the USA is a nation galvanised by professional sports, and that Paralympic sport is afforded minimal media coverage, the difficulties of strategically constructing a pathway from grass-roots participation through to high performance disability sport are salient. However, Darling considers the future of Para-rowing to be promising. Focusing specifically on progressive avenues for Paralympic talent identification, the investment in coach education and the strengthening of associations with US military organisations, this case study unpacks the methods in which community, resourcefulness and leadership are inspiring and driving the growth of Para-rowing in the USA.

Historical context of Paralympic rowing

When considering the overall landscape of sport, it is commonly acknowledged that, from the playground to the podium, competitive participation is stratified and categorised. This division of competitors allows for the optimum provision of a level playing field, with such parity providing greater opportunity for athletes to participate in, and achieve at, the peak level of human performance. Rowing consists of two technical styles – sweep (where competitors each use a single oar) and sculling (where competitors use two oars) – with a sub-division of these events including categories for open-weight and restricted-weight (lightweight) male or female athletes. In addition, the division of adaptive rowing is a further race category in both head of the river races (winter) and regatta races (summer) at domestic, national and international level. Further to this, adaptive rowing contains its own sub-categories of gender and ability. The term 'adaptive' rowing implies that the equipment is 'adapted' to the athlete rather than the sport being 'adapted' to the athlete. For many national governing bodies (NGBs) of sport, the term 'adaptive rowing' is adopted for recreational and domestic participation and competition, whereas 'Para-rowing' is used by the World Rowing Federation FISA (from the French, Fédération Internationale des Sociétés d'Aviron) for elite performance programmes and international competition (such as World Cups, World Championships and the Paralympic Games). Before we discuss the case-study coach in detail, let us first explore the origins and the growth of the sport, with particular attention on its development in the USA.

At the end of World War II, adaptive rowing had been employed as a small, participatory sport for the rehabilitation of injured service men, for people with visual impairments and for those recovering from polio. During the 1970s and 1980s the sport grew in popularity, and rather than focus on separation and segregation, the emphasis was to integrate adaptive rowing into readily established rowing clubs and programmes. When required, attempts were made to customise equipment to suit an individual rower's specific needs as they related to their disability, with boats holding a combination of both rowers with and rowers without disabilities. During this time in the USA, the town of Philadelphia hosted regular Army-versus-Navy adaptive rowing races for servicemen blinded in World War II, and in 1980 the first rowing club for people with disabilities was created – the Philadelphia Rowing Program for the Disabled (PRPD). Throughout the 1980s and 1990s the sport of adaptive rowing was gathering momentum, with stand-alone and integrated adaptive rowing programmes being supported by national governing bodies across the globe. By the early 1990s the noticeable growth in participation and competition was so encouraging to the World Rowing Federation that the first FISA recognised adaptive rowing World Cup event was held in the Netherlands in 1991, aided primarily by the development of the first adaptive rowing international classification system.

Over the succeeding decade, interest, support and participation in the sport continued to expand; with the classification system becoming increasingly refined and sophisticated in its approach to developing the medical and technical criteria for the elite programmes around the world. The popularity of the sport was as such that in 2002, adaptive rowing was added to the regular competition schedule for the FISA World Championships (with the USA winning three of the six available medals). At present, rowing is one of only a handful of sports that sees Para-athletes participate annually alongside able-bodied athletes, with this happening at both

World Rowing Cups and the World Rowing Championships. After being accepted into the Paralympic programme in 2005 by the International Paralympic Committee (IPC), the sport of Para-rowing was showcased at the Shunyi Olympic Rowing-Canoeing Park at the Beijing 2008 Paralympic Games. For the following cycle, the London 2012 Paralympic Games saw 23 countries, 48 boats and 96 rowers competing in (the newly named) Para-rowing consisting of four boat classes, with a total of 12 medals being won across nine countries (inclusive of the USA winning a bronze medal). In 2014, 26 countries competed in Para-rowing events at an international level – an increase from seven countries in 2002.

As aforementioned, the development of the classification system for Para-rowing has been shaped and professionalised over a number of years, with FISA releasing the latest classification manual in 2014. Upon meeting with a Technical Classifier and a Medical Classifier, athletes will be considered eligible for racing under one of three categories:

1. Legs, Trunk and Arms (LTA): Rowers are able to use a sliding seat and have function in their legs, trunk and arms to row. Athletes may have a visual or physical impairment, however it is not a requirement that a visually impaired athlete have a physical disability. Rowers with physical disabilities are categorised as LTA-PD. Sub categories for visually impaired rowers are indicated as LTA-B1/B2/B3, however in the interests of vision impairment equality, during races all visually impaired athletes wear black-out blindfolds.
2. Trunk and Arms (TA): Rowers have functional use of the trunk and arms but are not able to use the sliding seat to propel the boat because of significantly weakened function or mobility of the lower limbs. TA rowers use a fixed seat with a form of pelvic support which must adhere to FISA standards.
3. Arms and Shoulders (AS): Rowers who have minimal or no trunk function (i.e. shoulder function only), using a fixed seat and back support which adheres to FISA criteria.

The first adaptive-rowing World Championships in 2002 saw events for LTA (legs, trunk and arms), TA (trunk, arms), and A (arms-only) boats. Later, in 2009 the A category was replaced by AS (arms and shoulders), and an ID (intellectually disabled) category was added, however this was removed after the 2011 World Championships. With a new event added in 2013, Para-rowing is currently divided into five boat classes: LTAMix4+ (LTA mixed coxed four), LTAMix2x (LTA mixed double sculls), TAMix2x (TA mixed double sculls), ASW1x (AS women's single sculls), and ASM1x (AS men's single sculls). The LTA and TA are mixed gender boats and competitive regatta races are held over 1000 metres for all five events.

Historical context of Tom Darling

Tom Darling was appointed the US Rowing High Performance Director of Para-Rowing shortly after the London 2012 Paralympic Games. As a former Olympic rower himself, with a keen understanding of developing mutually beneficial partnerships, managing large budgets, and with experience in coaching adapted sports, his hiring to the position was inevitable. Tom described his role as a process of 'self-actualisation', and that pretty much everything he has achieved in his life up to the point of our meeting he 'fortuitously fell in to'. However, from what I have learnt about Tom and his achievements both in and out of sport, I consider this to be an exceptionally modest and humble self-reflection. Whilst he may not have actively sought a career in disability sport, Tom's strength of character, compassion for others and tenacity to seek performance solutions has without question led him to such a notable position.

Tom had a formidable athletic career spanning three Olympic cycles, representing the USA at Moscow 1980, Los Angeles 1984 and Seoul 1988, with his most successful Olympic performance being a member of the silver medal winning Men's Eight crew in 1984. During his rowing career, Tom excelled academically and graduated from Syracuse University, New York, in 1981 with a BA in Psychology and Economics – a qualification Tom admits contributes greatly to his position today in assisting him to 'understand my athletes and understand my numbers'. In addition to being a university graduate and Olympic medal winning athlete, Tom's CV also boasts being a two-time winner of the Americas Cup in 1987 and 1988 as a crew member of the 'Stars and Stripes' San Diego Yacht Club. Of particular note is that whilst Tom was achieving exceptional athletic accolades in both sailing and rowing, he was also enrolled on a seven year M.Ed. degree at Boston University from 1984, graduating in 1991.

Upon athletic retirement, Tom naturally found himself gravitating back towards rowing and in 1991 was appointed Head Coach of the Boston University Rowing team, leading the women's crew to national championship victory in both 1991 and 1992. After such successes in rowing, Tom decided to focus once more on sailing and was appointed the principle trainer for the 'Stars and Stripes' San Diego Yacht Club Americas Cup crew from 1994 to 1996, leading them to victory in 1995. After such athletic successes, Tom decided to move away from sports in 1997 and get a 'real job' working in the financial services sector in Boston, however he continued to do ad hoc coaching at local community rowing clubs around the city. In 2006 Community Rowing (a non-profit rowing club in Boston) approached Tom and asked for his help in developing an adapted rowing programme to run out of their boathouse on the River Charles. The Community Rowing programme seeks to offer multiple opportunities to learn to row – for example children with learning disabilities and wounded war veterans. From 2006 to 2012 Tom became increasingly involved with the programme both as a coach and as strategic lead for its development. As a result of his dedication to, and vision for, adapted rowing, the national governing body US Rowing approached Tom in 2012 to be appointed High Performance Director for Para-rowing. His remit going forward is to develop and grow the elite programme in time for the 2016 Rio Games and beyond.

The case study of Tom Darling

The high performance programme

Tom was appointed High Performance Director and Head Coach for US Para-rowing in June 2013, inheriting a programme that faced a number of physical, cultural and financial challenges, yet is tasked with delivering at least two out of the five medals available at the 2016 Rio Paralympic Games. It is evident that he is very much aware of the impediments this role will consistently encounter.

For example, the USA is dominated by the multi-million dollar industries of professional sports such as basketball, baseball and American football, it occupies a geographical space almost 40 times that of the United Kingdom and is a country which is yet to securely embed wider sporting provisions and opportunities for people with disabilities into its national policies or societal consciousness (Silvers & Wassermann, 2000; Shapiro et al., 2012; Misener & Darcy, 2014; Cottingham et al., 2014). These considerations, plus the addition of much wider debates concerning the socio-cultural, biological and political positioning of disability in the USA makes the priority of, enthusiasm for and co-ordination of a high performance Paralympic sports programme a phenomenal feat.

Funding (or lack thereof)

For the US Para-rowing programme, the primary funding stream is via the US Department of Veterans Affairs (VA) and their partnership with the USOC, and in January 2014 the sport successfully bid for $250k to run the entire adaptive rowing and Para-rowing programme. At present US Para-rowing sits within the remit of US Rowing (similar to how GB Para-rowing falls within the overall structure of GB Rowing), however Tom's budget of $250k means he can only afford to pay a salary to himself and one other member of staff – Programme Development Specialist Debbie Arnberg – the entire programme is operated through two full-time members of staff. In addition to the elite system, Tom must ensure that a proportion of the $250k is spent supporting the development of community adaptive-rowing programmes nationwide, all of which is done through the 'personal interests and good will of volunteers already in the rowing community'. I asked how this seemingly impossible task was being managed and I admit I was taken aback by the answer:

> We have a lady who is basically traveling around the country with her dog in a van, visiting nearly every community rowing programme and just asking 'hey, how would you like to start an adaptive programme?' She gets around $500 a month which doesn't even cover her gas.

The idea that Tom must oversee the development of an elite Para-rowing talent pathway to Rio 2016 whilst simultaneously facilitating the national development of the sport at grass-roots level seems utterly removed from the UK system. Responsible for the current elite athletes, the potential talented athletes, the community initiatives and the social responsibility attached to the funding grant, Tom is responsible for both performance and participation – and as we talked, the professional and moral tension experienced between the two priorities was evident. As he begins to reel off names of coaches within the community who volunteer their time to support new adaptive-rowing opportunities ('mainly women and masters rowers') the disparity of the programme is mirrored in his fragmented reflections:

> I really need to follow up on … I just remembered that I need to call/email … That's a good point, I need to chase that … That reminds that I haven't done [a task] yet … I'm just making notes to myself whilst we talk.

What is clear from the outset is that Tom is in a position in which the success of his role depends upon the extent to which he can rely on others outside of the performance environment. Indeed, the overall staffing structure of the Para-rowing programme runs in relative isolation to its able-bodied counterpart, with little practical collaboration or cross-over between practitioners in the two sports. Considering this reality as part of a much richer conversation within disability sport, Hums et al. (2003) ask the question of identity for Paralympic sports programmes; is it better for athletes with disabilities to host their own NGB with specific recognition (i.e. as GB Wheelchair Basketball is separate from GB Basketball), or to be subsumed into a larger NGB? They ask 'Does equality mean loss of identity as athletes with disabilities – and is that positive or negative?' (p.270). The deliberation of the binary of inclusion/exclusion within Paralympic discourse is pertinent, particularly within the area of governance, and is one that athletes and scholars, differently abled and not, have provided voice to. It is a rhizomatic problem with no obvious solution; yet for Tom, he is aware that in order to create a high performance disability sports programme, he must draw upon the knowledge and support of his colleagues working in able-bodied rowing.

> There is nobody to help me run this camp [in March] so I went to the national team manager in US Rowing and I was like 'what do you know about running adaptive camps?' and he gave me a list of things and I had to just say 'send me that information because guess what – you're the guy to help me run it!'

From camps to competitions, the nutritionist, the psychologist, the physiologist, even the physiotherapist, right through to the administrators and logistics co-ordinators are roles currently occupied by paid and voluntary staff outside of the US Para-rowing environment.

Talent identification

Whilst organising a training camp in Sarasota (Florida), Tom talked me through some of his concerns for a much-anticipated week of talent identification. He commented that his budget could not pay for the labour of classifiers, physical therapists, psychologists, coaches or technical support needed, let alone for their flights from across the country or for accommodation for them to stay in the area, and so the camp would only be possible if enough volunteers came forward to offer their time and expertise. All the members of staff attending were (as Tom put it) 'scrounging around' for finances to support a camp that could potentially unearth a new US Para-rowing medal winner. Talent identification is a huge priority for Tom, and from running the camp in March he hopes to be able to have at least one athlete physically robust and technically efficient enough to send to the World Rowing Championships at the end of August. Although the concept of talent identification is not new to academic research or able-bodied sport, it is largely an underdeveloped area in Paralympic sport which is gaining more attention in the field from both hard science and soft science research approaches.

Whilst most talent confirmation stages are conducted with athletes over a three- to six-month period, Tom hoped to take some individuals at his camp from talent identification to World Championship level in only five months. The speed at which an individual is to be transformed to an athlete may appear to be inauthentic or disingenuous at first, perhaps providing a derided nod to the standards of Para-rowers in the US, but Tom does not see it this way, commenting that:

> If we have an athlete who wins the national trial, and if they can fund themselves, then they can go over [to the world championships] and represent the USA, even if they're coming in 1.5 minutes behind the gold medal time – it's about participation and opportunity.

Tom's consideration of competing internationally may be unorthodox, there is method to his madness – his 'talent ID calendar' is saturated. Each week Tom finds himself travelling throughout the country to events that enable him to make use of staff and resources not readily available to him to find the new talent. From Gateway to Gold[1] events to the Valour Games,[2] from high-school regattas to community rowing coaching sessions, Tom understands the importance of consistently seeking out new talent if he is to grow the talent pool for US Para-rowing in the run up to 2016. He wants boat selection to be competitive. Yet this need for constant talent identification dovetails with a financial agenda. A caveat for the programme continuing to receive financial support from the VA is that Tom needs to report that every three months he has introduced 250 injured service men and women to the sport of rowing – be that on the water or on a rowing machine.

It would not be unfounded to comment that the USA is a patriotic country, with the historical and present day considerations of the military firmly embedded within the national culture. Indeed, for the London 2012 Paralympic Games, 20 out of the 227 Team USA athletes were former service men and women injured in combat.[3] The almost excessive desire for NGBs to fast track former members of the armed forces to become a Paralympian has been explored by numerous academics from multiple disciplines, with research pertaining to issues such as the disabled soldier/athlete body as a site for inscription of national fantasy (Batts & Andrews, 2011), the impact of sport and physical activity on well-being and rehabilitation (Hawkins et al., 2011; Brittain & Green, 2012; Caddick & Smith, 2014), the cyborging of the soldier athlete body (Wolff, 2011) to the social and medical transitioning of the 'warrior' (Cooper et al., 2013; Messinger, 2013). Parallels between military personnel and elite athletes are often drawn – diligent, dogmatic, self-disciplined and committed individuals, who professionally absorb orders and facilitate task cohesion; the allure of the injured service man or woman as a future Paralympic potential is attractive. However, none of the squad members who made the US Para-rowing team for the 2014 World Championships are former military.

Geographical and relational distance

With such an emphasis on talent identification currently galvanising his finite resources, I asked Tom about the current athletes he has on his programme and how the high performance programme currently operates under the constraints identified. The current ASM1x athlete is at law school in Ohio. He has his own coach and follows his own programme and whilst Tom has input into his training, their contact time is limited. Similarly, the ASW1x athlete trains independently in Massachusetts, whilst the two athletes that comprise the LTAMix2x train separately in Connecticut and Massachusetts. The LTAMix4+ boat consists of two college (university) students and two high-school (sixth form) students, all of whom are involved in their own rowing programmes where they live in four different states – Washington, Ohio, Michigan and Connecticut. Hundreds of miles separate the athletes from each other and from Tom, meaning that time spent in boats together, or simply in each other's company is minimal. It is not uncommon for NGBs to require athletes to relocate to a centralised environment once invited onto a high performance team, especially so in rowing. A fundamental concern that any rowing coach will contend is that it is critical for a crew to spend as much time in a boat together as possible. The issue of centralising is a concerted subject for Tom to negotiate:

> You can't put someone in a camp-like situation for years. They get bored; they have other lives to live so we just have to work with what we've got.

Reflecting on his own rowing career Tom recounted how during this time he was responsible for the physical programming of his crewmembers from 1985–1987.

> I knew what they were eating, I knew when they sleeping, I knew what they were feeling, I saw them every single day you know? I knew about injuries, and it was a great resource of course, but I don't have that luxury now – and you know what? It doesn't work anyway.

However, as is noted, Tom cannot do this. His main objective is to streamline communications between him and their coaches in regards to how he is updated on their physiological and technical progression. Unquestionably his objective is for the rowers to peak for the World Championships in late August – he is aware that their domestic coaches (especially those athletes in high school and college) will be working to different performance agendas; and whilst he posts programmes regularly to the US Para-rowing facebook page, Tom must relinquish some level of control in regards to regulating individual athlete progression:

> I ask them to follow the programmes on the concept 2 system[4] so that I can see they're doing the work, don't make excuses. If you do as I ask you to then in six to eight weeks we'll see improvement. If you don't do what I ask you to do then we're probably not going to be on the same team.

In October 2015, however, Tom was given a specific directive by the USOC – to qualify a TAMix2x boat in April 2016 that would race competitively at the Rio 2016 Games. Knowing the present system, it seems like such an overwhelmingly difficult task in such a short space of time with so much ground to cover. Tom needs to find a male and a female athlete who would both classify (medically and technically) for the TA boat, but who could also train together – and most importantly – row well together. To achieve this, Tom explains how he will need to be 'creative' with a recent $290k secondary grant from the VA.

> You see the VA gave the USOC that money to build a cross-country sustainable model of connecting local VA offices and reachouts to their local rowing programme, and so the money can't really be used for training camps or the likes, unless those camps specifically develop veterans into elite athletes.

Tom budgets a cost of approximately around $12k– $15k per week for an elite training camp to cover flights and accommodation for prospective athletes, volunteer support staff, and the cost of boat and facilites hire. Knowing that each camp could host approximately 25 athletes, I wondered what strategic monitoring had been implemented to ensure that from the invited athletes there would be two who could fill the seats in the boat. As we spoke it became clear that the selections were reliant on self-report data. The new objective would inevitably require a shift in the way Tom currently worked, acknowledging that he will need to undergo less 'head coaching' and more 'performance directing' if he is to achieve this extraordinary task of qualifying a TAMix2x.

And so, with budgetary constraints, limited athlete contact, a gigantic geographical space and one member of staff, how does Tom think he will be able to deliver on the challenging medal and participation targets set by the USOC and the VA respectively? By growing a culture of support and awareness and building effective partnerships and strong relationships with people already in the rowing community.

Building partnerships

One of Tom's first actions in post was to investigate if any of his 'old crew' contacts were still involved in rowing – and to ask for their help. The tendency for disability in the USA to be the adopted responsibility of community physical activity programmes for wounded soldiers often leaves elite programmes for Paralympic sports significantly lacking in visibility. As Tom put it there was 'no-one knocking down the door' to work with a Para-rowing wanting to develop as a practitioner (in whatever discipline). The development of the programme therefore is determined by the consistent need to rely on others. Fortunately for Tom, a former team mate had transitioned into a career as an engineer and agreed to (voluntarily) explore a more ergonomically enhanced design fixed seat for the TA and AS rowers to capitalise on marginal gains. In fact, Tom credits this new design of the ASM1x seat as a contributing factor to a 4th place finish at the 2014 World Rowing Championships. In addition, a collaborative relationship with the head coaches of Canadian and Australian Para-rowing has led to a better understanding of the international classification system and curriculums for coach education – the first of which is an online manual explaining the classification system for the sport. I considered this knowledge transfer partnership between nations to be something quite unorthodox, and so I asked Tom if he thought there was a distinct contrast between the adaptive community and the able-bodied community in elite sport:

> I think there is something bigger in adaptive coaching, it's like we understand the process and the requirements are bigger than ourselves, and whilst some coaches don't want to talk to me, it's my job to find the ones that do so I can learn.

Tom is honest about how much he has to learn in his new role. Often he finds himself needing to be the coach, the physiologist, the nutritionist, the psychologist and the handler at camps and most competitions if USOC staff are not available to help. The 2014 World Cup in Amsterdam was a steep learning curve for the programme, identifying a number of issues that had been overlooked such as the need for more 'buddy' staff[5] accreditations and that clothing for some of the athletes was insufficient. An exceptionally important consideration for coaches of spinal cord injured athletes or athletes with more than one amputation that the individual may have difficulties in detecting thermoregulatory changes during physical activity – for example, an inability for the body to detect dipsia (thirst), be unable to activate appropriate diaphoresis (sweating) or recognise sensations of hypothermia (cooling).

The coach–para-athlete relationship

Tom acknowledged that the physical distance between himself and the rowers over the course of the year had, at times, resulted in strained coach–athlete relationships at international competitions. He recounted an incident with the ASW1x athlete who presented with an injury during the World Cup 2014 in Amsterdam, and although the medical doctor had signed her off as being able to compete, Tom was apprehensive. Prior to the competition Tom had invested a lot of time learning about her condition, and despite expressing his concern for her physical well-being, the athlete chose to race. What emerged later was that Tom had not invested enough time in learning about *her* – her background, her family, her psychology.

The athlete was able to push herself so hard that she slipped a cervical disk during her final race.

Tom was happy to report that part of this VA funding had allowed for a performance psychologist to be at the forthcoming LTA camps. This was a huge benefit for the programme in terms of progression. As he took me through how he hoped the psychologist would deliver at the camps, there was a particular area of impact that Tom was most concerned with:

> Because I don't see my athletes one-on-one as much as I would hope, I feel I need to do more to develop the trust between us all. If we can develop those 'inner-voice' dialogues of trusting each other to be working towards the same goals, then we're getting closer as a team you know, despite the many different states we all live in

As such, Tom was reflective in his worries that the continued and consistent physical distance between him and his athletes could manifest mentally, disrupting not only their training, but also their relationship with him. Tom understood the need to remain psychologically close to his athletes, even when they were training thousands of miles away. The LTA training camp was the first step to overcoming this.

This paradoxical nature of the coach–Paralympic athlete relationship is one that Tom is aware of and whilst contemplating his position, he is conscious of the stratified concepts of authority and power akin to the role of head coach:

> I don't want them to think they did or didn't make [the team] because I do or don't like them … and on the other hand I don't want to get too into their personal lives because it's about performance.

Tom is right; Paralympic sport is about performance. It is not about participation, nor is it about pity. Despite the multiple duties, his primary objective is to find four men and four women who can contend for a medal position at the Rio 2016 Paralympics.

Finding the (controversial) future talents

At present, Tom relies on existing rowing programmes to identify (and flag to US Para-rowing) athletes within their system who may be eligible for Paralympic classification. Yet this pipeline for talent acquisition needs to be expanded at the source; once more Tom considers sharing knowledge and building relationships to be paramount:

> I want coaches to know that we are searching for athletes with minimal disabilities so when I see them at different college [rowing] events I can ask … I know some of them do, it's just that they don't have the information of what we're looking for.

Tom does not gloss over the importance of wanting to find 'athletes with minimal disabilities'. He is aware of the physiological and psychological advantage of transforming an already athletic individual into a technically competent rower, as was the Head Coach before him. In March 2011, an online talent identification process saw two former elite athletes and a former Navy Seal – all of whom had acquired their disabilities – be introduced to the sport of Para-rowing.[6] Five months later at the 2011 World Championships, each was at the start line of their respective events racing to qualify their boat category for the London 2012 Paralympic Games.

The notion of purposefully seeking out individuals with 'minimal disabilities' to supplement the talent group is a contentious issue. It causes practical questioning around selection and classification for both athletes and coaches – indeed, the entire classification system presents conceptual conundrum. As our conversation drew to a close, I asked Tom to reflect on his own journey in rowing and to expand on how he considers that his coaching philosophy will ensure that once he finds these athletes they will stay committed to the programme.

The coach

One of the first things Tom did upon coming into post was to sit on an indoor rowing ergometer and attempt to row 1000 metres using only his arms and shoulders. He felt it was important to get a physical blueprint (even if temporary and somewhat falsified) of what his AS1x athletes are required to do. Despite his physical conditioning and technical efficiency on the rower, he stopped after 250 metres. This was an important learning experience for Tom as the coach, immediately needing to reframe his ontological notions of 'knowing' what it felt like to row. This concept of the able-bodied coach being able to 'understand' the needs of the athlete with a disability for performance development is well researched (Tawse et al., 2012; Fitzgerald, 2013; Martin & Whalen, 2014). Alarmingly, within the UK only 6 per cent of registered qualified coaches across all sports (professional/ Olympic/Paralympic) self-identify as having a disability.[7] In turn, this indicates that the vast majority of those who participate in disability sport are coached by an able-bodied individual. Without question, the more coaches can understand about the pragmatic considerations of disability sports coaching the better – and this is an area Tom is keen to invest in.

Coach education

Recently Tom and Debbie Arnberg have completed a piece of work that has been in development for the past six months. Together they have created an online adaptive coaching manual of over 100 pages, which community coaches can access and download for free (http://www.usrowing.org/docs/default-source/adaptive-documents/2015-guide-to-adaptive-rowing.pdf?sfvrsn=0). The manual aims to introduce coaches to the technical aspects of the sport, the way that equipment needs to be adapted as well as providing information on how to best introduce an individual with a disability to the sport:

> It's basic advice like getting an individual with a visual impairment to feel the oar and the boat before getting onto the water, or if you have a person with a spinal cord injury they should sit in a boat with able-bodied rowers to get a sense of movement and imbalance on the water.

He explained how the development of the manual was in part due to Joy (the lady with the dog traveling the country) visiting as many clubs in the country as possible and asking the coaches what they would need in order to feel confident and competent in delivering to an adaptive athlete; she then reported this information back to Tom and Debbie. Taking advantage of his relationships with Head Coaches of other nations, Tom has been able to adopt and adapt information from multiple NGB coaching manuals and add an American stamp to it. The manual is important to Tom and he reflected that when he began as a volunteer adaptive coach he had no formal training, no documents to refer to and no one to ask; he had to learn about the sport – and about disability – session by session, just as the participants did. I asked Tom how the manual had been received so far:

> To be honest I don't really know. I mean I'm sure, no I should ask the IT guys to pull up stats [sic] on how many times it's been looked at but for now at least if anyone calls US Rowing to ask about adaptive we can point them to our web pages.

I was curious to understand what it was that prevented Tom from making contact with the clubs in his network, taking the manual to them as opposed to waiting for a phone call. After all, he and Debbie have a vested interest in ensuring more and more clubs are able to offer adaptive rowing both in terms of veteran/community level growth and also to develop a healthy talent pathway. Tom considered my suggestion for a moment and responded in earnest:

> If I could show you the list of things I have to do against the list of what I want to do … At the moment I can only respond to the need, not create the need. I have to find athletes for Rio.

However, Tom is the High Performance Director of US Para-rowing, not a university graduate entering into their first position; should community coach education really be part of his job role? And how much could it detract (as he pointed out) from finding his 2016 hopefuls?

Managing expectations

Tom admits that whilst reaching out for partnerships at the beginning of his role, he was surprised by the resistance expressed from others within the sport whom he 'assumed would be open minded'. This hinting at a shared empathy or enthusiasm towards people with disabilities is not uncommon amongst academics within the elite disability sport domain – the notion that increased awareness will inevitably lead to acceptance and therefore interest in disability seems yet to be challenged. Furthermore, it has been argued that whilst Paralympians are considered to gain empowerment from the Paralympic Games, their specific lifestyle choices and failure to identity as 'disabled' can actually be a limiting fact to the empowerment of others in the community who are not identifying as an 'athlete' (Purdue & Howe, 2012) and that the Paralympics has limited impact on the everyday lives of disabled people (in the UK at least) (Braye et al., 2013). In order for the programme to progress at a pace which pleases both the USOC and the VA, Tom is practical, almost business-like, in his approach. His staff, his funding and his time are finite and with the 2016 Paralympic Games within a little over 12 months, he feels he cannot afford to be too political about the position he occupies.

> If someone is not willing to support something I'm involved in then I'll go to the next person. I mean I'm not trying to change people's opinions about the disabled or working with the disabled.

It seems that despite being the High Performance Director for US Para-rowing, Tom does not see it as his role as being politically motivated towards championing disability sport.

Coaching philosophy

I found Tom's role as Head Coach and High Performance Director of US Para-rowing to be very far removed from my own understandings of how this job would operate within the Team GB system.[8] I was in awe of how he managed to do so much with so little (whilst still trying to be a present and good husband and father). He mentioned that he never intended to come back to high performance rowing. He had transitioned well out of his elite athlete career and whilst was happy to volunteer at his local club, his current position was not an anticipated future career move. I asked Tom why he chose to take the position, knowing the limitations that would be placed on the programme:

I enjoy getting people to that elite level because I did it. It's no different. The athlete has to put the time in, put the effort in, got to want to do it, but you have to have someone there saying 'I believe you can do it too'.

Reflecting on his own career, Tom postulated that former athletes develop a habitual style of coaching that mirrors how they best responded when they themselves were training. Tom defined himself as a 'compassionate' coach – a coach that listens and a coach that cares about the athlete beyond the medals table. Yet throughout our discussion, he was able to acknowledge that such sentimental behaviour may not always best serve the situation:

I don't think I push as hard as I could. I have to figure that one out you know? When is it time to put the hammer down and when to be the pat on the back kind of person.

I found his attitude to be both holistic and progressive. The concept that individuals who reflect on their own practices make for better leaders has been embedded in business management for a number of years. This idea of questioning our own performance before questioning the performance of others is slowly becoming an integral part of the development of elite sports coaches (Cruickshank & Collins, 2012; Frontiera, 2010; Kidman & Hanrahan, 2010).

Despite numerous successful case studies of interventions including supporting athletes to earn degrees, cope with family disruptions, transition healthily out of competitive sport and issues pertaining to mental health, the elite sports system in the UK has been slow to embrace the need for such support. However, recent studies within the domain of elite sport have grounded this need to support elite athletes beyond performance targets with the theoretical frameworks used in positive psychology. Considered a scientific exploration of the theoretical application of optimal functioning to human flourishing, the area examines the strengths and virtues which enables individuals and communities to thrive. The application of positive psychology to the elite sports domain is in an embryonic stage, however a handful of studies have explored the use of positive psychology in sports organisations (Wagstaff et al., 2012), the influence of using positive emotions in sports performance (McCarthy, 2011) and the relationship between hope and burnout in competitive sport (Gustafsson et al., 2010). As yet though, the extent to which high performance coaches understand and implement positive psychology to enhance the well-being of their athletes is yet to be determined. Tom leads me to believe that he would be an advocate of such approaches:

I've been involved in rowing for so long and have rowed all over the world at internationals. I would never want any athlete to feel that I had my thumb on them the whole time to win a gold medal … The bottom line is if the athlete doesn't want to row, you're not going to convince them to row. An elite will always put more pressure on themselves than you ever will – so if they're not doing what they need to, it's my job as the coach to question how much they want it, how much can they give?

Again, Tom positions himself as a coach who drives performance through facilitating and reflecting; he is not a dictator. Overall, Tom's coaching philosophy is one that nurtures – he constantly and consistently tends to the foundational bed of adaptive rowing in the USA, with conviction that over time talent will indisputably flourish and advance. Despite participation and integration being a financially rewarding objective for Tom, he contends that through the programme he is developing the USA will become one of the most competitive and decorated Para-rowing nations. He will create a culture where becoming a champion is inevitable.

> If you asked any gold medallist how they did it, not one will say it was because of the money or the perks. No. They'll talk about community, about the support structure, their friends, the club, the coaches you know? They will say it was a culture that made them champions. I plan to build this culture here.

Recommendations for Paralympic rowing coaching, education and practice

This chapter has highlighted that in the not too distant future, a reality those involved in high performance disability sport may need to consider is 'how can we do more with less?'. Certainly exploring Tom's role and the landscape of elite sport in the USA helps to shape an understanding of this. Whilst it is unlikely that elite sport in the UK will see a complete reduction in financial support, the gap between the funding allocations to participation and high performance will undoubtedly begin to narrow – preparation is paramount.

What lessons can be learnt, what information can be gleaned and what examples can be used on how to drive forward the anticipated success of a Paralympic sport with the smallest of budgets and minimal full time support staff? It would appear that UK Sport have already confirmed to NGBs a drop in funding post-2021, and are subtly filtering the message through to teams. As part of annual reviews conducted by the organisation, NGBs are expected to demonstrate how the provision of their elite sport services can be funded via self-sustaining business–case initiatives for the 2021 Olympic and Paralympic cycles onwards. I would argue that those hoping to enter employment into high performance sport (be that Paralympic or Olympic) during this time should anticipate two changes:

1. The route into a full-time, salaried role will be a lengthier process, with fewer opportunities being made available for entry-level practitioners. A reduction in funding is likely to create an emphasis on practitioners volunteering at more senior levels of sport, with an overall impact being that salaries will remain below the national rate of inflation.[9]

2. Sports will be seeking to appoint individuals who can fulfil a dual-purpose role, and this my fall within two particular areas – increasing participation (and therefore paid membership to supplement the elite structure) or increasing funding (to pay for support staff). Without question, a coach who will span both elite and participation will be preferable, as will team mangers that are able to increase sponsorship deals with corporate agencies. Going forward, practitioners may need to be conscious of sharing roles and responsibilities across the entire organisation, as opposed to working exclusively with the elite athletes.

Future practitioners may gain a competitive advantage by observing a number of practices adopted by other nations and explore how such alternatives could be adapted to suit National systems – such as the 'Adopt an Athlete' initiative driven by the Hellenic Olympic Committee to support the elite system, or by investing only in a small number of popular sports with high levels of medal expectation. Essentially, future practitioners should be exploring private-sector strategies and formulating business plans of how Team GB can remain as successful, supported and committed should elite sport fail to make the qualifiers for government spending priorities post-Rio 2016.

I asked Tom to tell me about the future of his role and the direction of US Para-rowing – how did he envision it transforming from a sports programme driven primarily by motivated and passionate individuals into an elite training system supported by paid staff and long term planning? His response was unequivocally that of a High Performance Director of sport:

> I have a plan but honestly, I couldn't say. Ask me again after the 2016 medal count comes in.

Additional resources

http://www.usrowing.org/domesticrowing/adaptiverowing
http://www.worldrowing.com/para-rowing/

Notes

1   Gateway to Gold is a USOC organised, multi-sport event held in different states across the USA which serves the dual purpose of encouraging veterans with disabilities to take up a Paralympic sport, and as potential fast-track Paralympic talent identification events.
2   The Valour Games aims to bring together disabled veterans and wounded, ill or injured service members and engages them in three days of Paralympic sport competition. It is held annually in various locations in the USA.
3   Since the commencement of the wars in Iraq and Afghanistan in 2001, over 35,000 American military personnel have returned home with serious physical and psychological wounds, including amputations, traumatic brain injuries and paralysis (Batts & Andrews, 2011).
4   Concept 2 is a rowing ergometer manufacturing company that has online systems for recording numerical data from erg sessions.

5   Many adaptive and Paralympics international sport events will allow each athlete to have an accredited 'buddy' who may not have an official role within the team but will provide additional assistance to the athlete.

6   One athlete was a former elite road cyclist who was knocked off her bike whilst on a training ride, resulting in complete paralysis from T4. The second athlete was a former nationally competitive marathon runner who contracted bacterial meningitis, resulting in the medical condition Stiff Persons Syndrome. The third athlete was a US Navy Seal who was involved in a traffic accident whilst on leave, resulting in partial paralysis from T7.

7   Email correspondence with sports coach, UK, April 2015.

8   Team GB Para-rowing received £3.8m towards elite development of the sport for the 2013–2017 Rio cycle. Funding amounts received by each Olympic and Paralympic sport can be viewed at www.uksport.gov.uk

9   National governing bodies of sport (and associated organisations) are defined as being within the public sector and are therefore subject to similar restrictions in pay increases and bonuses.

References

Batts, C. & Andrews, D.L. (2011). 'Tactical athletes': the United States Paralympic Military Program and the mobilization of the disabled soldier/athlete. *Sport in Society, 14*(5), 553–568.

Braye, S., Gibbons, T. & Dixon, K. (2013). Disability 'rights' or 'wrongs'? The claims of the International Paralympic Committee, the London 2012 Paralympics and disability rights in the UK. *Sociological Research Online, 18*(3), 16.

Brittain, I. & Green, S. (2012). Disability sport is going back to its roots: Rehabilitation of military personnel receiving sudden traumatic disabilities in the twenty-first century. *Qualitative Research in Sport, Exercise & Health, 4*(2), 244–264.

Caddick, N. & Smith, B. (2014). The impact of sport and physical activity on the well-being of combat veterans: A systematic review. *Psychology of Sport & Exercise, 15*(1), 9–18.

Cooper, R.A., Pasquina, P.F. & Drach, R. (2013). *Warrior transition leader: Medical rehabilitation handbook.* Houston, TX: Borden Institue/Government Printing Office.

Cottingham, M., Carroll, M.S., Phillips, D., Karadakis, K., Gearity, B.T. & Drane, D. (2014). Development and validation of the motivation scale for disability sport consumption. *Sport Management Review, 17*(1), 49 –64.

Cruickshank, A. & Collins, D. (2012). Culture change in elite sport performance teams: Examining and advancing effectiveness in the new era. *Journal of Applied Sport Psychology, 24*(3), 338–355.

Fitzgerald, H. (2013). *The coaching chain: Reflections of disabled athletes and coaches. A report for sports coach UK. Research institute for sport, physical activity and leisure.* Leeds Metropolitan University. Retrieved from: http://www.sportscoachuk.org/sites/default/files/Reflections%20of%20 disabled%20atheltes_0.pdf

Frontiera, J. (2010). Leadership and organizational culture transformation in professional sport. *Journal of Leadership & Organizational Studies, 17*(1), 71–86.

Gustafsson, H., Hassmén, P. & Podlog, L. (2010). Exploring the relationship between hope and burnout in competitive sport. *Journal of Sports Sciences, 28*(14), 1495–1504.

Hawkins, B., Cory, A. & Crowe, B. (2011). Effects of participation in a Paralympic military sports camp on injured service members. *Therapeutic Recreation Journal, 45*(4), 309–325.

Hums, M.A., Moorman, A.M. & Wolff, E.A. (2003). The inclusion of the Paralympics in the Olympic and Amateur Sports Act: Legal and policy implications for integration of athletes with disabilities into the United States Olympic Committee and National Governing Bodies. *Journal of Sport & Social Issues, 27*(3), 261–275.

Kidman, L. & Hanrahan, S.J. (2010). *The coaching process: A practical guide to becoming an effective sports coach*. London: Routledge.

McCarthy, P.J. (2011). Positive emotion in sport performance: current status and future directions. *International Review of Sport & Exercise Psychology, 4*(1), 50–69.

Martin, J. J. & Whalen, L. (2014). Effective practices of coaching disability sport. *European Journal of Adapted Physical Activity, 7*(2), 13–23.

Messinger, S.D. (2013). Sports, disability, and the reframing of the post-injury soldier. In N. Warren & L. Menerson (eds) *Reframing disability and quality of life* (pp. 163–178). Dordrecht: Springer Netherlands.

Misener, L. & Darcy, S. (2014). Managing disability sport: From athletes with disabilities to inclusive organisational perspectives. *Sport Management Review, 17*(1), 1–7.

Purdue, D.E. & Howe, P.D. (2012). Empower, inspire, achieve:(dis) empowerment and the Paralympic Games. *Disability & Society, 27*(7), 903–916.

Shapiro, D.R., Pitts, B.G., Hums, M. A. & Calloway, J. (2012). Infusing disability sport into the sport management curriculum. *Choregia, 8*(1), 101–118.

Silvers, A. & Wasserman, D. (2000). Convention and competence: Disability rights in sports and education. *Society, 37*(1) ,63–67.

Tawse, H., Bloom, G.A., Sabiston, C.M. & Reid, G. (2012). The role of coaches of wheelchair rugby in the development of athletes with a spinal cord injury. *Qualitative Research in Sport, Exercise & Health, 4*(2), 206–225.

Wagstaff, C., Fletcher, D. & Hanton, S. (2012). Positive organizational psychology in sport: An ethnography of organizational functioning in a national sport organization. *Journal of Applied Sport Psychology, 24*(1), 26–47.

Wolff, A. (2011). Prosthetics: Between man and machine. *Sports Illustrated, 115*(5), 50–53.

Editors' summary reflections

Campbell's articulation of Darling's experiences highlights a number of concerns shared among coaches working in high performance sport contexts (e.g. challenges with coach education pathways, resourcing, sustainability, programme management and talent identification). Such issues may form part of coaches' collective experiences, however, Darling's work within Para-rowing in the United States illustrates that for coaching in disability sport many of these issues are exacerbated, complicated and/or more nuanced. For example, limited resourcing and administrative support constrain opportunities for talent identification and the ability to overcome geographic barriers to support regular participation, competition and athlete development initiatives. Furthermore, high performance disability sport coaches working in some settings (at least in Darling's case) are confronted with unique challenges precipitated by the nature of their work and specific needs of athletes whose development and performance they support. Persistent terminology differences and distinctions among regional and national governing bodies, the lack of clear guidelines for high performance pathways from the international federation, and a lack of coaching and disability expertise, for example, have all influenced how Darling (not unlike other coaches represented in this book) fulfils his roles as a coach. The lack of government support and lottery funding (available to coaches within the United Kingdom, Australia, New Zealand and elsewhere) have also contoured Darling's coaching concerns and compounded the pressures he faces in ensuring high performance targets (for example, for the Rio 2016 Olympic Games) are successfully achieved.

As Campbell reveals, Darling has responded to these challenges and issues in a number of ways. The establishment of a supportive team culture appear, for Darling, instrumental in implementing a successful coaching programme. Such a culture is not only central to ensuring the effectiveness of the coaching programme and associated performance maxims, but also the efficiency and sustainability of organisational structures of the sport; which, in Tom's case (and in the case of other sports represented in this book) often rely on the most minimal of staff and financial support. Engendering a supportive culture within Para-rowing has also been made possible by Tom and his colleagues actively facilitating community engagement in the sport around the country, harnessing the generosity, goodwill and drive of volunteers, and seeking out avenues for partnership building to enable the sport to grow and develop. One effective mechanism in this regard, and perhaps reflective of the vitality of the military–sport–industry complex operating within the United States (Batts & Andrews, 2011), has been the connections established with the military services around the country. While the recruitment of soldiers with a disability into elite sport is not necessarily novel, Darling's story suggests that such a partnership can work in terms of fulfilling both talent identification and participation objectives. In addition to partnerships, one useful mechanism (born out of geographic adversities) has been the development of simple, straight-forward communication strategies (e.g. basic programmes communicated over email) which have aided Darling's ability to respond to the technical and physiological needs of his athletes and also manage expectations over the course of an athlete's sporting career.

Darling's responses may not, we recognise, be particularly unique to the general high performance setting or other peers working with disability athletes at this level. As we are beginning to discover, many coaches do not, necessarily, choose disability sport or even high performance sport as a career pathway. At least, as the case studies of Bates, Dantas, Sawicki and others demonstrate, high performance disability sport coaching is often an employment opportunity that follows personal passion, a conviction to the sport and its athletes, and/or a dedication to the coaching profession more generally. Darling is no different in this regard and his passion and commitment to the sport and to his athletes is a theme reiterated and shared by some of the coaches. Darling's excerpts crystallise, however, that an empathetic approach (characterised by humility, compassion, perseverance, generosity and determination) is a fundamental attribute for those working in the high performance sector (Annerstedt & Lindgren, 2014). While empathy matters, high performance disability sport coaches must also complement this with quite idiosyncratic technical expertise, pedagogical proficiency, a breadth and depth of medical knowledge, and a strong business acumen. As such, Darling's experiences, Campbell also importantly highlights, prompt us to consider whether the role of the coach at this level may necessitate a rethink.

Constant redefinition/conceptualisation of 'the coach', outcome-orientated demands driven by governing body funding, and the related complicated specifics regarding qualifying particular athletes for particular boats and particular events, for example, may be symptomatic of a shift in focus from (primarily athlete-centred) head coaching to (predominantly externally driven) performance directing. Such a shift, we acknowledge, may have already come to pass in able-bodied high performance sporting contexts. Yet Darling's story indicates that contemporaries in disability sport may be still engaged or about to engage in this transition. What might matter most is for disability and Para-sport programmes (within universities and those supported by national and international federations) to more readily recognise these concerns within their education initiatives, and better prepare and resource coaches for the challenges they may be confronted with and the numerous and varied roles the high performance contexts may require them to fulfil (Cushion et al., 2003).

References

Annerstedt, C. & Lindgren, E-C. (2014). Caring as an important foundation in coaching for social sustainability: A case study of a successful Swedish coach in high-performance sport. *Reflective Practice*, *15*(1), 27–39.

Batts, C. & Andrews, D. (2011). 'Tactical Athletes': The United States Paralympic military program and the mobilization of the disabled soldier/athlete. *Sport in Society*, *14*(5), 553–568.

Cushion, C.J., Armour, K.M. & Jones, R.L. (2003). Coach education and continuing professional development: Experience and learning to coach. *Quest*, *55*(3), 215–230.

3

COACHING ACROSS THE SPECIES BARRIER

Para-equestrian dressage

Georgina Holmes

Historical context of para-equestrian dressage

Equestrian sport has three Olympic disciplines: dressage, showjumping and eventing, of which only dressage is also a Paralympic discipline. Historically a competition for commissioned military officers to demonstrate the effective training of their battle steeds, the Olympic dressage competition became open to non-military riders in 1952.

At the Helsinki Olympics in 1952, Danish rider Lis Hartels participated in the dressage competition. Not only not a commissioned military officer, Ms Hartels was obviously also a woman – and, having had polio in 1944, she had limited use of her lower legs, arms and hands – therefore also being classified (in modern terms) as disabled. Lis Hartels won the individual silver medal and did so again at the 1956 Stockholm Olympics, thus establishing participation in equestrian sport on equal terms by women and men as well as proving disability need not be a barrier to successful equestrianism.

It was forty years later, in 1996, before dressage was given status as a Paralympic discipline and it swiftly became an area of strength for British sport. Team GB demonstrated the strength in its tradition and support for para-equestrian riders by winning team gold at every Olympic, World and European Championship since the sport of para-equestrian dressage began. Team GB dominated the London 2012 Paralympic Games achieving fourteen medals: five individual gold, five individual silver, one individual bronze and team gold. This chapter focusses on the career and philosophy of one coach who has been instrumental in achieving this success.

Participation in para-equestrian has increased across the world since Lis Hartels' victories and it is currently recognised as a mainstream sport in many countries. The benefits of horse riding as therapy for people with disabilities are well known (Bizub et al., 2003; Davies et al., 2009, amongst others) and many national organisations have established development pathways from therapy to sport for their riders. In the UK, the vast majority of opportunities are provided by the Riding for the Disabled Association (RDA), which spans the progression and provides competition opportunities for riders of all levels as well as coaching qualifications and training programmes. All of Team GB's para-equestrians at London 2012 began their riding careers with RDA. RDA is a member body of the British Equestrian Federation and works closely with British Dressage for coaching and competition through to higher and elite levels.

The RDA provides opportunities for people with disabilities to experience all kinds of equestrian activity, including driving, vaulting and showjumping as well as dressage. Their activities depend upon the level of ability and the instructor's assessment of potential risk as well as available horses and facilities. However, a competitive structure at international level exists only for para-dressage. This is primarily due to the perceived 'safer' nature of dressage riding, which does not involve the explosive thrust of the horse leaving the ground to jump fences, reduces the risk of falling and can be done at much lower speed than jumping. A rider's classification will dictate the paces at which they compete – the highest classifications (most disabled, in para-equestrian known as Grade 1A) competing walk-only tests, whilst the lowest (Grade IV) have trot and canter exercises in their tests.

There are World and Regional Championships run on a four-year cycle for both dressage and para-dressage, alongside the Olympic and Paralympic cycle.

Participation in Paralympic equestrian events has grown steadily since 1996; from 61 athletes (16 participating nations, 15 male and 46 females) in 1996 to 78 athletes (27 nations, 22 male and 56 females) in 2012 (Official Website of the Paralympic Movement). The growth in the number of participating nations is particularly encouraging for the inclusiveness of the sport although this necessarily means much greater competition for athlete places in the event. Equestrian is demanding of space for exercising horses as well as stabling, making the expansion of athlete numbers unpopular with competition organisers. Additionally, the time taken by the competition, which comprises separate individual and team tests for each athlete, mean that it is not possible to significantly increase the number of athletes participating in major championships. Nevertheless, the expansion of international participation at elite level is a positive trend in the sport.

Both RDA and British Dressage are fully signed up to the UK Coaching Certificate framework and require their accredited coaches to follow the structured training programmes towards certification (up to UKCC Level 3 in each case) in order to be recognised as RDA or British Dressage coaches. There are plans (at April 2015) to develop a specific framework for para-equestrian coaches. This is a departure from the equine industry's traditional approach of instructor training, which has focussed on the acquisition of technical skill. The UKCC has slowly gained traction in the industry, although there remains tension and overlap between the traditional (British Horse Society) qualifications and the UKCC, perhaps reducing the perceived value of both.

Reflecting the interrelated nature of therapy and sport, Clive Milkins, the subject of this chapter, has long held a role as manager of one of the largest RDA centres in the UK, providing riders of all levels with the opportunity to develop their skill. The advantage such centres provides is that they have access to a wide variety of horses and ponies on which potential high performance riders are able to develop their skills. It is within this framework that Clive and Sophie Christiansen OBE met and developed their strong and successful relationship: a relationship that would see Sophie moved from potential talent to repeat Olympic champion in the course of just a few years.

Sophie Christiansen OBE: Profile

- Team GB's most outstanding para-equestrian at London 2012 with three gold medals.
- Winner of individual gold and silver plus team gold at Paralympic Games in Beijing 2008.
- Winner of individual bronze medal at the Paralympic Games in Athens 2004, aged 16.
- Winner of three gold medals at 2005 European Para Dressage Championships.
- Individual gold and bronze medallist at the 2007 World Para Dressage Championships.
- Awarded an MBE in 2009 for services to disabled sport and then promoted to OBE in 2012.
- Individual gold and silver medallist and team gold medallist at 2009 European Para Dressage Championships.
- Individual gold and silver medallist and team silver medallist at 2011 European Para Dressage Championships.

(Source: British Dressage)

Historical context of Clive Milkins

Clive Milkins FRDA, BHS Int. Teach, ANCEBM

Professional Qualifications:
- 1988: National Certificate in Horse Management
- 1989: Advanced Nat. Cert. in Equine Business Management
- 1992: British Horse Society Intermediate Teaching Test
- 1999: Riding for the Disabled Association (RDA) Senior Coach
- 2008: UKCC Sports Coach Level 3
- 2009: Neuro Linguistic Programming Coach Practitioner
- 2012: Fellow of RDA
- 2013: RDA Level 3 Showjumping Coach

Awards:
- 2006: Frank Howell Award for Outstanding Past Student at Warwickshire College
- 2008: Buckinghamshire County Council, Coach of the Year
- 2008: British Dressage Volunteer of the Year

- 2010/12: Graduate of UK Sport Elite Coaching Programme
- 2012: Inducted to the UK Sport Hall of Fame
- 2012: Mussabini Coaching Award
- 2012: Horse and Country Television Unsung Hero Award

Nominated for:
- 2006: Queens Award for Equestrianism
- 2006: Kuster Groom of the Year

Case study of Clive Milkins

Developing an interest in coaching

Clive has no equine connection in his family background, and only started riding aged 13. He says there was no particular reason for wanting to ride – but given the choice between watching his newly relegated football team for another season and a new hobby; he fancied learning to sit on a horse. Riding quickly became a passion, and a formal education through the British Horse Society followed as soon as he could leave school. Many highly respected figures in the British horse world contributed to his education, and he considers himself privileged to have worked with experts who were generous with their time and expertise as well as pushing him to become the best he could be. He benefitted from always having 'someone to go to' and never being left on his own. During his early career, Clive gained general coaching and teaching experience through his time at an equine college. Despite 'hating' teaching practice, he was encouraged to begin teaching disabled riders and soon discovered the challenges of coaching for the Riding for the Disabled Association. Involvement with their teams followed until he was a travelling coach with the international team. However, fate dealt him a blow at a competition when he was badly injured by a loose horse. He was left with epilepsy and a head injury, the consequences of which ultimately led him to have a nervous breakdown.

His former mentors stood by him and helped his recovery through a structured and supported return to coaching. At this time, he became involved with the South Bucks RDA Group, gained his first 'elite' rider and began regularly coaching for National and International Championships. The particularities of equestrian sport, as explored below, meant that many of the elite para-riders came through the South Bucks centre during this period and Clive was able to further develop his coaching through working with these talented athletes. As Collins et al. (2013) suggest, just like athletes, coaches have to go through a maturation process to develop their style and expertise. Clive credits this period as being formative in his growth as a coach.

Without that experience of the accident, Clive says he would not have been so motivated to work with people with disability long term. He knew he would be a riding instructor or possibly a lecturer at an agricultural college. Teaching disabled athletes had never crossed his mind. He discovered the talent for it before he had his injury, and he was 'spotted' by his mentors long before he started teaching. He credits the 'process' of his life events as offering him the opportunities which have helped him to grow into the person he is today and says he wouldn't change anything, in spite of the personal challenges he has had to overcome to achieve his success.

His accident gave him first-hand experience of living a life dependent on legal drugs to function, the frustration that comes with injury and the challenges that this brings, especially related to psychological issues. He feels this has empowered him to work more effectively with athletes with cerebral palsy and head injuries especially because he has experienced challenges similar to those such athletes face. Discussing this, he suggested 'You would never say to somebody without legs, "Kick it!" [the horse], because the limb disability is obvious. When you have somebody that is neurologically impaired, it is very difficult to explain to other people what that means'.

Asked whether his rider winning so many international medals made him more comfortable in his own skin, he agreed. That has made him passionate about coaching and helping young people – and in the future he sees himself getting more involved with charity work, coaching and coach mentoring across other sports using the legacy of the equestrian work he's done.

Acknowledging what every competitive equestrian knows, but often fails to appreciate, the factors that differentiate equestrian from any other sport are related to the unique conditions faced by coaches in equestrian sport: the athlete is in fact a unit made up of two sentient beings, one human and one equine. The training required to succeed at any level of equestrian sport is made all the more fascinating because it requires both horse and rider to reach their mental and physical peak at the same time. The 'perfect' equestrian athlete should appear to be one body – that is, two beings moulded into one unit, performing without visible communication and in complete harmony. Training a horse to perform at international level takes a minimum 6–7 years of consistent skill and strengthening work, time and relationship building, whilst 'learning to ride' is a process that never stops, due to the individual nature, size, shape and movement of each horse a rider rides. Certainly, the level of learning becomes more and more refined as the athlete develops more experience and skill – but no elite rider works without a trainer (technical skill) as well as a coach (mental preparation). For some people, those complementary skills are found in the one person, for many they represent diverse skillsets which often require two people on the team of an elite equestrian, sometimes more.

Reflecting on this dichotomy, Clive speaks of the example of athletes from other sports who have moved into coaching, citing the example of Chris Newton, 'a great cyclist and someone who is becoming a very good coach'. After the end of his international career, he went on coaching courses and learned the skill of coaching.

Talking to colleagues from other sports influences Clive's practice a great deal. Whether they are diving people, cycling people or football managers, he is open to learning from them and considers this exchange of knowledge an essential contributor to the growth of himself and others as coaches. He is comfortable trying techniques from other sports, and asserts that coaching is a generic technique, specialised only for the technical detail of the sport. However, he acknowledges the specificities of equestrian sport when he says:

> Horses get in the way of coaching – with a horse you have your own way of doing it and if the athlete doesn't buy into what you say, you pull the rider off and do it [ride the horse] yourself. We should be using the judges a lot, and looking at performances from the judge's perspective. But I think we sometimes become arrogant because the horses give us an excuse against other sports. Real professionalisation of coaching [as has happened in other professional sports] is unlikely to happen overall – we're here because of horses [rather than purely because of the competitive or sport aspect of the activity].

Coaching in elite environments

For Clive, much of the coaching relationship is about looking at goals and planning for the long term – the relationship with the athlete over-rides everything else. Long-term planning allows the development of athletes without excess pressure and this is an element that Clive feels many other coaches within equestrian miss. The development of the long-term athlete plan is fairly recent within the sport. Within equestrian there is a tension between coaching the athlete and developing the technical skill of the rider as well as the physical and technical development of the horse. You can't just coach the mental aspects of performance because you also have to develop the technical skill. Clive recounts how, when he worked with the cycling coaches on the ECAP course, he learned that they don't teach – 'once you can ride a bike, you can ride a bike' – but they have emphasised the exercise science aspects of training to find competitive advantage. In equestrian, professional support teams have become an essential part of the success of athletes just as in other sports; there is perhaps a more complicated structure due to the duopoly of athletic demand of the equestrian 'unit': for every professional required by the rider, there is likely to be a corresponding requirement for the horse. The coaching/training tension is part of this dynamic too.

Reflecting on his position as an 'elite' coach, Clive suggests that the role is not for everyone. Riders' competition schedules mean coaches spend a lot of time away from home – leaving their 'job' or business to function without them, challenging personal relationships and requiring a high level of focus to be constantly available and present for their riders. They need to be diplomats, cheerleaders, negotiators and disciplinarians, often at the same time. As an elite coach, Clive feels the need to balance all the demands on his rider, controlling their environment to allow them to perform at their peak, even though this may place high levels of demand on his capacity too. He therefore highly values the support he is able to receive from his network of colleagues, family and friends and is clear that they also contribute significantly to his success – and that of his riders.

Clive's coaching philosophy

'Perfect planning prevents poor performance'

Clive defines his approach to his coaching as 'non-academic', meaning more practical than theoretical, although he is clearly a reflective coach (Winfield et al., 2013). He collects anecdotes to repeat to riders about focus, attention, development and meeting goals. In a sport where every movement in a competition test is scored out of 10, with typical winning scores between 70 and 80 per cent, the question for each day's training is 'how do we turn that 6 into a 7 (or that 7 into an 8)?'. He asserts that you only win a gold medal on gold medal winning day – meaning that the rider and the coach must see all other competitions and training sessions as a means to an end. In a sport where there are very few 'invitational' competitions and riders pay to enter, athletes who must earn a living from their horses need to win competitions to sustain their reputation and showcase the horses they ride, many of which are for sale. To see every competition except the medalling competition as a training exercise therefore is a significant departure from the normal 'equestrian' mind-set – yet this is what he demands from his athletes.

Before the 2008 Olympics, where the equestrian events took place in Hong Kong, Clive researched the climate and conditions for the competition and ensured he and Sophie were prepared for the heat and humidity – spending the summer in overheated houses, riding and training wearing several layers of clothes to mimic the climate they would meet at the competition. He notes that equestrian is the only sport in which athletes do not train in the same equipment as they compete in – casual riding wear is cooling, technical and in line with modern sportswear; competition dress requires formal coats which are dark in colour and often made from wool, formal shirt and tie (for the men) or cravat (for the ladies) and long, stiff leather boots designed to protect from iron-clad hooves and an enemy's sword rather than to allow the wearer to remain comfortable. Clive's approach of mimicking climatic conditions reflects contemporary thinking in the equestrian sports which have invested heavily in understanding methods of cooling horses and riders during and after competition. Leading trainers and coaches emphasise the importance of regularly using 'competition wear' to ensure that it is comfortable and familiar to the athlete. However, for many riders their competition wear is expensive, hard to maintain, seen as their 'best kit' and therefore only comes out during competition. Part of Clive's focus on preparation is to reduce this behaviour and ensure that all equipment is regularly used and familiar to both horse and rider.

Clive's background in equestrian eventing and early work experiences taught him to be ready for all eventualities and to take no chances with regard to equipment failure. He insists on planning every minute in the run-up to a competition, carrying several sets of spare equipment and attempting to control everything his rider and horse will experience before the competition. His approach echoes psychological management techniques which talk about 'controlling the controllables'. He plans 'obsessively', using graphs and sheets to plot the goals of the rider, planning to achieve that goal. He says,

> this is about the riders, but I could never let a rider down because I have a cold or can't cope with the heat

and continues

> Sophie won the medals. In order to help her with the medals, I had to give as big a performance as she did. I always have done, and I've been very lucky that I've been able to. As a coach you do have to deliver a performance and get yourself to a place physically and mentally when you're able to do that.

His commitment to supporting his riders in every way possible includes long-term planning over the competition cycle to include World and European Championships as well as the Olympics. His attention to detail encompasses an obsessive approach to routine and dedication, citing the example of 1980s decathlete Daley Thompson who was quoted as saying that he trained five times on Christmas Day because his key rival would only train four times. Although it is the rider who has to post the performance in the arena, Clive understands the role of the coach as the interlocutor between outside factors – both positive and negative – and the athlete, which protects the athlete and allows them to do what they have to do in order to win. The coach provides the environment for that performance to occur. This might be by creating space for the athlete to mentally prepare for competition, by supporting the athlete in training and living patterns to create best performance or by acting as mediator between the athlete and governing bodies, sponsors, competition organisers or family, for instance. The approach is commonly seen in other sports but the often fragmented nature of support teams for horse and rider in equestrian means such an integrated support role is rarely seen in equestrian.

Working with verbal pictures is important for Clive. As an example, he says,

> Coaching is like a jigsaw puzzle – how do we create the picture? Make the frame (lifestyle, career, culture, background) then collect all different pieces of the puzzle – put them together, realise there are blocks of pieces, can then take the more complicated pieces to put them together and then step back and realise what each bit represents. It's filling in the bits at the very end that balance everything else – they are the bits that make the picture. That image is a very strong one – how you put it all together to make what you want. I see the coach and coach's mentor as being the conductor or the chef, the person that orchestrates. They must know what the rider really wants to do. Understanding that allows coach to create process to get to success. To oversee the whole arrangement [organising the structures for the athlete] is the coach-mentor's role.

Citing Adrian Moorhouse as an inspiration, Clive identifies his philosophy of coaching as 'I want to be the best I can be with the talent that I have on any given day'. He asks, 'am I delivering the world-class performance as a coach every time I walk in the arena?', and says 'I believe my role is to create the environment where excellence is perceived as the norm. Coaching is a performance in the same way as standing on a stage and delivering a Shakespeare soliloquy. Be quiet and say less'. He works with 'bullet points', which he believes allows riders to better concentrate on what he is saying. He says this comes from working long term with riders so they understand what he means with the shorthand terms that develop in his vocabulary. Like any specialist discipline, there is a great deal of technical 'jargon' in equestrian; however, there are often several interpretations of words, so ensuring that coach and athlete understand each the same way enhances clear communication.

Clive's riders all get homework, and send him reports on their riding regularly, allowing him to make sure they understand what they are doing and why – so they are more likely to be able to replicate successful actions and patterns of training in the future, especially if circumstances dictate that they must ride without the coach there some of the time. With Sophie, Clive says that was never an issue: 'Sophie never rode unless I was there', but for many of the riders in his current role as Hong Kong para-equestrian coach, it is not possible for him to be present every time every rider rides and therefore he has had to develop these methods to encourage independent of learning.

Sport specific concerns and trajectories

Horses bring a unique dynamic to the athlete–coach relationship. The question which needs to stay at the forefront of any coach's mind is, 'are we coaching athletes or are we coaching the athlete–horse unit?' This draws on the differentiation between the traditional teaching approaches in the industry and modern coaching qualifications, referred to above, and is a key challenge for coaches in equestrian. Some coaches therefore focus more on the technical aspects of the horses' development; others, like Clive, follow a route through coach development, NLP and athlete-specific skills to work in a more holistic, team-focussed manner. Both have a role to play in the success of a rider.

As well as his focus on the athlete, Clive's expertise is putting the partnership together. Janeiro 6, Sophie's most successful horse to date, was a failed Grand Prix horse which was offered for sale to Clive by its trainer as a potential para-horse. Known to have a difficult temperament, Clive considers he took 'a hell of a risk' buying him for Sophie but was convinced that he and Sophie could produce the horse's talent to win at London 2012. This kind of faith in his decisions is typical of Clive's goal-focussed approach to coaching – he knew the talents of his rider, could spot the necessary predisposition in the horse and was confident in his ability to combine the two to produce a stated outcome. In this sense, Clive frames himself as an 'expert coach' (Berliner, 1994).

When asked whether there are enough coaches in para-equestrian, Clive demurs. He laments that many young people in the industry now don't have that structure of support and mentoring, although he notes the value of Facebook in providing a way of swapping material between coaches and varying sports, suggesting that such exchange has immense value in the development of effective coaching techniques. Such informal learning approaches are recognised in coaching theory and validated in other sports (Wright et al., 2007). He expressed the view that his background in multiple equestrian sports and the brain injury he experienced have given him a wide-reaching understanding of the para-rider, which others cannot share. He has concerns that the pressure put on para-riders may lead to higher-risk decisions being made about the suitability of horses – especially as the standard of competition increases with every major championship and the pressure for funding a very expensive sport also increases:

> We don't need more elite coaches, we need more elite advice. We only have ten elite riders in this country. It's very interesting that [World Class schemes] Start & Potential have set their benchmark on international level; that may not be the wrong thing, but it means every year they lose more riders who aren't coping with the pressure. Where are the kids coming from? We don't want elite coaches unless they are going to learn to build people up.

Instead, he says, more support teams are needed – people who understand disability sport – and more judges to support the growth of the sport.

Clive says the biggest issue in para-equestrian for Team GB currently is 'pressure'. With the history it has of near total domination of the sport, Team GB is expected to win every time they go out. But even more than other sports, equestrian is unpredictable, with many variable factors in performance, not least of which is the involvement of the horse. The nations which are growing their para-equestrian teams are investing heavily in horses, training and support. This is a good thing for the future of the sport, but some people are expressing concern that increasing pressure and performance levels also increase the risk of physical injury as horses become more powerful and highly-strung at higher levels of fitness and ability.

Para-equestrian has an approach to coaching which is very different to any other sport. In the majority of instances, there are shared coaches, funding, centres and competitions with able-bodied athletes. It also has its roots in therapy, like swimming. However, the profile of athletes is now changing – there are now fewer neurological problems seen, and more limb impairment, accidents and acquired neurological conditions such as multiple sclerosis. Clive fears that this change may cause the sport to change and lose the inclusivity which has always marked it out as something special in the sporting world.

Conclusions

Undoubtedly, many people have played a role in supporting Team GB's para-equestrian team to the huge success it has achieved to date. Clive Milkins has been a very influential part of that success through his association with Sophie Christiansen as well as other elite riders who came through South Bucks RDA. At the time of writing, however (2015), he has recently moved on to work in Hong Kong as manager and coach for the Chinese para-equestrian team. Reflecting his strong belief in personal growth and evolution – a belief which is clearly demonstrated through his approach to coaching – he intends this next period to allow him to create space to refine his identity further and explore the development of his coaching techniques. His career has gone from coaching to athlete team management and he is open to the possibilities of involvement in other activities as an offshoot of coaching and management in the future.

Recommendations for para-equestrian coaching, education and practice

Equestrian sport has always considered itself to be 'different' to other sports, and in many ways this view can be defended. Inevitably, however, a position of difference may also be a position of weakness and it is this that has led the British Equestrian Federation – as well as other international federations – to increasingly attempt to identify the similarities between their sport and others. With its roots in therapy rather than pure competitiveness, para-equestrian has a broad appeal. In terms of coach development and education, this gives a wide remit for skill requirements and – as highlighted in the sections above – there are considerable variations in skills for technical instructors, horse trainers and rider coaches.

The equestrian industry as a whole has embraced the UKCC programme in recent years and as work continues on a specific para-equestrian qualification, we look forward to seeing the growth of a strong base of para-coaches, some of whom will have the personal qualities and tenacity Clive speaks of to enable them to move to elite ranks. Additionally, the use of the UK Sport's Elite Coaching Apprenticeship Programme (ECAP) enhances the development of established coaches and encourages cross-fertilisation of ideas between sports. It is clear from talking to Clive how much benefit he gained from this programme in the language he uses and the examples he gives of his coaching. In a time of change for UK para-equestrian, where their dominant competitive position is increasingly being challenged, it is vitally important that the pool of coaches is continuously enhanced and new horse and rider combinations identified and encouraged.

Clive's contention that para-equestrian coaches must learn from the experiences of coaches in other sports is – in the view of the author – a very important contribution. His use of information technology to share ideas, encouragement and thinking is an example of open and transparent practice which is sadly not common enough in this sport currently.

Another factor which loomed large in the author's conversation with Clive for this chapter was the suggestion that the elite sport may be developing into one predominantly for athletes with acquired disability rather than birth disability. There are no statistics yet to support or negate this suggestion, but it may be an area which requires further research to consider the effect of intense competitive pressure as well as disability classification on the future of disability sport.

An issue of concern raised in this chapter is the influence of pressure on athletes and the concomitant risk of injury due to 'over-horsing' riders or over-preparation of the horses by able-bodied riders who train the horses to levels of energy and power which the para-rider may not be able to contain or sit to. Ultimately, horses are unpredictable, big and strong – and even the best, strongest and most able riders often fall off. This is one factor amongst many that makes equestrian a lifetime passion for many, but there should perhaps be caution sounded regarding the safety element of competition. In this regard, coaches must remain mindful of the limitations of their riders, ensuring – as all try to do at all times – that safety comes before success. This issue has clear parallels with sailing and many winter sports, for instance, where the sport deals with inherently unpredictable elements such as the weather conditions – but perhaps forms a discussion and learning point for wider deliberation in disability sport.

Although often seen as a 'minority' sport, there is no denying the importance of para-equestrian to Team GB's results and its role in creating opportunities for disabled people to experience more freedom, opportunity and competition at all levels. At an elite level, clearly para-equestrian has already got a great deal right. The challenge for the sport going forward is to harness all that is good about the sport and its heritage whilst utilising the technical, theoretical and academic progress being made in the world of coaching as a whole. The specifics of equestrian sport make it an interesting environment for coaching development, and demonstrate the need for translation of generic skills to particular environments. Given the progress in coaching development over the last few years, the increasing opportunities and funding available to talented coaches and athletes and the history of success for para-equestrian, the future looks very bright indeed.

Additional resources and supplementary material

Information about the UK Coaching Certificate in equestrian is available from this website (accessed 22/12/2015): http://www.equestrian-qualifications.org.uk/sports-coaching-uk-coaching-certificates.html

Further information about dressage, para-equestrian and coaching is available on the National Governing Body website: www.britishdressage.co.uk

Information about riding for people with disabilities is available from Riding for the Disabled Association: www.rda.org.uk

References

Berliner, D.C. (1994). Expertise: The wonder of exemplary performances. In Mangieri, J. & Block, C. (eds) *Creating powerful thinking in coaches and athletes: Diverse perspectives.* FortWorth, Texas: Harcourt Brace College.

Bizub, A., Joy, A. & Davidson, L. (2003). 'It's like being in another world': Demonstrating the benefits of therapeutic horseback riding for individuals with psychiatric disability. *Psychiatric Rehabilitation Journal, 26*(4), 377–384. http://dx.doi.org/10.2975/26.2003.377.384

British Dressage: rider biographies. Available at http://www.britishdressage.co.uk/our_ teams [accessed 27/7/2015].

Collins, D., Trower, J. & Cruickshank, A. (2013). *Coaching high performance athletes and the high performance team*. In Sotiraiadou, P. & de Bosscher, V. (eds) *Managing high performance sport*. Abingdon: Routledge.

Davis, E., Davies, B., Wolfe, R., Raadsveld, R., Heine, B., Thomason, P., Dobson, F. & Graham, H.K. (2009). A randomized controlled trial of the impact of therapeutic horse riding on the quality of life, health, and function of children with cerebral palsy. *Developmental Medicine & Child Neurology, 51*(2), 111–119.

Jones, R. (ed) (2006). *The sports coach as educator: Reconceptualising sports coaching*. Abingdon: Routledge.

Kidman, L. (ed) (2005). *Athlete-centred coaching: Developing inspired and inspiring people*. Christchurch, New Zealand: Innovative Print Communications.

Official Website of the Paralympic Movement http://www.paralympic.org/results/ historical [accessed 29/4/2015].

Winfield, J., Wiliams, J. & Dixon, M. (2013). The use of reflective practice to support mentoring of elite equestrian coaches. *International Journal of Evidence Based Coaching and Mentoring, 11*(1), 162–178.

Wright, T., Trudel, P. & Culver, D. (2007). Learning how to coach: The different learning situations reported by youth ice hockey coaches. *Physical Education and Sport Pedagogy, 12*(2), 127–144.

Editors' summary reflections

The case study of Milkins demonstrates that while the issues for coaches within para-equestrian sport are comparable with contemporaries working in other disability sport contexts (see the other chapters in this book for example), the very presence of the horse (and, specifically, the implications that this has for coaching) makes it a unique site for examination (Wolframm, 2014). In the first instance, para-equestrian coaches, who at least in Milkins' case have emerged via Riding for the Disabled Associations, have had similar experiences vis-à-vis serendipitous entrances into the sport, ad hoc coaching development and educational opportunities, struggles over resourcing, talent identification and development, and managing and sustaining high performance programmes in light of organisational imperatives and funding maxims. Yet while this has formed the coaching backdrop, as Holmes demonstrates, what makes Milkins' day-to-day work as a coach different is that he must also manage the horse. While the focus is on the athlete and their performance, the horse is an intrinsic part of the coach–athlete relationship. Indeed, Milkins suggests that getting the 'right' horse with performance potential is a key part of a creating an effective coaching environment. Moreover, that as the pressure within para-equestrian sport to continuously meet performance objectives increases, and as part of maximising value for money in what is by nature a very expensive sport, this partnership between horse and rider has become particularly paramount. Not unlike environmental conditions or equipment, horses can be unpredictable. This, too, can place added pressure on coaches and their athletes. For the para-equestrian coaches, the dynamics of coach–athlete–horse triad is part and parcel of the sport. However, as Milkins' experiences help to highlight, these horse-related complexities are perhaps not necessarily well acknowledged or understood outside of the sport or within the formal coaching education and development pathways.

Milkins' case is revealing in not only demonstrating how personal trajectories and experiences shape a coach's approach to their work, but also, how the coach's pedagogical development is borne out of informal and formal opportunities and frameworks (Rynne & Mallett, 2012). Milkins' story also, more specifically, raises questions about how well placed equestrian sport is to deal with its future. In particular, for example, how might national governing bodies and centralised funding schemes respond to the pleas of those within the para-equine industry to provide economic and development support? Given the noted shifts in the types of athletes now entering the sport (e.g. less neurological conditions and more limb impairment), in what ways might coach education programmes need to adapt? How might interdisciplinary, in addition to multi-sport, knowledge sharing and expertise be fostered within coaching pathways? How, too, are the split imperatives of high performance and participation/inclusion negotiated amid evermore commercial sport funding climates?

The need to address some of these sorts of specificities of coaching para-equestrian sport, and attempt to fortify the quality of coaching frameworks across all levels of riding for the disabled, have precipitated an industry move writ large toward improving coaches' engagement with national accreditation programmes and, specifically, knowledge and expertise sharing opportunities. Programmes such as UK Sport's Elite Coaching Apprenticeship Programme (ECAP), which as Holmes details encourages interaction among established coaches within and across varied sporting spheres, provide one example of interdisciplinarity in coach education which might be fostered. Herein lies some encouragement for other disability sport organisations; particularly those who lack resourcing and support for coach development, suitable networks or connections within their specific sports, or lack expertise in particular areas. Other case studies in this book, for example, have also raised the paucity of opportunities for sharing 'best' practices and the lack of provision of networks in which coaches' voices may be heard and given further agency. Schemes like ECAP might offer a mechanism in this regard.

However, such schemes are not yet universal, and (at least in the UK context) their existence remains predicated on the sustainability of government and/or national organisation funding whims and imperatives. Moreover, while it seems para-equestrian has made significant advances in terms of its profile and coach development beyond that of other sports, there is inevitably some scope to improve its investments in high performance. Within schemes like ECAP, for instance, there are possibilities for interdisciplinary discussion and education, however, the scheme is still by nature coach focused and there remains room to bring other parties, stakeholders, and significant others to the table from a range of disciplines. In so doing, formal coach education might be better tailored to the nuances of the sport, specificities of coaches' individual work, and the complexities of their athletes' lives.

References

Rynne, S.B. & Mallett, C.J. (2012). Understanding the work and learning of high performance coaches. *Physical Education and Sport Pedagogy*, *17*(5), 507–523.

Wolframm, I. (2014). *The science of equestrian sports: Theory, practice and performance of the equestrian rider*. New York: Routledge.

4

'JUST DOING IT'

A strength-based approach to coaching athletes

Tania Cassidy, Lisette Burrows, Raylene Bates and Joan Merrilees

Introduction

Nearly 30 years ago, DePauw (1986) highlighted that a research priority within disability sport was to understand the biography and development of coaches working with athletes with a disability. In the intervening years there has been increased attention on coach learning and development, yet there is still limited research on those coaches who work within the context of disability sport (McMaster et al., 2012) and even less focus on those coaches who work with elite athletes who have a disability (Tawse et al., 2012).

In the editorial for a Special Issue on the Paralympics and Disability Sport in *Qualitative Research in Sport, Exercise and Health* Smith (2012) suggests, 'when thinking about the Paralympics and disability sport, it is vital that the structural environment, history, disabled people's narratives, relationships, coaching experiences, motivation, emotions, impairment, the media, health policies and, for instance, everyday interactions with others are investigated' (2012: 174). In this chapter, we heed Smith's (2012) call, drawing predominantly on the perspective of one New Zealand track and field[1] coach; Raylene Bates. We agree with Smith (2012) in his desire for a more nuanced and holistic understanding of disabled sport and are hopeful that Raylene's narratives will afford a rich exposition of the personal, political, and of course, the inter-relational aspects of her life, contributing something to the mission Smith espouses above. In addition, we anticipate the narratives will contribute to a small but growing body of sports coaching literature that discusses and explores female coaches' work–life interface (Bruening et al., 2013), the emotional aspect of coaching (Cassidy et al., 2016; Nelson et al., 2014; Potrac & Marshall, 2011; Potrac et al., 2013) and the notion of the caring coach (Jones et al., 2004; Jones, 2009; Jones et al., 2013).

Historical context of athletics for athletes with a physical disability

International context

Athletics, initially in the form of a foot race, was part of the Ancient Olympic Games and was an event in the Games of the I Olympiad.[2] In the first half of the twentieth century some athletes with physical disabilities did compete in, and win gold medals at, the Olympic Games but not in athletics (Wallechinsky & Loucky, 2011). In 1924 the first ever games for athletes with a physical disability – the International Silent Games (now known as the Deaflympics[3]) – were held in Paris, France a few weeks after the city had hosted the 1924 Summer Olympic Games. Athletics was one of the seven inaugural events at these Games.

In 1948 an event, which was grandly called the World Wheelchair and Amputee Games, was run in Stoke Mandeville, England. At these 'Games', 16 participants competed in one sport – archery. The event was the initiative of Dr. Ludwig Guttmann, who had the aim of using sport to rehabilitate servicemen and women with spinal cord injuries.[4] The opening of these Games coincided with the opening day of the London 1948 Olympic Games and have subsequently been viewed as the precursor to the Paralympic Games. Yet it was to be another 12 years until the Paralympics were officially recognized. This occurred at the 1960 Stoke Mandeville Games, which were held in Rome and involved 400 athletes (with physical and visual disabilities), from 23 countries, competing in eight sports, one of which was athletics. Since then the Games have grown, so much so that at the 2012 London Paralympics 4, 237 athletes (with a wide range of physical disabilities) competed in 20 sports.

In the late 1980s and early 1990s various conversations were had, and agreements made, between the International Paralympic Committee (IPC), the International Committee of Sports for the Deaf, the Special Olympics movement and the International Olympic Committee (IOC). One structural alignment that did occur during this time was an agreement that the Olympic and Paralympic Games would be hosted in the same cities, just weeks apart. A consequence of this structural alignment is that some countries have increased the resources (coaching, technological and financial) for para-sport and able-bodied sport in their high performance systems.

National context

The integration of para-sport and able-bodied sport in New Zealand has had an inconsistent history. There have been individual success stories, for example Neroli Fairhall, an archer from Christchurch, was the first paraplegic competitor to participate in an Olympic Games. She participated in the 1984 Los Angeles Olympic Games, having previously won a gold medal in archery at the 1982 Brisbane Commonwealth Games. However, at a systemic level, the integration has not always been so successful. In 2006, Athletics New Zealand (the national sport organization responsible for track and field events) made initial attempts to integrate para-athletes with able-bodied athletes yet failed to gain any traction at the high performance level. This was despite the 2002 Commonwealth Games including para-athletes as full members of their national teams, making them the first fully inclusive international multi-sport games. In 2011, the former Athletics Australia Para Athlete Manager, Scott Goodman, was appointed as High Performance Director for Athletics New Zealand. The appointment of Goodman provided opportunities for further discussions to be had, and practices to change, at the high performance level regarding the integration of para- and able-bodied athletes. The ability of Goodman to facilitate change reflects the literature, which highlights the importance of micropolitics and key agents to the change process, especially when change requires the 'reculturing' as well as 'restructuring' of institutions and/or organizations (Hargreaves, 1997; Sparkes, 1990).

An outcome of the discussions facilitated by Goodman is that Athletics New Zealand is the only sport in New Zealand to have its elite para-programmes embedded in the able-bodied model. Arguably the move taken by Athletics New Zealand to integrate the support for para- and able-bodied athletes reflects the message that Sport New Zealand[5] conveys, implicitly and explicitly, that the New Zealand sporting and coaching communities have to work smarter than their international counterparts if New Zealand athletes are to be successful on the world stage. High Performance Sport New Zealand (HPSNZ) funds para-athletics via Paralympics New Zealand, who then gives an allocation to Athletics New Zealand. A consequence of this is that Athletic NZ coaches, events, education opportunities, and facilities are shared between all athletes and coaches thereby providing para-athletes, and coaches of para-athletes, greater opportunities and resources (financial and human) than if they were under the Paralympics NZ organizational structure. Another example of what integration means in practice is that Athletics New Zealand supported and funded a combined pre-camp for all athletes competing at the 2012 London Olympics and Paralympics. No other sporting body in New Zealand did the same. However, a lack of segregation can have unintended negative consequences on resourcing. For example, able-bodied athletes get 'carded'[6] at higher levels than the para-athletes because there is acknowledgement that, for example, when a para-shot putter becomes a World Champion they do so in one of several classifications against a limited number of athletes, whereas when an able-bodied shot putter becomes a World Champion they do so in one open event against maybe a hundred competitors. Had the para- and able-bodied-athletes been segregated, and judged against different criteria, it is possible that the able-bodied and para- World Champions would have got the same level of support.

Historical context of Raylene Bates

Until 2015 Raylene had been a coach for 27 years as a volunteer. When Raylene began to coach she was in her early 20s and still a competitive athlete (a New Zealand champion in the throwing events – i.e., hammer, discus and shot put – as well as an Oceania champion in the latter two). Raylene's entrée into coaching was not a planned move, rather it began as a consequence of a parent asking her to help their 10-year-old son who had been selected to represent New Zealand at the Pacific School Games. At those Games the boy won two gold medals, and for the next 11 years Raylene coached him. He went on to represent New Zealand in the decathlon at a Commonwealth Games. Not long after Raylene began coaching the 10-year-old her own coach asked her to help him with his squad of athletes.

After her coaching exploits in the Pacific School Games, and whilst still holding dual roles as athlete and coach, Raylene was invited to attend her first international coaching conference in Adelaide. It was an International Association of Athletics Federations (IAAF) Level 3 Javelin Throwing course facilitated by Margaret and Fatima Whitbread. When Raylene reflects on her invitation to attend that conference she considers it must have been a huge gamble by the then Coaching Director of Athletics New Zealand. Yet it was a gamble that paid off because Raylene described the experience as the platform for her subsequent coaching career. Being immersed in an environment with world leading athletes and coaches for that week, testing her own knowledge, and taking the opportunities to learn when the chances presented themselves, Raylene was inspired to continue learning, immerse herself in coaching, and transfer her skills from being an athlete to a coach. Another factor influencing her decision to embark on coaching was the birth of her two sons, explaining that they 'were brought up on the side of a track … everywhere I went they came with me'.

During the past 27 years Raylene has coached athletes to World Championships and Paralympic Games, as well as having been a Team Leader/Manager at the Olympic Games. She is an IAAF Level 5 coach in Throws, an International Paralympic Committee (IPC) coach facilitator, and the Head Coach/Athletics New Zealand-High Performance Para Athlete Manager. She has also graduated with a Bachelor of Applied Management (Sport Management and Business Change & Transformation). Her current squad of athletes comprise para-athletes as well as able-bodied athletes, who specialize predominately in throwing events. In the squad there are male and female athletes, varying in age and abilities, with some of the athletes having attended Paralympic Games, and having won medals at IPC World Championships and Commonwealth Games. Raylene organizes the squad on sporting ability rather than disability or gender (i.e., 'carded' and international athletes train together, national athletes work as a group, and the secondary school athletes train together). She explained that she organizes the squad this way because she does not view the para-athletes as 'having a disability'. She went onto say that 'I encourage them to try things/exercises that able-bodied athletes do and if they physically can't, then I find a solution to enable it to be done'.

Raylene has achieved numerous local, national and international awards for her coaching and contribution to athletics, such as Athletics Otago Coach of the Year, recipient of the IAAF Award for Contribution to Athletics, an Athletics New Zealand Award for dedication and contribution to the High Performance Programme, and is a life member of her club and provincial association. During much of the time Raylene was a volunteer coach she was employed in various administrative roles, some of which have were in the sport sector in High Performance Sport. For example, Raylene was the Business Manager for the NZ Academy of Sport South Island, an IPC Coaching Advisory Committee member and acting High Performance Director for Athletics New Zealand.

Narratives

Raylene's way

As mentioned above, Raylene's current squad of athletes are diverse in age and gender and comprise para-athletes as well as able-bodied athletes, predominately specializing in throwing events. The way Raylene organizes the squad is based on sporting ability rather than sorting athletes into disability or gender categories. This organizational practice runs contra to that described in much of the disability and sport literature, where gender, age and 'disability' have served individually, or in tandem, to mark individuals as different and as 'outsiders' (DePauw, 1997; Morrison, 2011). There are no 'outsiders' in Raylene's squad, rather individuals of varying ability. Ability rather than disability fuels her decisions.

DePauw (1997) writes of the cultural, social role and structural marginality that disabled athletes have historically experienced. She provides a surfeit of examples of the exclusion of disabled people from sport and physical activity and her analyses are supported by those who have conducted empirical work in educational contexts with young people (e.g. Fitzgerald, 2006; Holland, 2010; Morrison, 2011). While young people in the aforementioned studies routinely report feeling marginalized by teachers and coaches on account of assumptions (often faulty) about their capacity to move, Raylene regards athletes as athletes. Indeed, as will become evident throughout this chapter, she rarely thinks about disability, nor permits her athletes to be 'othered' on account of their impairments. For decades disability advocates, critical education scholars and 'inclusion' researchers have been urging professionals and the public to see the person, not the disability (see Ainscow, 1997; Higgins & Ballard, 2000; MacArthur et al., 2007; Slee, 2007) and this is reflected in Raylene's attitude of just getting on with it and regarding her athletes as 'able'.

Purdue & Howe (2012: 194) describe the situation many elite disabled athletes find themselves in as a 'Paralympic paradox'. That is, on the one hand, able-bodied audiences can revel in the athleticism displayed by the para-athletes, with their prowess serving to dissolve distinctions routinely made between abled and disabled athletes and empower disabled athletes themselves. On the other hand, when an athlete's impairment is de-emphasized it conceivably alienates them from the so-called disabled audience and also may trigger questions from able-bodied audiences who wish to ensure athletes are credibly participating in disability sport competitions (Purdue & Howe, 2012). We have no sense of how Raylene's athletes feel about this paradox, whether they experience the dual pressures or not, nor whether Raylene's focus on 'ability' vs disability shapes their response to broader forces such as these. Nevertheless, we can speculate that Raylene's disposition toward her athletes and her reluctance to sift or sort them along impairment lines will yield some affect in terms of how her athletes come to regard themselves and view their engagement in high-level disabled sport. Perhaps her athletes, and those who view their performances, may be more likely than some to regard the sport and athlete with disability couplet (DePauw, 1997) as nothing out of the ordinary. In so saying, as Purdue & Howe (2012: 202) suggest, it would seem important to appreciate both sport and disability rather than risk a 'simplistic subordination of one by the other which further disenfranchises individuals who wish to partake in sport, including those elite athletes with a disability competing at the Paralympic Games'.

Raylene's narratives provide plenty of examples of poor resourcing of athletes whose impairments necessitate extra support, a phenomenon regularly unearthed in disability sport studies (McMaster et al., 2012). She recalls there being no funds to take medical personnel with her team to the World Championships in 2013. In effect, this meant Raylene herself performed duties as coach, team leader, physiotherapist and massage therapist for two athletes. On other occasions she called upon her own family to help with her Paralympic teams when funding for a support team was not forthcoming. As signaled in the narratives shared later in this chapter, on another occasion, Raylene served as a professional cleaner, scrubbing floors and wheelchairs to alleviate the possibility of athlete infection in Dehli. While most coaches need to be competent at many tasks (Barker et al., 2004; Lyle, 2002) the extent to which Raylene has needed to re-invent herself as something so much more than a coach is extraordinary. In these instances more, not less, recognition of the ways an impairment configures resource needs would no doubt, be a welcome thing. The fact that Raylene just gets on with these tasks, quietly cleans the wheels of a chair or scrubs down an apartment without making a fuss, nor drawing attention to the extra burdens the para-athletes might place on her, speaks to her regard for *all* her athletes as athletes first and foremost. Yet with Raylene doing all this support work, on top of her coaching, it does raise questions as to the sustainability of the Paralympic athletic programme if she was no longer able, or willing, to coach.

Raylene's orientation towards her athletes is evident. In her words,

> [I] coach athletes on their strengths – especially para-athletes. I'm trying to make athletes resilient and resourceful. I'm always looking outside the square to get the best out of the athlete. Sometimes this means changing techniques to suit particular athletes, experimenting with different types of recovery.

While she adopts a strength-based approach to her coaching Raylene does not embrace an ideology of protectionism, a desire to 'protect' them from either emotional or physical harm (Withers & Batten, in Kelly, 1998). Nor does she consider the debates that occur in the literature regarding the merits of adopting a strength-based approach, or focusing on developing resilience or resourcefulness (Cassidy et al., 2014). Rather, her approach is grounded in building on athletes' existing strengths and resourcing them to progress in ways that work for them. In many ways, her approach mirrors that mooted by critical coach education scholars. For example, she adopts pedagogical strategies to fit the needs of the athlete rather than squeezing the athletes into pre-framed pedagogical models, and she starts from a place that recognizes what athletes can and want to do, rather than what they cannot and do not want to do. Moreover, she fosters resourcefulness amongst the athlete cohort, which are features that socially critical coach education scholars would advance as crucial (Armour, 2014; Cassidy et al., 2014). Raylene does not necessarily regard her practices as 'special' or extraordinary, yet the sport coaching, disability sport and physical education literature signals student- or athlete-centred practice is the exception rather than the norm (DePauw, 1997; Fitzgerald, 2006; Penney & Kidman, 2014).

In the narratives that follow, Raylene shares some poignant stories from her extensive repertoire, in an endeavor to shed some light on what, and who has shaped her particular orientation towards coaching and what characterizes her approach.

'Just doing it'

'After 27 years of coaching athletics in her own time Raylene Bates can finally say it is her job' (Van Royen, 2015). During those years Raylene coached athletes to World Championships and Paralympic Games, as well as being a Team Leader/ Manager at the Olympic Games. In many countries it would be unimaginable that someone with this degree of responsibility, and who had dedicated this amount of time and energy into coaching would still be a volunteer.

In the 27 years Raylene spent coaching, prior to it becoming 'her job', she did not regard her coaching as work, explaining that if she had done so she 'wouldn't be here, as simple as that'. Despite not regarding coaching as work, Raylene did say that her approach to coaching, and how she behaved as a coach, was 'professional like work'. Raylene pointed out that for her the difference between work and coaching was that

> [n]o matter how stressed I am in my paid employment, when I get onto the track and I start coaching I am completely a different person. I start relaxing and I just enjoy it so much. The biggest thing is I get so much pleasure out of seeing people achieve and it is not necessarily at elite level, it can also be at just beginner level. Just seeing them being able to achieve a goal or do something [like] a technique correctly, or achieve a personal best, that's what makes it all worthwhile.

Given Sport New Zealand's explicitly stated priority of getting 'more Kiwi winners on the world stage' (www.sportnz.org.nz/about-us/who-we-are/what-we-are-working-towards/), Raylene's pleasure at seeing beginners achieve, again, marks her departure from coaching norms and also helps us understand both the enduring nature of her career and her on-going passion for it. While those driven by external rewards (e.g. medals, numbers of athletes on the world stage) will presumably wax and wane in their coaching fortunes, when the driver is genuine pleasure at the achievement of others, no matter what their status, there are few impediments to feeling and experiencing satisfaction in the role.

Raylene lives and coaches in Dunedin, the second biggest city in the South Island of New Zealand, but 1400 kilometres away from Auckland, in the North Island, where the High Performance Sport New Zealand National Training is based. Other sports like cycling and rowing, while not based in Auckland have their centralized programmes in close proximity (approximately 150 kilometres south of Auckland). There are also regional high performance centres in Wellington, Christchurch, Dunedin and Wanaka. In recent years many sports organizations whose sports are targeted by Sport New Zealand have encouraged, or incentivized, their high performance athletes to relocate to the high performance centres. In the case of Athletics New Zealand these centres were either in Christchurch (500 kilometres north of Dunedin) or Auckland. If this practice was to become compulsory, and Raylene still lived in Dunedin, it would have a huge impact on who she was able to coach. Not surprisingly, she called the move towards centralizing the coaching of athletics as not necessary in all situations. She explained:

> when you have got individual athletes, it doesn't always work. If you look at the international studies and the international experience ... Australia for instance, they tried it, it did not work. You cannot take young teenage children away from their family and put them in an environment that they are not happy to be in unless they want to do that. You cannot force them to do it ... I have been in situations where I have had teenagers come away from their homes and it has been unsuccessful but others, when put with families, it has worked out. And actually it has been their choice, they had not been told they must do that, it has been offered as an opportunity. Here is an opportunity it is up to you whether you decide to do that or don't decide to do that. Here are the pros, here are the cons, you make the decision.
>
> I think that is the difference. There is a big difference between ... being told that you have to do it [relocate to a centralized coaching programme] as opposed to being given the choice of doing it. It is a bit different for senior athletes, but there again you know if you have got a coach who has brought an athlete through from being a young teenager to a senior and is actually obtaining international status and doing really well, who is to say they are not the best person for that athlete? ... We have 4.3 million people in this country with 1.3 of them sitting in Auckland but there is still 3 million people in the rest of New Zealand, and a large percentage of our athletes are rural-based athletes they are not city athletes, they cannot handle going into a city, they just do not survive.

And I think history shows, if you do a study of the number of athletes that have been in our international teams ... the majority of them have come from rural areas, and still do come from rural areas. There has been a vast majority of athletes that have gone to big cities and have never succeeded because of it.

While not situated in the sport of athletics, some recent research has found that rural communities appear to have positive influences on athletic development in New Zealand (Pennell, 2014) and Canada (Balish & Côté, 2014).

Over the years, Raylene and her family have had numerous athletes from her training squad come to live with them for various lengths of time, and for diverse reasons. One such athlete was 16 years old and from a small rural town. Some months prior to the athlete going to stay with Raylene and her family she had placed fifth in the javelin and seventh in the shot put in her first IPC World Championships. To improve as a javelin thrower the athlete and her family recognized that she had to move away from home. This athlete did not want to go to boarding school or board with a family she did not know so she decided to move to Dunedin to live with, and be coached by, Raylene. The athlete described the move to leave her friends and family as 'huge', but the possibility of making the London Paralympics and improving as a javelin thrower was 'too big to turn down' (http://www.voxy.co.nz/sport/london-paralympian-excited-about-ipc-athletics-world-champs/5/161839). The athlete went on to compete in London, and in the 2013 IPC World Championships she 'won a silver medal in the F46 class javelin with a throw of 34.37 metres', results her parents said 'vindicated' their decision to send the then 16-year-old to Dunedin to live and work with Raylene (Richens, 2013). Since then the athlete has gone on to break New Zealand records in the shot put and javelin and win a gold medal in the 2014 China IPC Athletics Grand Prix. The consequences of leaving home to be coached are not always predictable or sport related. One of the social benefits of the move for the athlete is that she now describes Raylene as being 'like a second mum' (http://www.voxy.co.nz/sport/london-paralympian-excited-about-ipc-athletics-world-champs/5/161839).

Raylene is not the first throwing coach to have one of her athletes live with her and develop a close bond. In the 1970s Fatima Whitbread (who became world champion, world record holder and two time Olympic medalist in the javelin) ended up living with her coach, Margaret Whitbread, who in time did legally become her mother (Williams, 2012). In the early 2000's Kirsten Hellier was the coach of Valerie Adams (the current two-time shot put Olympic gold medalist). Adams also ended up living with Hellier's family explaining that '[w]hen my Mum died I was 15, and Kirsten and Pat's house was like a second home to me. They took me, a teenager, in and really looked after me. In 2001 I lived fulltime with them for 12 months' (Adams with Gifford, 2012).

What Raylene has described thus far bears little resemblance to the analyses of work/home binaries presented by scholars in occupational studies. For example, Hochschild (1997) offers a sophisticated three-year study of the boundaries between work life and family life in a large corporation. Hochschild reports on the regularity with which her participants viewed work as 'an escape from the stresses of home' (1997: 37). Raylene, however, does not regard coaching as work. For her, the boundaries between home, work and, in her case, coaching are permeable at most, and at times, barely there. She is at once 'mum' to an athlete in the geographic space of her home, 'working' as cleaner, physio and/or confident in her pleasurable role as coach, and engaging her biological family in support of her athletes. To regard Raylene as possessing an ethic of care (Noddings, 2003) in relation to her athletes would be an understatement. Further, she is acutely aware of the gendered dimensions of the care 'work' women volunteer or (paid) coaches engage in, including the emotional labour (Hochschild, 1997) women are expected to undertake in the home, but also in relation to their coaching roles. Raylene explains that as far as she is concerned, female coaches:

> have to be prepared to sacrifice things within their own home … because a woman still is expected to bring up a family and look after a house and everything else. They have got to expect to do it [coach] for nothing and they have got to expect that it is not easy.

As Raylene signals in the next two narratives, negotiating family responsibilities and normative notions of what a mother can/should do in the home, is coupled with going the extra mile when travelling overseas with athletes. While we signalled some of the multiple tasks Raylene applies herself to in the context of her coaching earlier in this section, we devote the following vignettes to this theme, which, in our view, illuminates compellingly the moral and ethical underbelly of Raylene's approach to coaching.

Women's work is never done

> Dehli 2010 Commonwealth Games: When you have a fully integrated athletics team for the first time in a Commonwealth Games and those Games are in India you have to take precautions. Precautions because people in wheelchairs can't side step something on the ground and in fact they have no idea what is on the ground but they have to push their chairs and touch the wheels of the chair. Not only is there then a risk of those individuals getting sick but if something is picked up on the chair and that then gets spread through an apartment … we are in trouble.
>
> There had been horrendous media [about the condition of the athletes' village] prior to our departure to India and I knew that I could not blow the chance of having a fully integrated team going forward if I did not take every precaution with these athletes and team. To complicate the situation Jessica Hamill (a wheelchair athlete who won the silver medal in the seated shot put) was rooming with Val Adams (the then current World and Olympic shot put Champion). Val was to go on from the Commonwealth Games and compete in the Diamond league and could not afford to get sick.
>
> So I shipped cleaning products to India in preparation for my arrival and I went into the village a day prior to the team and cleaned all the apartments

from top to bottom including washing all the bedding to ensure that everything was clean. Then every night I washed the two wheelchairs down whilst the athletes were in the showers. I took every precaution with hand sanitizer with the athletes and ensured that everyone had wipes and sanitizer as a precaution.

Making house

Beijing 2008 Olympic Games: My first Olympics … to be in an apartment in the village that every other team was envious of, an apartment where every direction you looked there was something to remind you of home, posters, flags, street signs, even a barista! Bean bags, NZ lollies, always something to remind you of home. Artwork from children throughout NZ – everywhere you looked or walked was a reminder of Aotearoa[7]. I was so excited, proud and honoured to be part of this team. Other teams would come and sit outside our apartment just to get glimpse of the set up and watch the athletes relax, sit on their laptops, or just hang out together.

When I left the team in Beijing to head back to the Paralympic pre-camp I was so excited. I actually looked forward to going back to the village but was horribly disappointed and upset when I finally went back to the village and the NZ apartment. There was nothing – all the flags, murals, posters, signposts everything was gone. It was like a hospital – plain, sterile and bland. How could this happen? … Only two New Zealanders have been through an Olympic and Paralympic campaign so I took it upon myself to ensure this did not happen again.

As a result of collaboration between the New Zealand Olympic Committee (NZOC) and Paralympics New Zealand and the sharing of resources we saw a whole different experience in London. Whilst there is some NZOC specific resources that can't be shared, resources that could were, which resulted in feeling like a NZ set up once again.

The previous vignettes bring us up close to the politics, emotions, structural and environmental constraints as well as the relationships implicit in elite coaching. They also shed considerable light on the nature of Raylene's ethic of care. Noddings (2003) refers to a distinction between what she terms 'natural caring' – a kind of caring that does not necessarily require an ethical effort to motivate it, but rather has its roots in a person's (and often women's) experience, and 'caring about' which she describes as a form of caring arising from the public realm – a concern, for example, about the well-being of others and a desire to do something about it. In later work Noddings (2013) made a distinction between 'natural caring' and 'ethical caring'. The notion of ethical caring is informed by a deontological approach to ethics where actions are performed out of duty and obligation and what the philosopher Kant described as a 'categorical imperative' – i.e. I 'must' (Morgan, 2007). When explaining what governs our obligations, Noddings (2013:

701) points out it is linked to the value we place on the 'relatedness of caring'. For example, our obligation to care increases if there is 'capacity of the cared-for to respond' (2013: 703). Additionally, when there is a possibility of the relationship to be dynamic and for the relationship to 'grow with respect to reciprocity – then the possibility and degree of ... obligation also grows' (2013: 703). In Raylene's disposition and actions, there is evidence of Noddings' (2013) notions of 'natural caring', 'ethical caring', and 'caring for' and 'caring about'. Battling to preserve or re-create an environment infused with New Zealand culture for Paralympic athletes, when this happened as a matter of course for New Zealand Olympic athletes, is reflective of a 'caring about' and 'ethical caring' and simultaneously illustrative of a 'care for' and 'natural caring'. Her commitment to her athletes is unequivocal and her willingness to add political advocacy for a NZ house at the Paralympics to her considerable workload (although she doesn't think of it this way) as a coach speaks volumes about the ethical and moral foundations of her approach. Perhaps an ethical compass and capacity to 'live it' in one's coaching are not things that can be taught. Nevertheless in the next section we endeavor to tease out what may be useful from Raylene's story for others who are practicing coaches and/or coach educators.

Recommendations for para-athletics coaching, education and practice

At first reading of Raylene's narratives, and our analysis of these, it would be easy to think she is some kind of 'super coach' or 'superwoman' whose experiences with elite para- and able-bodied athletes have little relevance for the everyday coach or coach educator. Portraying Raylene and her story in this way has not been our intention. We have tried to say it straight, as Raylene does. 'Just doing it' is the key maxim we draw from her biography and her story. Translated as a recommendation for coaching practice this motto may not be very helpful. 'Just do what?' is the question we imagine our undergraduate coaching students asking. Nevertheless, we *do* think there are things to be learned from Raylene – things that may not fit everyone's style, personality or beliefs, but nonetheless notions that may afford inspiration for those wondering what makes a 'good' coach tick.

First, it is Raylene's enduring pleasure in her coaching practice that stands out in her narrative. To coach at the top level unpaid for 27 years, it must have been fun. Enjoying one's role would seem crucial if longevity in the profession is desired. Second, the relationships Raylene has with her athletes, her genuine care for them as people and as athletes seems pivotal to her success. They trust her enough to 'live' with her. They know she 'has their back' when she's battling Olympic bosses for resources and cleaning their apartments. Any good pedagogue knows that good relationships are at the heart of sound pedagogy. Raylene's story simply reinforces this. Third, her willingness to work across traditional boundaries of home, work and sport in ways that make a nonsense of their separate locations is striking. Not all will have the time, nor the inclination to do so, but in Raylene's case, with limited institutional support, working voluntarily and under-resourced, her capacity to draw family into sport, to dissolve work/home/play boundaries and re-frame thousands of hours of voluntary work as 'fun' renders her an extraordinary coach. Fourth, Raylene's wholehearted involvement in coaching and administration has left a legacy for para-athletics. Her contribution to the production of resources and curricular for Athletics NZ has meant that para-athletics has gained greater exposure. For example, questions about para-rules are now included in Athletic NZ's officials exams, and para-specific modules in its Performance Coaching Assessment (Qualification) system. The embedded nature of para-athletics in Athletics NZ has resulted in coaches being given opportunities to coach para- as well and able-bodied athletes, and as a consequence to extend themselves and become resilient. Finally, Raylene's 'I'm just doing it' ethos is interesting to reflect on, particularly given the contemporary push toward academic study for coaches and the drive for professionalization (Cassidy et al., 2016; Lyle & Cushion, 2010; Taylor & Garratt, 2010a, 2010b, 2013; Taylor et al., 2014). Raylene has, for the most part of her career, had little time to engage in theorizing coaching, or researching it. She operates from a place many fear to go. Raylene 'just does it' because she is unafraid of trying something new, is prepared to give things a go, as well as creatively approaching difficult situations, and challenging marginalizing rules and routines. We are not suggesting that reading, thinking, and studying coaching isn't helpful. Rather, all of this when combined with a pragmatic ethic of care, passion for coaching and respect for athletes and their worlds, should make for a delightful journey.

Additional resources and supplementary material

The Inclusion Club is a website aimed at promoting and sharing ideas and strategies around the inclusion of disabled children and adults in physical activity and sport. Peter Downs and Ken Black, both practitioners in inclusive physical activity and disability sport for a collective 60 years plus, launched the site at the International Symposium on Adapted Physical Activity in Paris in 2011. The Inclusion Club is designed to support best practice in this field and is free to join. Currently there are over 50 'episodes' with examples of innovations in inclusive sport and interactive discussions on the topic (http://www.theinclusionclub.com).

Notes

1 Subsequently, the term athletics will be used instead of track and field.
2 Also known as the 1896 Summer Olympic Games.
3 The Deaflympics has run every four years (except during World War II) making it the second longest running multi-sport event (http://www.deaflympics.com/sports.asp).
4 An interesting aside is that in the twenty-first century a number of western countries are still using sport to rehabilitate soldiers injured in the wars such as those occurring in Afghanistan and Iraq (Brittan & Green 2012).
5 Sport New Zealand is the government agency dedicated to getting: 1) 'more young people engaging in more sport and recreation'; 2) 'more adults engaging in more sport

and recreation'; and 3) 'more winners on the world stage' (http://www.sportnz.org.nz/about-us/who-we-are/what-were-working-towards/).

6   Carded athletes are those who have been identified as 'tracking towards podium finishes at Olympic Games, gold medals at Paralympic Games, and podium finishes for non-Olympic sports'. They are eligible for support services to enhance their performance (http://hpsnz.org.nz/athletes/carding).

7   Aotearoa is the Māori name for New Zealand.

References

Adams, V. with Gifford, P. (2012). *Valerie*. Auckland, N.Z.: Hachette New Zealand Ltd. Online. Available at http://www.stuff.co.nz/sport/other-sports/7873579/An-athlete-a-coach-the-parting-of-ways [accessed 10 June 2015].

Ainscow, M. (1997). *Understanding the development of inclusive schools*. London: Falmer Press.

Armour, K. (2014). *Pedagogical cases in physical education and youth sport*. London: Routledge.

Balish, S. & Côté, J. (2014). The influence of community of athletic development: An integrated case study'. *Qualitative Research in Sport, Exercise & Health, 6*(1), 98–120.

Barker, R., Saffery, G., Saipe, R., Sutton, L. & Miles, A. (2004). *Sports development and fitness options*. Oxford: Heinemann Educational Publishers.

Brittan, I. & Green, S. (2012). Disability sport is going back to its roots: Rehabilitation of military personnel receiving sudden traumatic disabilities in the twenty-first century. *Qualitative Research in Sport, Exercise and Health, 4*(2), 244–264, DOI: 10.1080/2159676X.2012.685100.

Bruening, J., Dixon, M., Burton, L. & Madsen, R. (2013). Women in coaching: The work-life interface, in P. Potrac, W. Gilbert and J. Denison (eds) *Routledge handbook of sports coaching*. London: Routledge.

Cassidy, T., Jones, R. & Potrac, P. (2016). *Understanding sports coaching: the pedagogical, social, and cultural foundations of sports practice* (3rd edition). London: Routledge.

Cassidy, T., Jackson, A-M., Miyahara, M. & Shemmell, J. (2014). Greta: Weaving strands to allow Greta to flourish as Greta. In K. Armour (ed) *Pedagogical cases in physical education and youth sport*. London: Routledge.

DePauw, K. (1986). Research on sport for athletes with disabilities. *Adapted Physical Activity Quarterly, 3*, 292–299.

DePauw, K. (1997). The (In)visibility of DisAbility: Cultural context and 'sporting bodies'. *Quest, 49*(4), 416–436.

Fitzgerald, H. (2006). Disability and physical education, in D. Kirk, D. Macdonald & M. O'Sullivan (eds) *The handbook of physical education*. London: Sage.

Hargreaves, A. (1997). Cultures of teaching and educational change, in B. Biddle, T. Good & I. Goodson (eds) *International handbook of teachers and teaching* (vol 3). Netherlands: Springer.

Higgins, N., & Ballard, K. (2000). Like everybody else? What seven New Zealand adults learned about blindness from the education system. *International Journal of Inclusive Education, 4*(2), 163–183.

Hochschild, A.R. (1997). *The time bind. When work becomes home and home becomes work*. New York: Metropolitan Books.

Holland, K. (2010). Discourse, 'disability' and physical culture: A story of a labelled life. Unpublished honours dissertation, University of Otago.

Jones, R. (2009). Coaching as caring (the smiling gallery): Accessing hidden knowledge. *Physical Education & Sport Pedagogy, 14*(4), 377–390.

Jones, R., Armour, K. & Potrac, P. (2004). *Sports coaching cultures. From practice to theory*. London: Routledge.

Jones, R., Bailey, J. & Santos, S. (2013), Coaching, caring and the politics of touch: A visual exploration. *Sport, Education and Society, 18*(5), 648–662, DOI:10.1080/13573322.2013 .769945.

Kelly, P. (1998). Risk and the regulation of youth(ful) identities in an age of manufactured uncertainty. Unpublished doctoral thesis, Deakin University, Australia.

Lyle, J. (2002). *Sports coaching concepts. A framework for coaches' behavior*. London: Routledge.

Lyle, J. & Cushion, C. (2010). *Sports coaching: Professionalism and practice*. London: Elsevier.

MacArthur, J, Sharp, S., Kelly B. & Gaffney, M. (2007). Disabled children negotiating school life: Agency, difference and teaching practice. *International Journal of Children's Rights, 15*(1), 99–120.

McMaster, S., Culver, P. & Werther, P. (2012). Coaches of athletes with a physical disability: A look at their learning experiences. *Qualitative Research in Sport, Exercise & Health 4*(2), 226–243.

Morgan, W. (2007). *Ethics in sport* (2nd ed). Champaign, Il: Human Kinetics.

Morrison, C. (2011). Disability, physical education and sport: Tom talks. Unpublished Master of Physical Education, University of Otago.

Nelson, L., Potrac, P., Gilbourne, D., Allanson, A., Gale, L. & Marshall, P. (2014). Thinking, feeling, acting: The case of a semi-professional soccer coach. *Sociology of Sport Journal, 19*(1), 19–40.

Noddings, N. (2003). *Happiness and education*. Cambridge, MA: Cambridge University Press.

Noddings, N. (2013). An ethic of caring, in R. Shafer-Landau (ed) *Ethical theory: An anthology* (2nd ed). Hoboken, NJ: John Wiley & Sons.

Pennell, K. (2014). A 'touch' of class: Investigating rural talent development. Unpublished honours dissertation, University of Otago.

Penney, D. & Kidman, L. (2014). Athlete centred coaching: A time for reflection on meanings, value and practice. *Journal of Athlete Centered Coaching, 1*(1), 2–5.

Potrac, P. & Marshall, P. (2011). Arlie Russell Hochschild: The managed heart, feeling rules, and emotional labour: Coaching as an emotional endeavour, in R. Jones, P. Potrac, C. Cushion & L. T. Ronglan (eds) *The sociology of sports coaching*. London: Routledge.

Potrac, P., Jones, R., Purdy, L., Nelson, L. & Marshall, P. (2013). Towards an emotional understanding of coaching: A suggested research agenda, in P. Potrac, W. Gilbert & J. Denison (eds) *Routledge handbook of sports coaching*. London: Routledge.

Purdue, D. & Howe, P. (2012). See the sport, not the disability: Exploring the Paralympic paradox. *Qualitative Research in Sport, Exercise & Health, 4*(2), 189–205, DOI: 10.1080/2159676X.2012.685102.

Richens, M. (2013). Record-breaker Holly just getting started. Online. Available at http:// www.stuff.co.nz/sport/other-sports/8955182/Record-breaker-Holly-just-getting-started> [accessed 10 June 2015].

Slee, R. (2007). Inclusive schooling as a means and end of education?, in L. Florian (ed), *The SAGE handbook of special education*. London: SAGE.

Smith, B. (2012). Editorial. *Qualitative Research in Sport, Exercise & Health, 4*(2), 173–174, DOI:10.1080/2159676X.2012.693030.

Sparkes, A. (1990). *Curriculum change and physical education. Towards a micropolitical understanding*. Geelong: Deakin University Press.

Tawse, H., Bloom, G., Sabiston, C. & Reid, G. (2012). The role of coaches of wheelchair rugby in the development of athletes with a spinal cord injury. *Qualitative Research in Sport, Exercise & Health, 4*(2), 206–225, DOI: 10.1080/2159676X.2012.685104.

Taylor, B. & Garratt, D. (2010a). The professionalisation of sports coaching: Relations of power, resistance and compliance. *Sport, Education and Society, 15*(1), 121–139.

Taylor, B. & Garratt, D. (2010b). The professionalisation of sports coaching: Definitions, challenges and critiques, in J. Lyle & C. Cushion (eds) *Sports coaching: professionalism and practice*. London: Elsevier.

Taylor, W. & Garratt, D. (2013). Coaching and professionalisation, in P. Potrac, W. Gilbert & J. Denison (eds) *Routledge handbook of sports coaching*. London: Routledge.

Taylor, W.G., Piper, H. & Garratt, D. (2014). Sports coaches as dangerous individuals: Practice as governmentality. *Sport, Education and Society*, DOI:10.1080/13573322.2014.899492, 1–19.

Van Royen, R. (2015). Coaching finally a paid job for Bates, *Otago Daily Times*, 4 February.

Wallechinsky, D. & Loucky, J. (2011). *The book of Olympic lists: A treasure-trove of 116 years of Olympic trivia*. London: Aurum Press.

Williams, A. (2012). Fatima Whitbread: Sport was my savior after a turbulent childhood. Online. Available at http://metro.co.uk/2012/08/07/fatima-whitbread-sport-was-my-saviour-after-turbulent-childhood-527182/ [accessed 10 June 2015].

Editors' summary reflections

Coaches' roles may be primarily orientated around athlete development and sporting performance; however, in many cases (and certainly at the high performance level it seems), coaches' work may frequently transcend these objectives. As a consequence, the notion of 'the coach' may subsequently become to be ambiguously defined and/or embody a variety of roles (e.g. carer, educator, mentor, health assistant, support worker, parent/guardian, financial advisor and friend) (Inglis et al., 2000; Lyle & Cushion, 2010; Pope et al., 2014). A coach may take on these roles willingly or otherwise, but in many ways they may become fundamental to the individual coach's experience, their work ethos and politics, and, importantly, the athlete–coach relationship. Cassidy et al.'s examination of Bates' experience as a high performance coach reveals how a coach's personality and identity, politics and history drive their coaching philosophy and practice. For Bates in particular though, not unlike other coaches in this book, a notion of genuine care (characterized by a close concern and empathy for athletes' needs and welfare) has underscored her ethos and sustained tenacity and conviction to disability sport and its constituents.

Cassidy et al.'s exploration of Bates is revealing in that it demonstrates the messy confluence of coach's 'work' and 'life' domains and balance. Beyond this, however, we learn much from Bates in regards to how coaches (particularly those with limited resources) can utilize their own agency to respond to and overcome some of the structural issues and adversities they are routinely confronted with as part of high performance and/or disability sport (e.g. geographic dispersal of athletes, lack of funding, staff and administrative support, and political tension). Over the course of Bates' career her agency has been driven by an innate desire to provide athletes with a positive, caring, and emotionally supporting environment in the first instance. A consequence, in turn, is that this has been particularly conducive to a good coaching relationship, effecting good pedagogical outcomes for the athlete in their sports, and, ultimately enabled successful performance. This may not be particularly unique (indeed it reflects the attitudes of coaches like Ferguson,

Sawicki, Fivash and Pohlman in this book). However, Bates' approach has led to blurred lines between family, work, home, coaching and play underpinned by a clear gender politics. Although recognizing her roles as distinct, for Bates these distinctions have become subsidiary to her motivations to 'just doing it' (whatever the roles happened to be). It is evident from the case study that for Bates utilizing her multifarious skills as a woman and mother (for example, by undertaking 'mother's work' and demonstrating motherly duty and care) helps frame and support her coaching experience. Whether a caring instinct is predominantly gendered a feminine trait is a moot point; however, clearly for Bates her broad conceptualization as a coach/mother/carer/woman are philosophically and pragmatically entwined and inherently linked to her identity and the way she frames her work and relationship with her athletes.

Bates' experience here also echoes that of coaches in others chapters who transitioned into disability sport and/or the high performance disability sport context in unplanned, coincidental, or accidental ways. In Bates' case, an active athletic background, general motivation for the sport, genuine passion for people, steadfast determination, and a sustained commitment to supporting the industry have been key parts of her coaching identity and journey. As demonstrated in the narrative vignettes, this has led Bates to instinctively mobilize a level of care in her relationship with high performance disability athletes that, we might argue, go beyond a regular coaching remit. Although other coaches in able-bodied sports might operate the same way, what we learn from Bates is that what constitutes a 'good', 'effective', and/or 'successful' coach in the high performance disability sport setting does not, necessarily or exclusively begin or end with professional qualifications and educational development (though this can be valuable), but requires much more from an individual than might be or could be envisioned at the outset. Thus, reiterating the experiences of Milkins, Darling and Tromans, Bates' experiences here might provide an impetus to continually question how the professional sport industries' education and development structures might better support coaches by not only addressing their pragmatic concerns but also accounting for their multi-dimensional roles and entangled identities.

References

Inglis, S., Danylchuk, K.E. & Pastore, D.L. (2000). Multiple realities of women's work experiences in coaching and athletic management. *Women in Sport & Physical Activity Journal, 9*(2), 1–26.

Lyle, J. & Cushion, C. (2010). *Sports coaching: Professionalisation and practice.* Edinburgh: Churchill Livingstone/Elsevier Health Sciences.

Pope, J.P., Hall, C.R. & Tobin, D. (2014). How do coaches identify with their roles as a coach? Exploring coach identity through a role identity lens. *Identity, 14*(2), 136–152.

5

ON THE WAY TO RIO 2016

Coaching Paralympic volleyball in Brazil

Carla Filomena Silva

Introduction

Sitting volleyball is relatively young in the Paralympic sport storyline. It is a pioneer in the fact that it is the first multi-impairment sport to have been included in the Paralympic schedule.

In Brazil, volleyball enjoys similar popularity to football, and for that reason, the task of coaching elite sitting volleyball is imbued with great cultural and social significance. This chapter focuses upon the personal experience of the coach in charge of leading the women's team to glory in the 2016 Paralympic Games, analysing philosophical, cultural and social issues surrounding his trajectory, role and the sporting context in which he operates. The theoretical background used is one of convergence of coaching literature, sociology of sport and disability studies. In agreement with Bowes & Jones (2006), coaching is herein conceptually understood as a complex, interpersonal system, defying the adoption of any simplistic framework of interpretation. Such complexity is further accentuated by the contested and volatile nature of disability, in particular in the elite context, where physical prowess and athletic 'perfection' are glorified. In this sense, this theoretical miscellany seems adequate.

Historical context of sitting volleyball

The sitting variant of volleyball was developed initially in the Netherlands, adapted from a German sport played on the floor: sitzball, also called fistball (De Haan, 1986). To create a more dynamic game, in the 1950s, under the auspice of the society of Dutch Military War Victims, sitzball and volleyball were combined into sitting volleyball (SV) (De Haan, 1986).

The most significant benchmarks in SV development are the organisation of the first international SV tournament ratified by the International Sport Organisations for the Disabled (ISODs) in Haarlem, Netherlands, in 1979, and its inclusion in the 1980 Arnhem Paralympics (men's event). For international legitimacy, SV also developed codified regulations, a classification system and gained membership within the existent ISODs. This membership was somewhat problematic as the ISODs were divided by categories of impairment, whereas SV was played by athletes with various types of impairments. In 1977, the creation of 'Les Autres' – covering all impairments not yet included – granted volleyball, both standing and sitting, its formal acceptance in the international disability sport movement. In 1992, an International Volleyball Committee was established within the existent ISOD. After that, SV developed fast, justifying the formation of an independent world organisation in 1996: the World Organisation Volleyball for the Disabled (WOVD), presently World ParaVolley. From this moment European bi-annual championships started in 1981 for men and for women in 1993. World Championships have been held for men since 1983 and for women since 1994 (Kwok, 2012).

Sitting volleyball has been the Paralympic version of volleyball since 2004. Before that, both sitting and standing volleyball were part of the Paralympic schedule from 1976 (Toronto) through to the Sydney 2000 Games, when the standing variant lost its Paralympic status. Relying on personal communications with several actors from the field (Silva, 2014), it seems that sitting volleyball was considered a more inclusive sport, allowing for the participation of athletes with a wider range of impairments. Sitting volleyball brought to the Paralympic scene an innovative sport on many fronts: an unusual movement habitus, as it was played from a seated position, sliding on the buttocks; it did not require any additional equipment, and included players with diverse impairments. Presently, SV is well established as a dynamic and popular team sport spreading to more nations, attracting more participants and funding, mainly due to its Paralympic status. Regarding the future development of the sport, it is difficult to sketch a clear picture, due to scarce information internationally and the volatility of disability sport policies across nations.

From personal conversations with several actors from the field (Silva, 2014), and in particular with the Chairman of the World ParaVolley Coaches' Commission and former coach of the Dutch Men's Team, Mr. Jouke De Haan, it became apparent that a few critical factors must be considered when examining the status quo of the sport.

First, nations hosting the Olympic/Paralympic Games tend to develop teams to compete in sitting volleyball, even if the sport was previously non-existent (e.g. Spain, Greece and more recently, Great Britain). This rapid development frequently lacks a solid infrastructure and grassroots participation, essential for a sustainable long-term growth. Secondly, the integration of SV into mainstream volleyball structures and mainstream education would benefit the sport. This is widely defended by personalities within mainstream volleyball culture, although it may be disputed by disability institutions and actors who have come to know the sport through other avenues. Thirdly, the national sporting policy in relation to disability sport is also a key predictor of development, as the flow of funding for disability sport usually originates from government sources. Lastly, important advancements in the development of SV seem to be very much dependent on the individual action of key charismatic figures in the national and international sporting landscape, rather than being the product of well-planned policies. In other words, it is very difficult to describe or predict the development status of the sport, as there are many, and unstable, variables to consider.

European teams, such as the Netherlands and Germany, dominated the competitive landscape during the early 1980s, but around 1985 Iran appeared on the international scene as one of the strongest nations in SV, alongside other nations involved in armed conflict, such as some former Yugoslavian republics (e.g. Croatia and Bosnia Herzegovina), Iraq and Egypt. Nations where volleyball itself and disability sport hold some popularity and tradition, such as Brazil, Russia, Ukraine and USA are also raising their profile in SV. Sitting volleyball has not yet reached a degree of development similar to other Paralympic team sports such as wheelchair basketball or wheelchair rugby. According to Jouke De Haan, the number of nations holding regular SV leagues (e.g. Netherlands, Croatia and Bosnia Herzegovina) are quite low and some other nations organise national competitions happening only sparsely throughout the year (Great Britain, Germany, Brazil). Furthermore, although World ParaVolley affiliated nations spread over four regions: Africa, Asia-Oceania, Europe and Pan-America, there seems to be no detailed knowledge of their development status.

Coach education in SV is also rather blurred and has been characterised by a high degree of informality and sparse actions instead of structured programmes. The available coaching pathways are also conditioned by the SV institutional and social context in each nation. In countries where the sport is under the responsibility of the mainstream Volleyball Federation, such as the Netherlands, UK and Portugal, some form of education/content on SV is provided within the mainstream volleyball courses or, as happens in the UK, under Volleyball England responsibility, elementary courses/workshops are available for delivery when requested. In Brazil, where SV is institutionally separated from the mainstream volleyball association, and included within a Paralympic Academy education, the first coaching courses started to be delivered only in 2014. Formal coaching education in SV is unavailable in most nations.

In sum, a formalised and well-coordinated institutionalised framework for SV coaches' education is yet to develop. It was only recently, after the World championships in Leblag, Poland (2014), that World ParaVolley appointed Jouke De Haan as the chairperson to lead an international commission on SV coaching education. In personal communication, Mr. De Haan unveiled the intention of World ParaVolley to organise and provide a Level 1 coaching course, as the foundational step to the development of a coaching certification.

An important benchmark in the organisation of an initial repository of resources and tools devoted to SV coaching was the set-up of an SV-dedicated educational website[1], under the leadership of Matt Rogers (former UK SV development manager). The construction of this website and of the resources therein is a result of a voluntary collaboration between suitably skilled and experienced people from around the world. World ParaVolley adopted VolleySLIDE as their education programme and recognised their package of resources as a knowledge basis for future coaches, what they refer to as a Level 0 course[2].

Historical context of José Antônio Guedes Dantas

José Antônio Guedes Dantas was born on the 4th September 1974 in a small town called Picuí, in Paraíba, Brazil. Raised and educated in a rural, impoverished area of Brazil, José learned the sports traditionally taught in school: handball, football, futsal, and athletics among others. Although volleyball was quite an important sport in Brazil, it was not taken as seriously in his school, but he played it informally until his entry into university. At university, he studied physical education and learned a vast array of sports at a theoretical and practical level. José's engagement in the professional world happened almost immediately on his entry into university, as there were several work opportunities available for physical education students. As a 1st year student, and being among the last students to choose, the only existing opportunities were in the field of adapted sports, specifically in athletics and swimming. His acquaintance with sitting volleyball happened in 2003, when, participating in a swimming competition in São Paulo, José observed the SV national team's training. José's personal curiosity, interest and determination led him to learn more about the sport. After a brief account of the most relevant dates, roles and events in José's personal and professional trajectory, a more developed account of his trajectory and approach to SV coaching follows.

Academic education

- 2000–2004: graduation in Physical Education.
- 2005: specialisation in Special Education.

Professional roles outside sitting volleyball

- 2000–2004: Athletics Coach for people with intellectual impairments.
- 2005: Swimming coach for people with disabilities.
- 2015: Physical education teacher.

Roles in sitting volleyball

- 2004–2010: Sitting volleyball coach of a men's team (national club).
- 2004–2014: Sitting volleyball coach of a women's team (national club).
- 2008–2009: Head coach of the Brazilian junior men's SV team.
- 2013 up to present: Head coach of the Brazilian SV women's team.
- 2014: Coordinator of SV coaching education at the Brazilian Paralympic Academy.

Important events/milestones

- 2002: Participation in the Special Olympics in Brazil, as an athletics coach.
- 2003: First contact with sitting volleyball in a national competition for people with intellectual and physical disabilities.
- 2004: José starts to coach an SV group in his town and since then he participates in all Brazilian National Championships leading either a men's team, a women's team or both.
- 2006: Participation in a sitting volleyball workshop, promoted by the World Organisation Volleyball for the Disabled (WOVD).
- 2007: Participation in the Para Pan-American Games in Rio de Janeiro as the Head Manager of the Training Centre.
- 2008: World sitting volleyball Junior Championship in Iran (Men).
- 2014: World Championships in Elblag, Poland.

Awards/relevant classifications

- 2005: 1st place in the SV women's National Championship, always finishing 2nd or 3rd in the other editions.
- 2007: Elected best coach of the Brazilian Sitting Volleyball Championship by his peers.
- 2009: 5th place in World Sitting Volleyball Junior Championship in Iran.
- 2014: 5th place in the women's event at the World Championships in Elblag, Poland.

The case study of José Antônio Guedes Dantas

Coaching trajectory and experience

This section provides an examination of the trajectory and experience of an elite sitting volleyball (SV) coach in Brazil, focusing upon the genesis of his engagement in disability sport, his learning/development and coaching experience in the elite environment. It has been widely acknowledged that the specific social and cultural context in which coaching takes places significantly affects the process (Cassidy, Jones & Potrac, 2008; Denison, 2007; Lyle, 2002). As such, a reflection on the concept of 'disability sport paradox' and a general overview of the social, cultural and institutional context of disability sport in Brazil introduce this section.

Disability sport paradox

Although the Paralympics are gaining increased social recognition (Howe, 2013), in many ways disability sport still constitutes a cultural paradox. The cultural parameters associated with sport such as prowess and excellence seem to be incompatible with the prevailing understanding of disability as lack of ability, dependence and inferiority

(DePauw & Gavron, 2005; Howe, 2008, 2012; Tweedy & Howe, 2011). It is therefore critical to understand that the cultural ethos of disability sport in each nation reflects distinct social perspectives on disability; varying from the complete lack of sporting opportunities, to segregated practices, to more inclusive opportunities, integrated in regular sporting contexts (Nixon, 2007). In Brazil, for instance, the provision of sitting volleyball is strongly attached to disability institutions. Furthermore, the SV national governing body (Brazilian Association of Sitting Volleyball) is distinct from the mainstream volleyball federation. This connection with disability institutions was explained by José in one of our conversations. During a period of military dictatorship, which lasted until 1985, opportunities for citizens to freely associate were non-existent. Influenced by the United Nations initiative of declaring 1981 as the International Year of Disabled Persons, a period of intense activism of people with disability coincided with the development of a democratic regime and several associations for people with disabilities emerged, and invested in sporting opportunities. This context, in which disability sport is segregated from the mainstream structures, suggests that Brazil's organisation of disability sport operates within what Reid (2003) calls a service-based paradigm, focused on the provision of specialised services, intended mainly to rehabilitate and reintegrate individuals in mainstream society.

It is within this context that the separation of SV from the mainstream volleyball structures needs to be understood. When disability services are segregated from mainstream provision, the social perception of disability as 'Otherness' (Davis, 1995; Smith, 2008) is accentuated and therefore it is not surprising that people 'do not consider Paralympic sport as elite sport. They still think that Paralympic sport is inclusive and is for people who could not do any other sport', as José affirms. There is also a general perception that 'I am doing charity. I am the coach of the national team, but what I am doing is charity and I am going to heaven, because I am teaching people with disabilities how to play volleyball'. He proceeds to explain, 'disability sport in Brazil is very recent. The first governing body for disability sport was formed in the 70's, and even presently, at the university level, there is no discussion on the problematic nature of disability and sport. They are not interested. There is only one university in the whole of Brazil which offers postgraduate studies in disability sport'. Referring to the relation of the SV community with the mainstream volleyball community, José recalled how volleyball people have been congratulating him, without attempting to truly engage with the sport: 'No volleyball club ever expressed any interest in forming a SV team'.

In other words, it is imperative to realise that disability sport in Brazil constitutes a segregated sporting culture fighting for its credibility as a high performance sport. While the women's national SV team enjoy some of the perks associated with high performance contexts, for instance a government grant and the support of technical and medical staff, José also recognises that it still lacks the performance delineation required by the elite level: 'Paralympic sport is still quite inclusive, because it allows a person who has never practised the sport to be playing alongside an international player. That would never happen in Olympic sport. I know that in other countries, this is not possible, but it still is in Brazil'.

This preamble intends to stress that while a coach trajectory, development, practice and roles are always idiosyncratic (Werthner & Trudel, 2009), in disability sport the coaching path is additionally conditioned by how each nation 'deals' with disability. Thus, although the content that follows is first and foremost informed by a series of conversations with José, it needs to be framed against this contextual background.

Entering the disability sport field

José's engagement with disability sport was more circumstantial than a true choice:

> When I was looking for a working opportunity, at the end of my 1st year studies in Physical Education and Sport, I was faced with the possibility of working with people with disabilities. Because the more advanced students could choose first, these were basically the only working opportunities left.

The seeds of José's interest and later engagement with SV started again quite incidentally when in 2003, participating as an athletics and swimming coach in a national competition for people with intellectual and physical disabilities, he could observe the SV national teams training:

> I was at this competition and the national teams were practising for the Pan-American Games, which would happen later that year, in Mar de la Plata, Argentina. They were finishing and I couldn't see much, but one of the girls was from my city, so I contacted her afterwards. At the time, they had as a goal that each team member of the national team started a team in the town where they lived. And some of my athletes told me that they would come and play, if I decided to start a team. A local association for people with disabilities (Association of People with Physical Disabilities in Goiáis) have agreed to host this team and invited me to coach and I started coaching in 2004. In two months, I had formed a men's and a women's team.

Development as coach

As noted before, formal opportunities in coaching sitting volleyball were (and still are) quite rare across most nations. When José started, they were completely non-existent in Brazil. His development process was a process of self-discovery, based on personal agency, interest and proactivity. This process started with José's recognition that he did not know enough about SV and he accepted the need to work in partnership with others, including his players, to gain expertise:

> In the beginning, the person who trained the team was Caritas, the girl playing for the national team. She would tell me how they practised in the national team and we would do the same. At the end of the training, I would

gather the group and I listened to the feedback from the players. I thought that I should teach the foundations of volleyball and that we would progress from there. But Caritas would say: 'No, Guedes, the displacement, the movement is very important'. And so, I started to work more on the displacements, evolving as a coach alongside my players.

This process of learning and discovery through observation, communication and experience extended to all available opportunities, which were proactively chased:

I always took all opportunities to learn more about the sport. When I arrived at championships, I would observe the teams, how they played and the exercises they did and I would collect some exercises and ideas to develop with my team. In 2005, only one year after I started, I managed to win the competition with the women's team. And that was very good, because people started to know sitting volleyball, which was gaining visibility. And I started to have more opportunities to talk with other people, to exchange views and knowledge.

The organisation of the SV world junior championship in 2007 justified the organisation of a coaching course promoted by the then WOVD at the end of 2006, as there was a perceived need for SV coaches. This was the only formal course in SV available in Brazil. Yet, this course was quite uncommon, as, instead of obeying a formal structure, it had a very practical character:

The best 40 players of Brazil came for that course and they were divided in four teams. A team of two coaches trained and coached those teams in a competition. This was a very good way of administering the course, as we could try different things and at the end of the game, the instructors would come and tell us what they thought. It was a very interactive course, as we learned with each other, with the players themselves and with the instructors.

In recalling his development as a coach, the role of self-directed learning and informal learning is evident. In this particular case, it was not that formal opportunities for development were considered unimportant (some literature suggests that coaches devalue the role of formal coaching courses (Gilbert, Côté & Mallett, 2006)), but that they were simply non-existent. Also, the often valuable coaches' community of practice was available only occasionally. SV national competition happened only during one weekend, during which the SV coaches were opponents and obviously did not exchange useful knowledge with each other. It seems then, that for this particular coach, informal learning was not an option, but a contingency. José continued to literally chase opportunities to learn more about SV:

When we hosted the Junior World Championship, in Rio, I was offered accommodation, so I got on a bus and I went there to watch and learn. I observed Russia, Iran, all fantastic teams. I realised for instance how the physical abilities of the Iranian players were so determinant in the game. And again, after observing those teams, I changed completely my practices and started to work on drills which prioritised movement and physical strength.

In that same year, the Pan-American Games were happening in Rio. I sent my curriculum to apply to be the manager of training facilities, and I was accepted. My actual goal was to be able to observe some other teams. I was able to observe the USA, who never allowed anyone to watch, but as the manager, I had to be there. Also, Canada, who were a weaker team but with excellent technical skills. I learned as much as I could and I went back to my coaching and tried to apply what I have learned … Same thing with Iran. I was lucky enough to be invited to train the junior team which represented Brazil in the 2008 World Championship and there I could observe many other teams, which trained and played differently. I have filmed many games but I would also go early in the morning for instance to see the team of Iran, the best in the world, training. I have learned a lot by participating in that competition.

Another form of learning which appears to have been significant in the development pathway of this coach is the learning facilitated by the athletes themselves: 'In 2010, 10 of the 12 players of the women's national team who competed in Holland, in the World Championship, were coached by me. They were also a source of knowledge for me, as they would come back and tell me about their experiences'. This interchange of knowledge between athletes and coaches happened also in another competition, named 'Copa do Brazil', where the 40 best SV players were invited to participate. They would be divided in four different teams and randomly allocated a different coach or team of coaches. 'That experience in the Copa Brazil offered me the opportunity to coach athletes who had been at the Beijing Games, and we could all learn from the experience: the players who were not international players yet, but also the coaches, who were confronted with different ways of doing things', said José.

Making sense of José's words, it is quite clear that the learning process of coaching is never ending. When questioned on what personal attributes he finds critical to perform his role well, he points out the ability to value, reflect and act upon the input provided by his own technical and medical team, as well as the players:

> My technical team possess full freedom to express themselves. They may say that something is wrong, justify their opinion and we discuss the matter further. They work with other coaches as well, they are very experienced. One of them is Spencer Lee, a very well-respected name in mainstream volleyball. And the same with the medical staff. What they have to contribute to the team, I consider pertinent and important to the team.

Evident in this account is that the career trajectory of José was less driven by choice and more by contextual circumstances. After the initial learning provided in university, the learning pathway to develop as a SV coach was for the most, internally driven and managed, without however being a solitary enterprise. Werthner & Trudel's (2006) categorisation of learning processes (mediated, unmediated and internal) drawing upon Moon's theory of learning helps to identify the particular process hereby described as predominantly an unmediated process, in which the coach was the main agent, creating his own opportunities and choosing the content of his learning. Key to this process was also the existence (though irregular) of sporting communities of practice (Culver & Trudel, 2008) which operated as learning networks (Werthner & Trudel, 2006). These communities not only acted as informal and rich sources of meaningful knowledge, as they also offered a space for collective reflection and a stimulus for individual and collective reflection, which this particular coach valued. A critical element in this process was the involvement of the players themselves as sources of knowledge, suggesting a process of shared learning and power.

For this particular coach, the entrance in the elite stream of SV happened after some years of participation in the national championships with both male and female teams, during which he explored all available opportunities to learn about the sport; namely from athletes and coaches from other countries. This is coincident with others' views on disability sport, characterised by a high degree of creativity and use of self-discovery, reflection and informal resources (DePauw & Gavron, 2005; McMaster et al., 2012; Taylor et al., 2015) due to the low level of resources available (Cregan et al., 2007; DePauw & Gavron, 2005) and perhaps for the same reason, characterised also by a strong reliance on a community of practice (Taylor et al., 2015). By doing so and by valuing the input from people around, José not only learned the 'craft' of the role, as, and perhaps more importantly, he positioned himself within the SV national and international community. Decisive in the opportunities offered to him at an elite level seemed to have been his early professional experience in other disability sports and disability institutions, granting him the necessary cultural, social and professional capital to later perform his role as an elite coach.

The SV coach's knowledge and skill

What might be the types of knowledge and skills that a successful SV elite coach needs to possess? Since disability is an important factor in this context, what emphasis must be placed upon it? What are the attributes of a good elite SV coach? What are your best attributes as an elite coach? These are some of the questions further explored in the conversations with José, on the topic of coaching types of knowledge and skills.

Disability

The presence of impairment is a central matter in sporting contexts. Historically, physical education, physical activity and sports develop in accordance with the assumption of a standardised human body (DePauw, 1997; Shogan, 1998). Some would even argue that these practices are disciplining mechanisms intended to help regulate human bodies according to a hegemonic normative ideal (Markula-Denison & Pringle, 2007; Shogan, 2003). There is ongoing discussion within adapted physical activity regarding how much emphasis should be given to difference and adaptation, considering that such a focus may be even detrimental for inclusion and empowerment (Reid, 2003; Silva & Howe, 2012).

In this sense, what should be the importance given to knowledge of disability and impairment within a SV elite context? For José, a distinction ought to be made between the participation and the performance sporting context. When the coach is operating within the former, they need sufficient knowledge about impairment. He needs to know about the history of the condition, how it was acquired, and in what specific ways the impairment influences the sporting performance and vice versa. At the grassroots level, this knowledge is critical for another reason:

> so that you can direct the person to the sport that is best suited for his/her impairment. Once a young man, who had a congenital impairment came to me wanting to play SV. I actually told him that SV would not be an interesting option for him and I advised him to try wheelchair basketball. So, it is important to know well the Paralympic sports and the main characteristic of different impairments so that you are able to provide good advice.

In José's opinion, as the coach distances himself from the grassroots level and progresses towards an elite level, the knowledge of disability is less and less important, as athletes will be already socialised in the sporting culture and quite independent and knowledgeable about their own impairment and sporting practice. Yet, he also acknowledges that at the elite level 'it is still important to have a minimal knowledge of the limitations and possibilities imposed by each impairment, because they condition the exercises you will be able to do'. He proceeds then to explain how each sport is naturally exclusionary of certain types of bodies. At the Paralympic level, the process of 'natural' selection will have played its part and the disability profile of the athletes participating will not constitute a determinant factor in the coach's work, at least in elite SV. However, because Paralympic sport is often still viewed as rehabilitative and inclusive in nature, rather than as performance sport (Howe, 2008); for the outsider disability is seen as a critical factor, which may discourage some mainstream coaches from engaging in disability sport. For José, impairment is non-controllable and individualised, therefore there is no intention to 'cure' or 'remediate', rather a concern that the athlete's health is not compromised by the sporting practice while hoping to maximise his/her sporting performance:

> Conversations about disability are not frequent. We also do not have many restrictions related with impairment, except for some abrasions on their stumps. Sometimes, athletes use something related with their impairment to

justify their absence at training or some limitations in training and my response is always: 'do what it takes to not compromise your health'. I am concerned with their general well-being, but also in terms of performance. I also know that if not solved, heath-related problems can keep the athlete away for longer.

Despite the aura of inclusivity surrounding disability sport, the exclusionary nature of the Paralympic Games have been previously explored in literature (Howe, 2008; Howe & Jones, 2006). In many ways, coaching elite disability sport requires individuals to be aware of what is real and fabricated in the rhetoric of inclusion and equality surrounding disability sport. For instance, the exclusionary character of SV comes to the forefront as, although SV is a multi-impairment sport, the most common disability amongst SV players is amputation. Because SV rules do not stipulate (as in wheelchair basketball) regulations concerning the diversity of players' impairment and its severity, the representation of other impairment is minimal, simply because athletes with leg amputations will be better able to move, while possessing the coordination and strength indispensable to play the sport at a high level.

Operating at the elite level: Crucial types of knowledge and skills

First of all, it is important to note that in Brazil, in many sports, the coach directing the team in competition and the coach training the team are not necessarily the same. There are important specificities attached to each of these roles. This would be the case in mainstream volleyball, in most top teams. However, given the more incipient level of development and funding associated, in SV these two roles conflate. Talking about his role as a competition manager, José explains:

> An excellent coach during the match will be one who will be able to quickly undertake a correct reading of what is happening in the game, use the statistical data he has available, listen to his technical team and have the capacity to make fast decisions and act accordingly. In practice, this also means having an excellent perception of what is the appropriate timing to stop the game, to use a motivating and tranquilising discourse, or to otherwise be more incisive and if needed more aggressive in the communication.

Elaborating on what it takes to gain this knowledge in content but also the timing of interventions, the importance of the practical experience of competition was emphasised 'this can only happen with many, many games … a lot of time spent on court having to read the game and make these decisions', confirming previous findings in coaching literature (Erickson, Côté & Fraser-Thomas, 2007). Sport-specific knowledge was another type of knowledge identified as critical:

> For the most, the best coaches are former elite volleyball players, at least here in Brazil. They need to have an excellent understanding of the sport, they

need to know how it is done, in practice. This is even more important in volleyball, which is probably the most difficult collective sport, in terms of technique. You ought to have an excellent knowledge of the sport.

Knowledge of physical conditioning and training methodology was also referred to as vital to 'make sure that you are not doing anything that may be detrimental for the athlete's health. I need to know the basics about these issues and keep communicating with the other technical staff'.

The importance of respect

In the face of what was already described, it is unsurprising that the capacity to communicate and interpersonal skills were the chosen critical skill to have: 'I think it is my capacity to communicate, to connect and to truly listen'. This capacity to communicate is grounded in key principles guiding his coaching practice. The most important of these is respect:

> I hold some principles to perform my role which are essential. The first one is that the athlete deserves my full respect as a human being. I treat them with an extreme respect and cultivate a very friendly relation. This means for instance that I will not use offensive terms to talk with them, or raise my voice to intimidate.

The topic of respect in disability sport is particularly important because the association of disability with dependence has traditionally increased the power differential between disability-related professionals and their public (Albrecht, 1992); but also because often the individuals involved in a Paralympic team are often beginners in terms of their sporting career, and as such frequently they are not sufficiently aware of the ethos of elite competition (Silva, 2014; Silva & Howe, 2012). José used the term respect in two fundamental ways. First, in terms of respect for the players' individuality, for instance, in defining the boundaries of the coach–athlete interaction: 'it is up to the players to decide what to talk about and when. Each one will create a different communication channel and I will respect that. Some athletes like to talk more about personal life, some like to talk more about volleyball. That is their space of personal freedom'. This respect also means respecting their state of being: 'sometimes, one player will come to me and say: "today, I am not feeling ok". And I will try to take it easier on her that day. But this is not a personal privilege. I will have the same attitude towards any of them'.

Secondly, he elaborates on how the athletes' respect for his authority as a coach is not inherent to his formal role, it is something which has to be earned:

> to earn their trust I need to truly listen to them, be genuinely interested in their well-being and fully respect them as human beings. Only by doing that can I succeed as a coach. If I don't have their trust, I will not be able to

influence them. Also, I need to earn their respect. And this means in the essential do my job as a coach very well. For instance, in a week of training with me, I need to help them to improve. There has to be some type of evolution which is visible, otherwise I am not doing my job.

Finally, respect is also framed in terms of clear negotiation of shared goals, clear expectations and the duty to provide the best support possible to achieve the team's goals: 'I do not demand anything from them that they did not show me already. So, if I know she can do it, I will demand it from her. If she fails to perform it again, I make sure we will work on it, until the performance is there again'. Although limited in space to elaborate further on this topic, respect relates to many other useful concepts in coaching literature such as coaching style, coaching philosophy and ethics, as presented by Markula et al. (2007).

In alignment with other authors (Markula et al., 2007; Potrac et al., 2002), it is clear from our conversations that José's approach to coaching respects a philosophy of 'Athletes first – winning second' which is implemented through an investment in open, honest and individualised communication channels. This communication factor may be even more fundamental in elite disability sport contexts, where athletes may try to 'hide' important matters related with their impairment, for fear of de-selection from the national teams (Silva, 2014).

Recommendations for coaching, education and practice

Despite advances in the international acknowledgement of the equal rights of people with disabilities in leisure activities (e.g. Art. 30.5 of the 2006 Convention on the Rights of People with Disabilities), meaningful sporting opportunities for people with disabilities are still to be developed to the same extent as mainstream opportunities. Meaningful opportunities imply the option to choose a sporting practice amongst a range of possibilities at an appropriate level of practice, which may benefit the person holistically (Silva & Howe, 2012). While this may seem distant from elite Paralympic sport, it is actually closely related, because without extensive participation in sport and strong grassroots, the development of an elite strand will most likely be occasional and inconsequential for the overall development of the sport. For instance, while the case study presented illustrates an elite sport context, there are several points which invite us to reflect upon the status quo of disability sport and SV in particular. Though Brazil is, arguably, one of the nations where sport, in particular volleyball is culturally and socially more valued, SV is still very incipient, with most of the teams concentrated in just one of the 27 provinces (São Paulo). Furthermore, the sport is still perceived within a charity's ethos, very much akin with the prevalence of a disability sport paradox (Howe, 2008). Although this chapter depicts the trajectory and experience of a national team coach operating at the highest level of the competition (Brazil was 5th in the last SV World Championships), culturally, the elite status of the sport is not cemented. In this sense, this chapter ends up being as much about grassroots as it is about the elite realm, as the two are closely related. Focusing on coaching paths and trajectories, at least in disability sport, it is highly unlikely that a coach may be involved at an elite level, without knowledge and experience of the grassroots level.

Examining José's engagement in coaching, one of the initial points to emphasise is the role that personal agency played to create his own working opportunities. SV was non-existent in his hometown and José engaged actively in making sure that an SV club would develop; finding players and keeping them engaged, even though the national competition only took place once a year. Also, though his knowledge of the sport was quite limited, he actively pursued various sources of learning. The first lesson to retain from this example is the importance of getting involved, of not being afraid of *the difference that disability makes* (Michalko, 2002) and develop the openness and courage to learn along the way, in close collaboration with the athletes. Due to a tradition of dependence from health professionals, it is often forgotten that the most important source of knowledge on disability are the individuals themselves. José's openness to dialogue and honest appreciation of his players as complex human beings first and foremost seems to have been essential in his path.

Even though, as he explains, disability-specific knowledge was not part of his curriculum in his physical education degree, in many ways the foundations he received in his formal education were equally valid in disability sport. Other essential coaching attributes seem to be more characteristic of personal philosophy than the result of formal instruction. The principle of respect, encompassing the understanding that the coach's authority is not an entitlement, but needs to be conquered in every interaction stands out as essential. Respecting the alterity of others, especially when the other is (at least apparently) different, requires qualities of empathetic understanding (Smith, 2008) and self-reflection and awareness which can be practised in any context involving human interactions. In part, this empathetic understanding also requires that the coach sits down and plays the game, not only to demonstrate a specific skill, but to talk with athletes at the same level and to demonstrate that he 'knows' the sport, not only cognitively, but phenomenologically, that he knows how it 'feels' to play SV. Previous research suggests that coaches who do this are better respected by players (Silva, 2014). The critical importance of healthy and clear communication was also evident, not only because it is essential to enact the principle of respect, but also because the most important contexts of learning stemmed from José's communication with people with similar drive and passion (communities of practice).

For anyone interested in engaging in disability sport, a second important lesson to retain is the need to understand the institutional context within which disability sport is developed. Whereas in Brazil coaching positions are offered by disability institutions, in other countries similar opportunities may occur within mainstream settings as well. In both cases, future coaches will be likely to face additional obstacles to their practice: issues of access and mobility are still prevalent; often people with disabilities do not believe that there are opportunities available, that they have the ability to play sport or they may lack the financial means to participate (French & Hainsworth, 2001; DePauw & Gavron, 2005; Rimmer, 2005). It is important that the future coach anticipates and embraces some of these challenges.

Lastly, while the elite context is regulated by a classification system which restricts participation, it is important to stress that in most countries, the national competitions are open to all interested players, regardless of their embodiment. This inclusive participation not only increases the number of teams but more importantly, attenuates the cultural and social separation between the 'disabled' and the 'able-bodied' and the perception of disability as 'otherness'. Such separation is artificial and detrimental for the construction of a more inclusive society. In this case, the coach will manage a heterogeneous group, with individuals with different characteristics and backgrounds (with and without impairments, with and without sporting experience, volleyball players and beginners) and will have to be sensitive to possible conflicts deriving from this heterogeneity.

In sum, while there may be different challenges to face in coaching sitting volleyball, the scope for development is immense. The lack of formal coaching pathways should not prevent from engaging in the sport, as, following José's examples, opportunities for coaching, but more importantly, opportunities for people with disabilities to play sport, are still to be created. Coaching in disability sport, at this moment in time and for the most demands passion, drive and political engagement to reduce the unfair inequality of opportunities in sport for people with disabilities (Sherrill, 2007).

Additional resources and supplementary material

Governing bodies

- Sitting volleyball world governing body: http://www.worldparavolley.org/
- Brazilian Paralympic Committee: http://www.cpb.org.br/
- Confederacão Brasileira de voleibol sentado (Brazilian Sitting Volleyball Confederation): http://www.abvp.com.br/
- UK Volleyball Federation, sitting volleyball page: https://volleyballengland. org/sitting

Sitting volleyball resources

- VolleySlide, the World ParaVolley official website to support the development of the sport: http://volleyslide.net/
- Games for Sitting Volleyball, Volleyball Canada Development model: http://www.vcdm.org/teachers/resources/games-for-sitting-volleyball
- Videos of drills, exercises, information on sitting volleyball (TeamUSA): http://www.teamusa.org/USA-Volleyball/Video/2014/02/05/Sitting-Volleyball

Sitting volleyball manuals

- Vute, R. (2009). *Teaching and coaching volleyball for the disabled: Foundation course handbook.* Faculty of Education. Available at http://www.pef.uni-lj.si/fileadmin/Datoteke/Zalozba/pdf/Vute_WOVD_Handbook.pdf
- Learn to train manual, Ontario Volleyball instructor resources: http://webcache.googleusercontent.com/search?q=cache:oZiV89sVvA4J:www.ontariovolleyball.org/sites/default/files/SPIKES%2520Sitting%2520Volleyball%2520Manual.pdf+&cd=10&hl=en&ct=clnk&gl=uk

Interesting to watch

- Women's Sitting Volleyball – Slovenia v Brazil – London 2012 Paralympics: https://www.youtube.com/watch?v=9fNO0M3uICw
- TV piece (TV Cultura) interviewing José Dantas (in Portuguese) and some players: https://www.youtube.com/watch?v=UotOfLn9ax4

Recreational level

- Ontario Volleyball Association: https://www.youtube.com/watch?v=zrBnuBPTDsc
- Have you heard about sitting volleyball? (Volleyball England) Scenes from the national competition: https://youtu.be/7akkrRxgZ_g

Basic knowledge

- Sport A–Z Sitting Volleyball (Paralympic Games): https://youtube/HgbsGXrovl8
- How to Play Sitting Volleyball: https://youtube/_ui4OwUW7ko

Equipment

- Matt Rogers gives some suggestions on equipment (VolleySlide): http://volleyslide.tumblr.com/post/42088651353/sitting-volleyball-equipment-where-to-start

Notes

1   http://www.volleyslide.net/
2   http://www.worldparavolley.org/development/overview/

References

Albrecht, G. (1992). *The disability business: Rehabilitation in America.* London: Sage.

Bowes, I. & Jones, R. (2006). Working at the edge of chaos: Understanding coaching as a complex, interpersonal system. *Sport Psychologist, 20*(2), 235–245.

Cassidy, T., Jones, R. & Potrac, P. (2008). *Understanding sports coaching: The social, cultural and pedagogical foundations of coaching practice.* Abingdon: Routledge.

Cregan, K., Bloom, G. & Reid, G. (2007). Career evolution and knowledge of elite coaches of swimmers with a physical disability. *Research Quarterly for Exercise & sport, 78*(4), 339–350.

Culver, D. & Trudel, P. (2008). Clarifying the concept of communities of practice in sport. *International Journal of Sports Science & Coaching, 3*(1), 1–10.

Davis, L.J. (1995). *Enforcing normalcy disability, deafness, and the body.* New York: Verso.

De Haan, J. (1986). *Sitting volleyball.* Den Haag: Uitgeverij De Vrieseborch.

Denison, J. (2007). *Coaching knowledges: Understanding the dynamics of sport performance.* London: A. & C. Black.

DePauw, K.P. (1997). The (In)visibility of DisAbility: Cultural contexts and 'sporting bodies'. *Quest, 49,* 416–430.

DePauw, K. & Gavron, S. (2005). *Disability sport.* Champaign, IL: Human Kinetics.

Erickson, K., Côté, J. & Fraser-Thomas, J. (2007). Sport experiences, milestones, and educational activities associated with high-performance coaches' development. *The Sport Psychologist, 21*(3), 302–316.

French, D. & Hainsworth, J. (2001). "There aren't any buses and the swimming pool is always cold!": Obstacles and opportunities in the provision of sport for disabled people. *Managing Leisure, 6*(1), 35–49.

Gilbert, W., Côté, J. & Mallett, C. (2006). Developmental paths and activities of successful sport coaches. *International Sports Science & Coaching, 1*(1), 69–76

Howe, P.D. (2008). *The cultural politics of the paralympic movement.* London; New York: Routledge.

Howe, P.D. (2012). Children of a lesser god: Paralympics and high-performance sport. In J.P. Sugden & A. Tomlinson (eds). *Watching the Olympics: Politics, power and representation,* (pp. 162–178). Abingdon: Routledge.

Howe, P.D. (2013). Supercrips, cyborgs and the unreal Paralympian. In M. Perryman (ed). *London 2012: How was it for us?* (pp. 130–141). London: Lawrence & Wishart.

Howe, P.D. & Jones, C. (2006). Classification of disabled athletes: (Dis)empowering the paralympic practice community. *Sociology of Sport Journal, 23*(1), 29–46.

Kwok, N. (2012). *When sitting is not resting: Sitting volleyball.* Bloomington, IN: Authorhouse.

Lyle, J. (2002). *Sports coaching concepts: A framework for coaches' behaviour.* London: Routledge.

Markula, P., Martin, M. & Denison, J. (2007). Ethical coaching: Gaining respect in the field. In Denison J. (ed). *Understanding the dynamics of sports performance.* London: A. & C. Black.

Markula-Denison, P. & Pringle, R. (2007). *Foucault, sport and exercise: Power, knowledge and transforming the self.* London: Routledge.

McMaster, S., Culver, D. & Werthner, P. (2012). Coaches of athletes with a physical disability: A look at their learning experiences. *Qualitative Research in Sport, Exercise & Health, 4*(2), 226–243.

Michalko, R. (2002). *The difference that disability makes.* Philadelphia, PA: Temple University Press.

Nixon, H.L. (2007). Constructing diverse sports opportunities for people with disabilities. *Journal of Sport & Social Issues, 31*(4), 417–433.

Potrac, P., Jones, R. & Armour, K. (2002). "It's all about getting respect": The coaching behaviors of an expert English soccer coach. *Sport, Education and Society, 7*(2), 183–202.

Reid, G. (2003). Moving toward inclusion. In R.D.Steadward, G. D. Wheeler & E.J.Watkinson (eds). *Adapted physical activity,* (pp. 131–147). Edmonton: University of Alberta Press.

Rimmer, J. (2005). The conspicuous absence of people with disabilities in public fitness and recreation facilities: Lack of interest or lack of access? *American Journal of Health Promotion. 19*(5), 327–329.

Sherrill, C. (2007). The passion of science: Research and creativity in adapted physical activity. *Sobama Journal, 12*(1), 1–5.

Shogan, D. (1998). The social construction of disability: The impact of statistics and technology. *Adapted Physical Activity Quarterly, 15*, 269–277.

Shogan, D. (2003). The social construction of disability in a society of normalization. In R. D. Steadward, G. D. Wheeler & E. J. Watkinson (eds) *Adapted physical activity,* (pp. 65–73). Edmonton: University of Alberta Press.

Silva, C.F. (2014). Forbidden to stand: The impact of sitting volleyball participation on the lives of players with impairments. Unpublished doctoral thesis. Loughborough University, Loughborough, UK.

Silva, C.F. & Howe, P.D. (2012). Difference, adapted physical activity and human development: Potential contribution of capabilities approach. *Adapted Physical Activity Quarterly, 29*(1), 25–43.

Smith, B. (2008). Imagining being disabled through playing sport: The body and alterity as limits to imagining others' lives. *Sports Ethics and Philosophy, 2*(2), 142–157.

Taylor, S., Werthner, P., Culver, D. & Callary, B. (2015). The importance of reflection for coaches in parasport. *Reflective Practice, 16*(2), 269–284.

Tweedy, S. & Howe, P.D. (2011). Introduction to the Paralympic Movement. In Y. Vanlandewijck & W. R. Thompson (eds). *The paralympic athlete: handbook of sports medicine and science* (pp. 3–30). Chichester, West Sussex, UK; Hoboken, NJ: Wiley-Blackwell.

Werthner, P. & Trudel, P. (2006). A new theoretical perspective for understanding how coaches learn to coach. *Sport Psychologist, 20*(2), 198–212.

Werthner, P. & Trudel, P. (2009). Investigating the idiosyncratic learning paths of elite Canadian coaches. *International Journal of Sports Science and Coaching, 4*(3), 433–449.

Editors' summary reflections

High performance sport can be a fickle industry. Not only is it a necessity for coaches to continually ensure the routine, and often exponentially increasing, success of athletes and national teams, the very existence of the sport in the upper echelons is contingent upon goal-orientated funding maxims and organisational politics, or central government and/or parent body priorities. The constant revision of sports, and specific events, on the Olympic and Paralympic programmes and competitive national sport funding regimes at work around the world are good examples in this regard. Coaches do not, of course, work in isolation. Rather, they are connected to their athletes and to their organisations and other stakeholders, and beyond this to the broader social, economic, political and cultural contexts. This said, and given the impact of broader forces on their coaching, an awareness of the wider milieu in which they work, may be of some value.

As Filomena Silva reveals, the development of coaches within sitting volleyball has not been impervious to these forces. Indeed, in the efforts to move sitting volleyball from a participatory/inclusion sport to a credible and legitimate high performance sport it has encountered considerable difficulties. For instance, and like Fivash, Milkins, Darling and Tromans, gaining and maintaining official recognition and funding streams, fostering constructive relationships with the able-bodied organisation, and reacting to disability policy changes that have emerged as a result of Brazil's specific social and cultural progression, have all contoured the context in which sitting volleyball coaches now work. As the experience of Dantas highlights, a consequence of this historical confluence of forces has been that coaches operating at the highest levels of the sport have persistently struggled for recognition for the sport, their roles and the performances of their athletes. Dantas' exasperations over how the growth of the sport at the upper level has been stymied is comparable to other high performance disability sport coaches. Yet Dantas' experiences, similar to Pohlman's career in the Czech Republic, also highlights how the influence of overarching discourses of disability and social integration/ inferiority, which are entrenched within the national political and public ether, have come to bear on the perceptions of the sport and opportunities available for coach and athlete development therein.

Notwithstanding coaches' personal motivations and emotional dedication to their work and improving the lives of athletes (Dantas' story, indeed, reflects the passion and humility seemingly endemic to many coaches in disability and para-sport), their ability to do their job effectively is ultimately compounded by historical and prevailing attitudes toward disability, athletes with disabilities and disability sport. In Brazil, and not unlike countries elsewhere, disability has been constrained by discourses of 'otherness' that have, essentially, served to marginalise, disenfranchise, stereotype and limit the agency of people with disabilities. Within the context of sport, conservative social and cultural assumptions around what disabilities are and what athletes with disabilities can do still abound. As Filomena Silva identifies, even within the sport industry misunderstanding and misconception can be seen in the relationship between disability sport organisations and their able-bodied counterparts. This has, Filomena Silva articulates, been problematic not only for the profile of sitting volleyball but for the sustainability of the sport at the upper levels; which, of course, has implications for coach development pathways and the continuity of athletic performance. In Dantas' case, while he (and others within the sport) have had success in driving participation and achieving quality performances, work still remains to challenge the perception of the team and its national profile.

Dantas' story is evidence that effective coaching is a melange of personal conviction, informal and formal educational opportunities, good networks, and a mix of personal skills and expertise knowledge. While each coach's approach to their work can be highly individualised, as Filomena Silva's and Dantas' conversations suggest, and in agreement with other contributors to this book, the future of disability sports could be advanced significantly through development of better sport-specific formal education and coach development pathways (Christensen, 2013; Koh, Mallett & Wang, 2011). While this is no doubt important, given the comments above and the persistence of assumptions within sitting volleyball, one challenge might be to ensure that such pathways better account for some of the contextual complexities that emerge within countries *and* ensure coaches can be better equipped to challenge problematic discourses of disability that limit progression of their sports and their athletes *in situ*. It is evident, certainly from the coach case studies provided here, that some individuals and groups are already doing this successfully. However, the situation and experiences of coaches like Dantas serve as a reminder that collectively the sport industry and societies more generally still have a way to go.

References

Christensen, M.K. (2013). Outlining a typology of sports coaching careers: Paradigmatic trajectories and ideal career types among high-performance sports coaches. *Sports Coaching Review*, 2(2), 98–113.

Koh, K.T., Mallet, C.J. & Wang, C.K.J. (2011). Developmental pathways of Singapore's high performance basketball coaches. *International Journal of Sport & Exercise Psychology*, 9(4), 338–353.

6

COACHING WHEELCHAIR BASKETBALL PLAYERS

From the beginning to the top

Hana Válková, Jakub Válek and Štěpán Válek

Introduction

The development of wheelchair basketball (WB) as a Paralympic sport within the Czech Republic is explored in this chapter. The case study coach is Rostislav Pohlman, an excellent athlete in discus and javelin throwing, subsequently an elite wheelchair basketball player, and most recently coach of the Czech National Wheelchair Basketball Team. His life-span trajectory, from after his injury up to success at the world Paralympic level is described against the background of pre- and post-1990 political-socio-economic changes in the Czech Republic (CZ). Of particular focus are the lack of systematic preparation and international contacts, strong intrinsic motivation of the Czech Paralympians and their coaches who were provided with more opportunities and better technologies after 1990, but also confronted with losing the enthusiasm of athletes as the limited systematic support for Paralympic sports still prevailed.

Historical context of wheelchair basketball

The development of sports for people with physical disabilities accelerated after World War II, as a pragmatic response to both the increased number of people with war injuries and suffering from poor health care. The sports for handicapped people were limited, in particular to an economic-political situation behind a so-called 'iron curtain' within the Czech Republic. The first official association was established in 1961 through the enthusiasm of medical doctors and/or educators (formerly an Association of Invalid Sports whose pioneers were Messrs Srdečný, Kříž, Smetana, Gronský, Stark). The first popular sports were athletics (track and field) and standing volleyball. During the 1980s the situation after the Soviet occupation became less restricted. Para-sports information from abroad was received through the media and through the experiences of several competitors who had had the chance to travel and compete abroad. Such exposures influenced the interests of more athletes with disability. Several further good sport results at European or World levels were also achieved due to enthusiastic intrinsic motivation of the participants who competed without a systematic network of governmental support. Their participation was due solely to the efforts of those few individuals that they were on top at that time in events such as cross-country skiing, alpine skiing, swimming, and cycling.

In the CZ Basketball is without doubt one of the most popular team sports (after football and ice-hockey) which made wheelchair basketball (WB) an attractive adapted sport too. Rare international contact between volleyball players and athletes helped share basic information about what wheelchair basketball was like, how to start and how to apply its rules.

In the late 1970s, WB was incorporated as a complementary part of rehabilitation processes in the programmes at two leading rehabilitation centres in distinct geographical locations (Kladruby in Bohemian and Hrabyne in Moravia). The programmes were optional, spontaneous, oriented around a leisure time activity and designed for fun and the social development of their patients.

When the acute rehabilitation process had finished, and thanks to the enthusiasm of the wheelchair users when returning home, sports clubs were established. Wheelchair basketball became an activity using an ambulatory wheelchair that had no official regulation and was played for fun.

The first attempt to make WB into a competitive sport for potential athletes as well as for the public is associated with Jan Šisler (Fér, 2002). Jan founded the first amateur WB group in 1983 in Praha. After just one year the club organized an international tournament involving teams from Budapest, Hungary and Leipzig, East Germany (neighbour countries from the 'socialist' bloc). The Czech team was dramatically beaten but continued with better organized training with a great WB promoter, Josef Kábele, who helped turn attention to the sport (Pokorný, 1994).

Thus, official WB history commenced in 1984 at an official tournament in Prague with the Mlada Fronta Cup, which later included an annual REHA exhibition. The only three clubs in CZ at that time (META Praha – later USK Praha; Moravia Brno – later Hobit Brno; Hrabyne – later Frýdek-Místek) participated in the tournament. The National Championships then consisted of three tournaments a year and the clubs were included in an official competitive WB league in spite of the fact that only three or four clubs used to participate regularly.

Knapek's Trophy in the cities of Hrabyne and Ostrava played an important part in handicapped sports. The Trophy, an annual international competition in various sports (athletics, table tennis, basketball), had developed since the early 1980s. The tournament was open to top competitors from neighbouring countries such as Austria, East Germany, Poland and Slovenia, as well as to beginners. The event included an opportunity to participate for competitors, spectators and fans, that was a great chance for all of them to be 'in' within the four-day event, and encouraged their future sport motivation, involvement and patronage.

After the political and economic social changes in 1989, public attention towards disabled sport increased. The drive for inclusion in the European Union stressed the need to demonstrate equal rights for minorities, which influenced a more intense focus on sports. More foreign knowledge was gained, more international contacts were made, more civic organizations focused on this issue and more people from these organizations and/or from popular sports were interested in this domain. It was positive from one side as the motivation, quality of equipment and training knowledge could rapidly improve. However, amid political uncertainties some of the agents polluted this domain focusing only on their personal benefits, privatisation medialization and exploiting potential sponsorship. As handicapped sports became more and more economically, technically and organizationally demanding, and the system of social care and rehabilitation care was changed, the Knapek Trophy moved to the city of Olomouc in 1996 with the sole focus on WB. Again, only three Czech teams plus teams from Poland and Austria used to participate regularly. This tournament played an important role in that time as preparation for international competitions and the Czech national representative team camp.

Within the next period, the club Hobit Brno developed a new approach in WB competitions and organized a REHA Cup in the city of Brno. Technical and personal conditions were on a higher level than before, and since then the REHA Cup European Championships, Division A, have been held in this city three times (2000, 2003, 2014). The best results of the Czech men's WB team were in the European Championships, Division A, in Sardinia, Italy, 2003 (10th place); Paris, France, 2005 (12th place and subsequent relegation to Division B); and the last achievement – a move to Division A, in Worcester, Great Britain, in 2015.

Since the beginning of the 1980s six coaches have coached the national team. None of them were specially educated in WB, none were fully paid and all of them were equipped only with practical knowledge. As there is no women's team in the national competitions, the team is organized on a coeducational basis (however only four females are engaged on the competitive level). Voluntary participation of players or team supporters (nobody is fully paid) is a great challenge for the future.

Despite the fact that the CZ WB Federation has recently risen higher than ever before, unfortunately the financial infrastructure is not enough to sustain daily life for the players or staff. The amateur concept and environment have remained (e.g. while there are three WB clubs in CZ, there are more than 100 clubs in Germany, and there is no youth WB in CZ). In comparison to the best world WB countries like Australia, Canada, Great Britain, USA and Netherlands the conditions in the CZ are totally different. This creates strong motivation for good para-athletes to leave the Czech para-sport environment and move to practice and play in better conditions in terms of finance, equipment, coach support and expertise in other countries, such as Austria, Italy, Germany or Turkey.

The lack of good competition among the three amateur WB clubs has resulted in the inclusion of two Austrian teams in the league system since 2005, bringing with it higher levels of sponsorship and public following. In terms of this situation the journey from the beginning up to the European Championship, Division A, is seen to be an enormous achievement.

Historical context of Rostislav Pohlman

After his severe injury, Rostislav Pohlman started as the 'pioneer' wheelchair basketball player in the Czech Republic. Alongside his foreign professional basketball contracts in Germany, Austria and Italy he also became a top level athlete in discus and javelin. More recently he has been the coach of the Czech National Wheelchair Basketball Team and managed to raise the previously rather poor team up to the European Championship in 2014 and beyond.

Rosta (his familiar given name) was born in 1964 in the small city of Litovel, located in the centre of the Moravian region along the river Morava. The region is a typical producer of agricultural commodities such as sugar beet, hops, barley and beer, with famous urban architecture around the Morava river, called Moravian Venice, and a great sports atmosphere in the city where the world-famous wrestler Gustav Fristensky lived (1879–1957).

It was natural that Rosta passed secondary school with leaving exams ('maturita') oriented on agriculture. Similar to other youngsters of his age he was involved in recreation and school sport. Just a couple of months before his 20th birthday, in 1984, he suffered a spinal cord injury (3rd–4th vertebrae) during recreational sport. The time he then spent in the rehabilitation centre at Hrabyne was important both for his health and physiotherapy care, and for its social aspects, for it was there that he encountered contacts that gave him chances for sport participation. The fact that he received his ambulatory wheelchair after only three months was a very important point. It was quite common at that time to have to wait six months or even 12 months to obtain a personal wheelchair. After intensive rehabilitation he was employed as a receptionist and then a technician – step-by-step he was becoming attracted to competitive sport. Milestones in his early professional sport trajectory in the period of 1991–1994 include him receiving his first professional contract in an Austrian basketball club (RSV Baskets Salzbourg), and his participation in the World Championship in Berlin where he won his first bronze medal in the javelin throw. His intrinsic motivation 'to achieve what is possible' was the main goal in his life as well as to attain economic stability for his family (a wife and two children). In the Czech Republic even if there have been a lot of proclamations or charters purporting to support Paralympic sport, the real state is that these words do not speak loud for action. The difference between the period before 1990 and recent times seems only in the increased opportunity to travel abroad and to obtain professional contracts legally with sports clubs in other countries, which was not possible before 1990.

Rosta has represented the Czech Wheelchair Basketball Team for more than 20 years. The team oscillates between A and B European Championship groups (mostly in group B), and Rosta has served as the captain of the team for more than ten years. Since 2012 he has operated as the coach of the Czech National Wheelchair

Basketball team. In that time (after the Paralympic Games in London) he stopped his own athletic career due to both the new system of classification and to concentrate on WB coaching – but he added participation in floorball for fitness and fun!

The course of his wheelchair basketball career – 4.0 point classification:

- 1984   META Hrabyne (CZ)
- 1984–1990   SKV Frýdek Místek (CZ)
- 1990–1991   Hobit Brno (CZ)
- 1992–1994   RSV Salzburg (AUT) – Austrian Champion
- 1994–1995   Cantu (ITA)
- 1995–1996   Hobit Brno (CZ)
- 1996–1997   Santo Stefano (ITA) – Italian Champion
- 1997–2000   RSV Salzburg (AUT)
- 2000–   Rollis Zwickau (GER) – German Champion several times

The course of his athletic career:

Paralympic Games:

- 1996: Atlanta – silver, javelin
- 2000: Sydney – silver, javelin
- 2004: Athens – gold, discus; bronze, javelin
- 2008: Beijing – bronze, discus: bronze, javelin
- 2012: London – silver, javelin

World Championship:

- 1994: Berlin – bronze, javelin
- 1998: Birmingham – silver, javelin; silver, discus; bronze, shot-put
- 2002: Lille – silver, javelin; gold, discus
- 2006: Assen – silver, discus; gold, javelin

The case study of Rostislav Pohlman

A small city, Litovel has been known for its sports atmosphere, with a famous wrestler (Gustav Frištenský) established as an iconic of sportsman. Schools educated students to respect his moral legacy – hard work and fair play. Students in Litovel, generally, had chances to participate in all-round school sports, and sports in local clubs, especially oriented around handball (which was the first competitive sport of our coach). Top running men's basketball was played in nearby Olomouc (in its club called Dukla) and its players were considered as ambassadors of basketball. Consequently, the younger generation around this town including suburbs like Litovel (20 km from Olomouc) chose basketball. The somatic parameters of our coach (his height being nearly 200cm) had predetermined him for basketball, even if he had never played the game on a competitive level. After his accident he was unexpectedly facing a life crossing: What about me? What to do? What is the reason to live? How can I live? However he mentioned some good luck arose from his bad luck. After basic treatment he was transported to the rehabilitation centre in Hrabyne, which gave him a chance to participate in a lot of physical activities. He met the best wheelchair athletes there, who would come back to the centre for additional rehabilitation (e.g. Jirí Véle, Dana Véleová, Tomáš Dvořák, Dana Lučanová, Vojta Vašíček). Personal contacts among these Paralympic ambassadors played a crucial role for a future direction in his life; namely, to become involved in sports as these people had. His decision was based on his inner motivation developed from the credo of his father: *be brave, be honest, work hard.* Having only experienced school-level handball before injury, Rosta's first sport was athletics, both because the Paralympic ambassadors were mostly oriented on this sport and on the advice of his medical doctor Včelařová. Individual athletic preparation was more simple to manage for him than team management duties at that time.

Discus and javelin throws became his favourite events at the beginning of his new life career. These individual sports corresponded with his nature – to be responsible for himself. A chance to go to top international competitions and to achieve gradually better results became a great challenge for him.

Over the years Rosta has been considered one of the best wheelchair athletes in the foreign context (several gold, silver and bronze medals, and records in European and World Championships, and Paralympic Games from 1992 up until today). He considers the fact that he was selected as the flag bearer at the Paralympic Games in Sydney a very emotional award.

In spite of various outstanding results in individual events and his declared preferences of individual achievements, the social team cohesion of WB has been more attractive to his extrovert nature. Rapid WB development in CZ as well as in neighbouring countries, his participation in the tournaments such as Knapek, REHA, Hobit, etc., strengthened his decision for full involvement in WB. Our coach was keen on team sports, his somatic parameters and point ranking in WB were more than substantial too. In combination with hard training, his efforts led to a high level of performance. It was not a coincidence that WB happened to be the place he encountered his future wife, and consequently established a long-term life together, with two now nearly adult children, in their own house fully adapted for family needs.

One of the important motivations was an opportunity to provide substantial economic security. This important desire to combine love for sports, skills, knowledge and economic status only became possible within an international professional environment: since 1992 he has travelled and played in several clubs in Austria, Italy and Germany (up until today, alongside athletics too). Nevertheless, the participation in the CZ context has been a part of his intrinsic motivation as well as his personal challenge.

Rosta's coaching career began in 2012 after an unsuccessful presentation in the European Championship, Division B in Slovenia (he did not participate either as a player or as a coach) when he was called by the players and WB management to the team. He accepted the post of the coach of the CZ national team for two reasons, as he mentioned in the personal interview with the author of this article:

> as I received support for life and sports career – it is my responsibility to open the chances for others.

> as I am competitive I'll try to transmit the competitiveness to players.

In spite of the amateur conditions in WB training at the time the team jumped up to the European Championship, Division A in 2014, which can be considered a great success. Unfortunately, history repeated itself, and the team subsequently fell down back to Division B without a winning game. No matter, Rosta decided to continue with a stronger focus not only on daily training of players but also on changing the system of conditions for WB development.

There is no officially recognized position as a sports coach for the disabled in CZ yet, despite the intention of the Czech Paralympic Committee to improve the situation in this domain, including its financial system. The first 'fast track' cohort of disabled sport supporters (including coaches) came into being spontaneously; post-1990 – people seeking predominantly their own self-profit were gradually and naturally substituted with real working enthusiasts.

Yet, still coaches of disabled sports have been recruited from professional or amateur (volunteer) able-bodied coaches. It was a small wonder how many Czech Paralympians ranked at the world top level in individual sports, particularly in athletic disciplines such as throwing, swimming, table tennis and cycling. Within, CZ, individual sports are more developed because the athletes can be prepared in home local clubs in cooperation with able-bodied clubs and their coaches. Still, for some time a lot of athletes have gone to foreign countries' clubs (handbikers, formula drivers, tennis players, etc.). Apart from wheelchair rugby, basketball is currently the only wheelchair team sport in CZ, while wheelchair floorball is rapidly developing (our coach participates in it on occasion to keep his physical condition and for strategy refreshment).

The first coach of the WB national team was Jaroslav Šíp, a former excellent running basketball player in the period 1951–1959. He applied standard training methods and structure of training, but above all training behaviour: personal involvement, responsibility, intrinsic motivation, individual skills preparation and team cohesion. Following Jaroslav's success, two years ago Rosta was asked to become Head Coach of the national team. An acceptance of his own coaching philosophy, and the inclusion of his own support team was his prerequisite before he said 'yes'. Even if he felt doubtful about the accompanying professional conditions, he believed in the interest and efforts of all team members – the aim to move up at least from the European Division B to Division A.

Rosta's personal decision was supported by long-term experience in both athletic and WB training, even though he had not passed any special sport training education either before or after his injury (having only graduated from general secondary school). An objective reason for that was that there is no specialized education for competitive wheelchair sports (just a general adapted physical activity university study).The secondary reason, in Rosta's view is that experience and practice with real sports are far more useful than any theoretical university study. As there is no demand from clubs or individuals for this type of education (there are only two regular WB clubs in CZ now: Hobit Brno, WB Studanka/Spring Pardubice), no actions have been taken to compile WB study curricula. Basic information about WB is included in an A licence course of the CZ running basketball federation, and WB short presentations have been used in various workshops for future social workers, volunteers, for children's inclusive games, company event promotion days, business team-buildings days, and so on. These activities are important for public awareness about the skills of the disabled athletes and their social inclusion. On the other hand, the activities tend to be abused for private profit.

Long-term training and competition practice in running basketball can help the training system to engage all four common training parts of WB basketball: general fitness; skills; team strategies; coach behaviour and approaches.

Even if all these common parts are essential for the coach's job, some of the principles cannot be purely transferred to WB. The content and intensity needs to be modified. Modifications should respect both categorical and environmental approaches (Sherrill, 2004). The categorical approach represents modifications relevant to sitting position, propulsion strength and rhythm, according to WB regulations. The environmental approach addresses every player's need to develop his skills individually, tailored with respect to the trunk height in a sitting position, length of arms, hands and trunk mobility according to the IWB point classification ranking, etc. Functional cardiovascular and breathing capacities are different in amputee and paraplegic players, too, which influence their conditioning training. Practical experience cannot be verbally transferred. It is the reason Rosta does not believe in translating academic knowledge from running basketball. Another reason is that there is very little available practical literature suited for training, no matter that WB basketball came into being after World War II (Frogley, 2010, p. 120). In addition to Czech, Rosta can only communicate in German, in which language only one relevant piece of literature can be found (Strohkendl et al., 1996). Alternatively, he has to use Czech sources, where there are no available manuals for training practice specifically oriented on WB, except some old fashioned general descriptions of wheelchair sports (Kábele, 1992; Kábele & Válková, 1996; Válek & Kudláček, 2007). He spontaneously expressed the idea of Frogley (2010, p.120) even if he has never read his book:

> most coaches and players of wheelchair basketball have taken what they learned from the running game of basketball and tried to adapt it to wheelchair basketball with varying degrees of success. Some of what is taught in the

running game of basketball can be transferred to wheelchair basketball; however, the different levels of muscle function present in wheelchair basketball and the different movements resulting from using a wheelchair present some unique skills.

In spite of these language difficulties Rosta has tried to read some books in coaching, in particular Martens' very popular book (Martens, 1997), however he believes more in visual information, such as short video shots oriented on the knowledge of skill training (on YouTube), which he finds useful and very illustrative. Rosta recommends such clips for individual home training, but WB is not only about the skills. The coach's team strategy, cooperation during offence–defence with respect to the IWB point system is crucial. Rosta believes that the best experience for him has come from high-level professional club coaches where he had been involved as a player (e.g. Italy and Germany). As he strived for excellence he saved notes and materials from his own personal trainings, and is now using them as the Head Coach of the Czech National Wheelchair Basketball Team.

A great perceived problem in coaching seems to be the confusion of amateur and semi-professional job positions of players. Basic systematic support (due to special regulations of the Ministry of Education, Youth and Sports and Czech Paralympic Committee) is oriented towards providing the national team's training camps and national league and international competitions. However the main needs lie in the players' personal input (individual preparation, transport to training centres – usually 150–250 km from their homes, and job reimbursement), which are hard to cover. These circumstances negatively affect the players' motivation and their efforts. Nearly all of them can go training only after work, and the coach has to respect their individual life situations. Especially our coach, who was in a similar situation at the beginning of his sport career before his first professional contract in 1992. This is why he understands his players' life priorities of having a good family life and job above all, and he sees sports in the third place in one's life ranking. Seemingly sad about the team's achievement, Rosta is a matter-of-fact person and knows he has to accept this situation. Why? The first important outcome was that the majority of players were independent, active people with different types of job (IT and computer experts, wheelchair equipment agents, insurance or financial advisors, etc.). They have set up homes and have families and children. This can be considered as the prime victory, thanks to basketball. This is why even a vision of Rio Paralympic Games attendance is perceived as unrealistic by some of the mature players. Managing team harmony among more or less ambitious players is one of the most difficult but most important tasks of our coach, because a single absence of a player in a preparation camp or at a tournament has a considerable impact, and this has already happened several times. Regarding realistic team self-evaluation, for Rosta the set goal is to be a permanent participant of the European A Division would be great.

Rosta's and his players' priorities are in relation to the CZ social care system: the primary support is oriented on medical and social care, and then come other priorities such as education and job access. In spite of this, the team's wheelchair equipment is comparable with other top WB countries. Although there is a great difference between the situation in the early 1990s and the current situation, there is still a lack of appropriate playgrounds for training and tournaments with accessible services (these are available only in two cities – Brno and Pardubice), which causes problems regarding distances and number of participants. The National Olympic Centre is partially accessible (in the city of Nymburk), with a vision to improve conditions for team sports.

Rosta's post is very similar to the situation of his players: it is not luxurious from an economic aspect, but in combination with a position as a player in Germany it is enough for his family life needs. The coach feels external problems but his former competitiveness and love of basketball go beyond these issues. His devotion acts as an 'infection' for his team. The team management consists recently of four part-time paid posts. Besides the coach there is a walking coach assistant (a skilful enthusiast from a new progressive team in Pardubice), a secretary (with administration responsibilities including public relations), an accountant (with economic and sponsorship responsibilities). The team is passionate and works well. For Rosta, good relationships within the team foster a good atmosphere in the team management, based on informal respect toward the coach due to his long-term experience and achievements in WB and athletics. Rosta has gone through a good deal of personal development. In 1999, when he was top of player rankings, the coach of the Dutch team replied to a question to a Czech reporter 'Would you like to include him in your team?' with the response, 'No, as he is very impulsive and emotional, uncontrollable. It is not O.K. for the team cohesion'.

Due to his long-term sports experience, as well as the wisdom age brings and his own personal experience, he has changed himself from a very spontaneous, emotional, angry player into a more responsible, rational and realistic man. The general life experience and playing knowledge the coach has is important, as it has been shown in able-bodied coaching to moderate poor behaviour and reinforce social responsibility in several coaching contexts (Davis & Davis, 2015).

The management of a positive atmosphere enables the coach to be free to focus only on training, competition issues and team cohesion. It is necessary to underline here that the team balance regarding the structure of IWB point classification is a crucial part of coach's skills. One has to bear in mind there is a great difference in offence or defence compared to running basketball. No walking coach can understand this if she or he has no actual experience of this game. This experience is verbally non-transferable, so having played the game is, in our view, an essential prerequisite for a high performance WB coach.

After his injury, Rosta was confronted with a new life situation, which acted as a new challenge (much like many other Paralympians). His new life situation regarding his family background (*be brave, be honest, work hard*) led him into a new active trajectory, formulated in our coach's sentence: 'we are not exotic animals – we are athletes'.

Recommendations for coaching, education and practice

'As a Coach we take on so many roles (teacher, leader, mentor, parent figure, friend, confidant, adviser, motivator, first aid person, transport manager, disciplinarian, cheerleader, etc. … well above just turning up to coach the team' (Walker, 2010, p.3).

As evidenced in Rosta's experience, coaching is about players' formation, and formation of himself/herself over the course of many years. During this time Rosta has had to accept a lot of roles depending on internal/external circumstances. External influence heavily determines team development, from a team's beginning to the European top level.

Rosta's example illustrates wheelchair basketball development in three distinct chronological timeframes:

a)   Non-systematic development before the 1990s, based on inner effort and motivation with randomly gained information. In spite of the limits in international contacts, quality of equipment or governmental attention, the roots of sports were laid by dint of enthusiastic patrons. Amateur coaches were no exception and as such they should be imprinted in the minds of the current generation.

b)   Spontaneous development in the early 1990s, with strong social orientation on the phenomenon of 'disability' as quite a new attractive domain. New fresh political atmosphere led toward more intensive support in legislation, social care, equipment quality, fast appropriate information, communication with foreign sports clubs, etc. These conditions initiated media interest, research orientation, a new generation of athletes and volunteers, new organizers and supporters including coaches (some of them with an approach to athletes' prosperity, some of them with an approach to private prosperity). Intrinsic motivation and personal enthusiasm of athletes were crucial, though.

c)   The current period, when professionalism in a top disabled sport is necessary. As the recent conditions are solved in a typical 'Czech way', which is 'something between', only a limited number of athletes remain in regular competitive activities. These athletes are either well supported, based on good living conditions, or they are enthusiasts with a personal vision to go over to a professional ranking. The system of support in CZ is only on a 'semi-professional' level, while elsewhere in the world para-sport is more likely to be supported on a fully professional level. This may be one of the reasons why the previous CZ successes (in skiing, swimming and athletics) are now less prevalent than before.

Thus, as Rosta's story exemplifies, coaches have to make up their minds which route to take, i.e. either focus only on their own team's achievements, or on the system of sport as a whole. which will inevitably affect the team's curve of performance. A coach's approach should be spontaneously 'holistic' as only a healthy, motivated player satisfied with his or her job and family environment can cope with the demands of training and competition in high performance sport to gain future success (Hall et al., 2015). A long-term systematic and strategic vision is crucial and should be based on:

a) recruiting new younger wheelchair users, providing them with information about sport participation in the early period after a trauma to initiate their intrinsic motivation for sports as part of their social and personal life development. Meetings with sports ambassadors, and establishing chances to participate in camps with sports icons (both wheelchair and able-bodied) which are an important part of such motivation;

b) providing high-quality pre-training of youngsters in youth clubs, oriented on sports mobility and later on WB. There is general apprehension that beginners' practice has to be modified, that beginners do not perform well among excellent players and that as a result both may become unmotivated;

c) systematic support of a habitually active lifestyle as a general component of one's life (such support is a base for both recreational and competitive levels, albeit with a different economic focus at the top level of competitive sport): decent living and family conditions as well as sports conditions (that can also increase the number of sports groups available to athletes, recruitment of athletes, family environment support, untroubled orientation on performance, and last but not least – players' responsibility and discipline);

d) the same systematic support and opportunities offered to trainers and coaches, including the chance to be in more frequent contact with excellent WB countries and their coaches.

Rosta's life-long motto comes from the running basketball coach Eddie Robinson: 'Coaching is a profession of love. You can't coach people unless you love them.' (Robinson, in Walker, 2010, p.3). Rosta's philosophy in a nutshell can be summed up in several principles:

- fair play in the playground – fair play in your life;
- long-term experience as a WB player (both as a wheelchair user and an able-bodied WB player);
- fair collaboration between the coach and his coach assistant, one of them a wheelchair user; both of them with knowledge and skills of the four basic training components;
- a good atmosphere within team management, with clearly delegated responsibilities with the head coach's sole role to coach the team;
- coach's knowledge and skills in maximizing team structure, roles, cohesion and ultimately success within the IWB point classification system;
- regular intensive team training with emphasis on and alignment with individual training programmes of players in their local clubs;
- understanding players' personal situation in accord with training requirements; and
- discipline, motivation and passion.

Rosta gave his consent to publishing his personal and sport story. He realizes that he is not a god with a halo around his head. He has gone through periods of despair during his first sport steps, and later on through a period of being a hot-tempered sport star, progressing up to a mature figure with an advanced coaching philosophy, having a balanced home environment, a love of sport, and the will to overcome barriers to achieve the best results as the WB national team coach. It is worth repeating his credo from the introduction: '… as I received support for life and sports career – it is my responsibility to open the chances for others…'.

Acknowledgments

- To Rostislav Pohlman, who spent a long time with me during several interviews in his nice garden surrounding his marvellous house, fully equipped for family needs, and for allowing me to use his website information.
- To his extreme efforts in his life activities, sports achievements and coaching.
- To his parents and family members, who keep supporting him and have formed him into a brave sports ambassador.

References

Davis, P.A. & Davis, L. (2015). Emotions and emotion regulation in coaching. In P. A. Davis (ed), *The psychology of effective coaching and management* (pp. 285–306). New York: Nova Science Publishers.

Fér, O. (2002). *Pomáhat se dá i na káře.* [Support is worth even on push-cart.] Newspaper Ekonomický deník.

Frogley, M. (2010). Wheelchair basketball. In V. Goosey–Tolfrey (ed), *Wheelchair sport: A complete guide for athletes, coaches, and teachers.* Part II (pp. 120–127). Champaign, IL: Human Kinetics.

Hall, E.T., Gray, S., Kelly, J. Martindale. A. & Sproule, J. (2015). A holistic model of the coaching process: Conceptualising the challenge of effectiveness in practice. In P. A. Davis (ed), *The psychology of effective coaching and management* (pp. 13–34). New York: Nova Science Publishers.

Kábele, J. (1992). *Sport vozíčkářů.* [Sports of wheelchair users.] Praha:Olympia.

Kábele, J. & Válková, H. (1996). *Basketbal na vozíku.* [Wheelchair basketball.] Olomouc: Univerzita Palackého.

Martens, R. (1997). *Successful coaching.* New York: Human Kinetics.

Pokorný, S. (1994). Pod českou vlajkou v Berlíně. [Under Czech flag in Berlin.] *Basket 1,* 24.

Sherrill, C. (2004). *Adapted physical activity, recreation and sport* (6th Ed.). Boston: WBC/McGraw-Hill.

Strohkendl, H., Thiboutot, A. & Craven, P. (1996). *The 50th anniversary of wheelchair basketball: A history.* Münster: Waxmann.

Válek, J. & Kudláček, M. (2007). *Basketbal na vozíku.* [Wheelchair basketball.] Olomouc: Palacký University.

Walker, M. (2010). *Wheelchair basketball: manual for coaching.* Available at: www.thebasketballedge.net/wheelchair-basketball.html [accessed 15th June, 2015].

Editors' summary reflections

One commonality among some of the coaches examined in this book is in coming to the high performance disability coaching profession following from previous involvement and/or success as an athlete and/or coach within an able-bodied sporting environment. Entry into the disability sport context, as many of the coaches articulated, was in this case rather serendipitous and occasionally also fortuitous. For Pohlman, a successful athlete and basketball player, this was also the case. However, in distinction to his coaching contemporaries, his physicality (or more specifically, changes to his physicality after his accident) influenced his decision to pursue a coaching career. For Pohlman, sport provided an important mechanism for rehabilitation, and in turn rehabilitation afforded opportunities for establishing coaching and participation networks and opportunities. Moreover, transitioning into disability sport, and eventually into high performance disability sport and coaching afforded him a means to continue the participation at the elite level that he had come to experience and enjoy as an able-bodied competitor. Like other coaches (e.g., Bates, Fivash, Dantas and Ferguson), Pohlman's transition into high performance disability coaching was also driven by an internal passion for sport and competition and a genuine altruism to help advance the lives and opportunities of others. What eventually followed Pohlman's transition, and a consequence of his coaching work ethic, was a greater profile for the sport and its participants, a degree of national, continental and international success, a recognized reputation as a successful coach, and respect among the sporting fraternity. To this end, Pohlman's story echoes the others coaches in this book and elsewhere. However, what makes his particular trajectory unique is the geo-political and cultural context in which he has gone about his work.

In Pohlman's case, his life as coach can be read against the backdrop of the separation of Czechoslovakia in 1989 and the political reorganization and social change that ensued in the Czech Republic in the following decades. The communist regime that presided over Czechoslovakia prior to 1989 had not produced favourable sport development conditions, let alone support for people with disabilities, or those individuals who wished to participate in sport (Numerato & Flemr, 2013). As Válková et al. note, fledging clubs did exist, however, opportunities for growth and coach development beyond the country were significantly limited and were largely entrenched within the constraints of a bio-medical discourse that compartmentalized and segregated disability sport and distanced its athletes and coaches from mainstream sporting organizations and their support opportunities. Although, post-1989, conditions in the Czech Republic changed (in Pohlman's case, by opening up sporting competition, raising disability awareness, and providing coach networking and development opportunities), being a disability sport coach still presented considerable difficulties (for example, mitigating the effects brought about by the unchecked introduction of professionalization and commercialization, and political uncertainty over the administration of the sport at the national level). Such conditions contoured Pohlman's early coaching experiences, but also invariably necessitated the development of strategies to ensure the success of his players, his teams and himself as a coach.

Pohlman's experience with limited coaching support during the communist era, for example, had honed his ability to work with extremely marginal resources (e.g.

equipment, tactical expertise, administrative and practical support, organizational infrastructure and financial aid). A familiar story perhaps for many disability and high performance disability sport coaches. This said, and recalling the encouragement of Hassanin & Light (2014), Penney & McMahon (2016) and Schinke et. al. (2015) to better understand coaching contexts, it is the geo-political forces contouring Pohlman's approach to coaching that should prompt us to consider the lives, work and experiences of other coaches working in non-Western settings. For Pohlman, for example, trying circumstances, and the uncertainty of national organization or governmental support in the early 1990s, meant that the maintenance and development of continental networks (many of which had been forged in his early years as a coach and player) were of particular importance. What also made Pohlman a successful, or at least seemingly very determined coach, during this time was his entrepreneurialism (at least within the Czech context) in utilizing the patronage, structure and coaching networks of existing able-bodied clubs (for example, existing basketball and athletic clubs) to build support, resourcing and a coaching base. In addition, Pohlman has also effectively utilized a wide range of able-bodied athletes and coaches, and non-basketball specialists, to further grow the sport. Though not necessarily unique (indeed, many emergent high performance disability sport teams are affiliated with/part of larger able-bodied franchises), given the constraints of the national Paralympic body in helping sustain a high performance coaching programme or infrastructure, Pohlman's efforts here are commendable. Pohlman's experience also, again, fortifies the undeniable resourcefulness of coaches who continue to work against trying sets of conditions. By examining stories like Pohlman's, and appreciating the distinct historical and geo-political spaces in the which coaches' work is played out, we might, hopefully, better come to understand and appreciate the nuances of the profession and its utility.

References

Hassanin, R. & Light, R. (2014). The influence of cultural context on rugby coaches' beliefs about coaching. *Sports Coaching Review, 3*(2), 132–144.

Numerato, D. & Flemr, L. (2013). The Czech Republic. In O'Boyle, I. & Bradbury, T. (eds) *Sport governance: International case studies* (pp.229–242). Oxon: Routledge.

Penney, D. & McMahon, J. (2016). High-performance sport, learning and culture: New horizons for sport pedagogues? *Physical Education & Sport Pedagogy, 21*(1), 81–88.

Schinke, R.J., McGannon, K.R., Yukelson, D., Cummings, J. & Parro, W. (2015). Helping with the acculturation of immigrant elite coaches in Canadian sport contexts. *Journal of Sport Psychology in Action, 6*(1), 17–27.

7

COACHING IN THE FLAGSHIP PARALYMPIC SPORT

A tale from trackside

P. David Howe

Historical context of Paralympic athletics

Without question, the sport of track and field athletics is one of the leading sports of the modern Olympic Games. This is fitting since track and field pursuits take centre stage in the historical record of the ancient games held in Greece over two thousand years ago. When the Olympic Games were revived by Pierre de Coubertin at the end of the nineteenth century, athletics once again took centre stage (MacAloon, 1981). The first Para-athletics competition was held in 1952 when wheelchair racing was part of the Stoke Mandeville Games which were organised for World War II veterans. It was one of eight sports included at the first Paralympic Games in 1960 which were held in Rome, Italy (Tweedy & Howe, 2011).

Over the next 20 years, additional impairment groups were added to Paralympic competition and today the sport is practised by athletes in over 120 countries, making it the most widely practised Paralympic Sport. Just like the Olympics, in the Paralympics, athletics is the flagship sport. The sport prior to 1989, when the International Paralympic Committee (IPC) was formed, was a collection of International Organisations of Sport for the Disabled (IOSD) who were the institutions with the power in disability sport, but gradually the IPC has whittled this away. Over the last decade Para-athletics has gained more attention, in part due to the development of the 'crossover supercrip' (Howe, 2011) Oscar Pistorius, who competed in both the London 2012 Olympic and Paralympic Games and has garnished much media attention (both positive and negative). At the London 2012 Paralympic Games, 1,100 athletes competed in 170 medal events.

Sports equipment

Many athletics events require specific sports equipment (for example, the discus, shot or javelin). In addition, athletes may use certain assistive devices as specified in the IPC Athletics rules (IPC, 2014). The rules for the practice of track and field athletics within IPC competitions draw mainly upon the rules and regulations that govern mainstream athletics – in other words the rulebook of the International Association of Athletics Federations (IAAF). As a result, the rules and regulations governing IPC athletics competitions are drawn from the IAAF rulebook with an addendum in the form of the IPC rules. These rules highlight how the IAAF's rules have been adapted to suit the diversity of abilities that the IPC are mandated to support (see Purdue & Howe, 2013).

Aerodynamic and lightweight wheelchairs and technologically advanced prosthetic running limbs are the most obvious forms of sports equipment used in Paralympic athletics. The dimensions and features of racing and platform wheelchairs, used in throwing events for athletes with spinal cord injuries or more severe cerebral palsy are outlined in the IPC Athletics rulebook.

Prosthetic devices, such as the carbon fibre blades made famous by Oscar Pistorius, may be used by amputees. These have been specifically developed to withstand the demands of sports competition and have catapulted IPC athletics into the media spotlight (Howe, 2011). Leg amputee athletes can either compete using prostheses or from a seated position of a wheelchair. The choice of the latter was the product of poor technology in the past, and more recently athletes with lower limb amputations have increasingly, in the developed world, chosen to compete using prostheses. Another form of sporting equipment that is unique to Paralympic athletics is the use of guide runners. Athletes with no usable vision, known in IPC terms as Class T11[1] use guides when they are racing on the track and they can be offered directional assistance while engaging in field events. Here the same athlete would be classified F11. Athletes with less than 5 per cent vision have an option of using a guide while competing on the track in the T12 classification. Athletes either run with a rope tether or other device to link with their sighted guides, but the visually impaired runner must cross the finish line before their guide. Acoustic devices (or a sighted 'caller') may be used to indicate take-off in jumping events, throwing target areas, etc.

Competition description

The events on the Paralympic programme include the vast majority of events catered for in mainstream athletics.

Track events include: sprint (100m, 200m, 400m); middle distance (800m, 1,500m); long distance (5,000m, 10,000m) and relay races (4x100m, 4x400m). On the road athletes can compete in the marathon.

Field events include: high jump, long jump, triple jump, discus, shot put, javelin, and some athletes compete in combined events in the case of the IPC in the form of a pentathlon. There are two notable absences from the IPC athletics programme, one on the track and one in the field. To date there is no Paralympic competition over 3,000m steeplechase or in the pole vault. As we shall see, the coach at the centre of this case study, while trained primarily as a long-distance running coach, has from time to time and with success turned his hand to all athletic disciplines.

Unlike the other case studies in this book the coach at the heart of this chapter did not see added value in being named. His coaching approach has been constructed by both listening and observing coaches and athletes through decades of involvement with athletics, a sport he is still passionate about today. As a result he is not named here as we feel it provides no benefit to the reader. Other coaching volumes (Jones et al., 2004; Walton, 1992) have named coaches, but it is felt that the act of naming an individual might lead future coaches to believe that by replicating the coaching methods of a particular individual they can somehow reproduce their success. Both the author and the coach involved in this chapter do not believe this to be the case.

The case-study coach – background

Born during World War II and raised on the edge of a large urban centre in the West of Scotland, the coach that is central to this chapter attended university in the mid-1960s and became a successful runner at the regional level. After graduation he turned first to the field of publishing before finding his vocation as a university lecturer. He began coaching when his daughter started training with the local athletics club when he realised the knowledge base at the club could have been harmful to his child.

In 1983 he was asked by the national coach of the visually impaired sportsmen and women to become a regional coach for athletics, and the following year he was the national athletics team manager at the Paralympic Games. At the 1984 Paralympic Games he was elected to the international board of the International Blind Sport Association (IBSA) in part because of his 'attention to detail and his ability as a problem solver'. By the early 1990s the development of the fledgling International Paralympic Committee (IPC) required the coach and now technical official to brandish all of his abilities to negotiate purposefully with the new organisation responsible for overseeing international development of pan-disability sport.

On domestic soil he was continually working on improving the infrastructure around athletes who wished to engage in Para-athletics at all levels. In the early 2000s he took a role within British Athletics where his role entailed supporting athletes and coaches to access high-quality medical treatment, such as physiotherapy and massage, as well as strength and conditioning experts in their home environments. He continued this role until just after the 2004 Paralympic Games, but in the background of this more high-profile position he was still working tirelessly with his own athletes. In the 1980s the coach had gained the reputation as arguably the best able-bodied women's distance running coach in the country, but by the turn of the millennium he had turned his attention to what high performance Paralympians needed regardless of which event they were involved in. After retirement from his academic post in 2002 he turned his considerable energy to helping all the athletes around him get the best out of themselves.

In 2005 he became employed by UK Athletics in charge of the Paralympic Potential Programme in the lead up to the Beijing Paralympic Games, where his bountiful energy led to many of the athletes on this programme gaining Paralympic selection, and in some cases gaining medals as well. Many of the athletes that went through the Potential Programme led by this coach became 'household' names in 2012.

The case-study coach – reflections

The coach at the heart of this chapter was instrumental in helping me in my own Paralympic career even though I am a Canadian citizen. As an exchange student at his university in the north of England, during the academic year 1986/87, I got to know the coach very well. His understanding of the simple attention to detail, and his ability to learn from others and both mimic and transform their coaching practice make him exceptional. The coach, let's call him Jimmy, is a humble man and his own humility about learning made him unusual in coaching, which is often full of ego-centric know it alls (Duda and Balaguer, 2007). This is to say that the reflection that follows is based on almost 30 years of friendship.

Habitus, sediment and the art of coaching

I now turn to focus upon the concept of embodiment to gain an insight in to how Jimmy actively engages with his athletic charges to produce an increased potential for sporting success. In order to fully understand performance coaching the concept of embodiment needs to be brought into the analysis since a coach must be able to translate their knowledge to the athletes with whom they are working. Kimayer has suggested that:

> Embodiment works against the tendency to treat bodies simply as property (my body and yours) or as vehicles entirely subordinate to our will. The essential insight of embodiment is that the body has a life of its own and that social worlds become inscribed on, or sedimented in, body physiology, habitus, and experience (2003: 285).

Over the last two decades the social investigation of sport coaching has placed increased importance upon the study of sporting embodiment. This work has been influenced by French social theory, particularly the writings of Bourdieu (Howe, 2006) and Foucault (Denison, 2010; Denison & Mills, 2014). From a methodological perspective embodiment postulates that the body is not an object to be studied in relation to the cultural world but is the subject of culture or the existential ground of culture (Csordas, 2002). In other words, the performance sporting body is (re) produced within and by the social environment. In the context of Paralympic performance sporting bodies influenced by Jimmy, the athletes can be disciplined through the creation of habit by the repetitive rudimentary drills that are set down by him to enhance the efficiency with which the body works when engaged in sporting practices. As Denison suggests 'effective coaching in track and field is largely understood to be a quest for order and control, as coaches continually strive to develop more detailed and predictable ways to manage and organize their athlete's training.' (2010:2). This conceptualisation of refinement has been, in one form or other, perhaps unconsciously, a focus for coaches' training procedures for generations (Howe, 2006). Therefore, training regimes that work on the body can be related to the theory of practice developed by Bourdieu (1977, 1984, 1990a) including in particular the concept of habitus. As a result this position may be adopted to explore the performance body and how this can be transformed by coaching practice (Howe, in press).

An athlete's habitus is continually being transformed through time and is the embodied sediment of every encounter they have had with the social world (Bourdieu, 1977, 1984, 1990a, 1990b) and in particular their encounters with their coaches. As a result, the physical actions of athletes are strategic and planned (Denison, 2010; Denison & Mills, 2014), and the better they are the more embodied cultural capital or physical capital a performer possesses. Qualities that are associated with performance athletes within the Paralympic games bodies, such as speed, strength and stamina are all part of what is required for an athlete to achieve physical capital within the culture of track and field athletics where these physical attributes are revered. Bourdieu's concept of habitus is closely linked to Merleau-Ponty's (1962) corporeal schema that articulates nicely the embodied agency of an athlete both as an individual and as a member of the social environment surrounding training and competition (Howe, in press). The corporeal schema comprises the skills required for the performance and the practical understanding of the competition that may be transformed depending on the action of other athletes. Development of an athletic habitus entails the continual modification of corporeal schema through the process of sedimentation that athletes undergo when they engage in variegated training regimes.

This conceptualisation of corporeal schema is of importance when trying to determine how athletes and coaches make the decisions they do without really thinking about them. When an athlete makes a strategic move in a race they do not have to think about running or accelerating; in a sense they 'know without knowing'. According to Crossley, 'the corporeal schema is an incorporated bodily know-how and practical sense; a perspectival grasp upon the world from the "point of view" of the body' (2001: 123). Corporeal schema, and the embodied knowledge that it entails, therefore need to be excavated in order to establish how the relationship between a particular coach and the bodies they train become performance athletes. This know-how gives the coach–athlete team the raw material to turn into habit and hopefully over time enable them to become more proficient at their chosen athletic discipline.

Physical action that becomes embodied in certain situations may be seen as habitual and these acts are often drilled into an athlete through countless repetition that lacks imagination. Habitual acts that are further developed by improvisation can be considered dispositions (Ryle, 1949). The disposition is the embodied ability to put the habitual training together in such a way that it can be quickly adapted to suit any situation. When an athlete goes through the training regime required of a high performance athlete, his or her body habitually knows things such as the 'race-pace' simply by the 'feel' of the body – there is no need to rely upon a stopwatch. Changes that occur within a race in terms of the tactics of the other competitors and the ability of the athlete to respond are directly linked to the disposition or the ability to improvise that the athlete innately has developed through physical training and lived experiences more generally (Howe, 2006: 328). Disposition can be used in the present to mould perception, thought and action to the extent that it has an important role to play in decisions that an agent might make in future encounters. In this sense high performance Paralympic athletes are manipulated by the coaches specifically, and can be seen not simply to follow rules but also to bend them in much the same way as Merleau-Ponty (1965) conceptualises improvisation as being fundamental to an individual's disposition. Therefore, the creation of habit through the discipline of training and competition undertaken by athletes may lead to the development of a flexible disposition that is central to performance athletics.

Coaching habit 'creating' embodied high performance athletes

Jimmy has almost 50 years of coaching development under his belt and an unsurpassed understanding of the need to enhance the bodily performance of his charges. His central philosophy is that it is the things that are currently not habitual that need to be worked upon. He also realises that the athletes with an impairment that he has turned into Paralympic medallists have distinctive understandings of their bodies. While this is the case with all athletes and is part of the coach's job in an individual sport such as athletics, it is made more complex because of the nature and varying degree of impairment. For example, for an athlete with visual impairment, teaching the fundamentals of good running technique through the application of various drills can be very challenging. As Jimmy suggests:

> When I first started working with visually impaired athletes I was a little bit lost. It is not straight forward to teach things such as good running technique let alone how to coach relatively more complex movements such as spin movements in discus or shot put. Getting to grips with how this was done took me a lot of time and patience.

It required the coach to re-evaluate his own know-how, because until he started to work with athletes with visual impairments he was always able to 'show' athletes in the conventional manner of demonstration. However he did eventually establish a robust method to train the habit required in athletics.

> I began to realise that people with visual impairment, even B1s (those athletes with no usable vision), are able to learn complex movements by mimicking

the movements that they feel. Today of course you have to be careful when you physically touch an athlete (as we all should have been in the past) but I have always done it in the presence of other people so that there is a realisation that there is nothing untoward.

By gently touching each part of the body that is required to move and naming it, the visually impaired athlete is able to mimic oral instruction. Such a process is often time consuming and requires a great deal of patience on both the part of the coach and the athlete. What is clear however is that with the success of the athletes under his charge who had visual impairment over the years his skill in transferring his coaching know-how to generations of high profile Paralympians is unsurpassed in Britain.

The same methods could be used with other impairment groups, but often visual representation was enough to reinforce good training practices, although from time to time the desire to coach athletes with learning difficulties required a very similar approach. As he stated:

> Sometimes in my experience the 'hands-on' approach to train or drilling running bodies works well with athletes who have a learning difficulty or even if they lack physical literacy. In other words I have adaptive coaching methods, but this is the product of decades of experience. I certainly did not have all the tools I have now when I started – only the simple feeling that I could do a better more informed job than those I saw coaching at my local club.

While the coach's desire was to help his charges go 'higher, faster and stronger' his own disposition and his sense of justice pulled him into the realm of the cultural politics of the Paralympic Games (see Howe, 2008). His work both in the UK and at the international level of Paralympic sport was a bonus for those who championed 'a better lot' for the visually impaired, but a good deal of traveling meant that training his athletes, from time to time, took a back seat and certainly led to a chaotic existence (Bowes & Jones, 2006).

> Sometimes my desire to fight for the injustice I felt was directed toward the [impairment group] overwhelmed me and I would charge in like Don Quixote in order to do my best to save them from what I thought was the tyranny of the IPC. But as a coach this was not always in the best interest of my athletes. Injustice is something that I have fought against since my youth, but unless one of my personal athlete's classification was being cut or realigned then my charging to defend the whole impairment group most certainly was counterproductive to my athletes' development.

Jimmy's disposition meant that throughout his career he has both fought for the underdog and tried to, at one and the same time, enhance his own athletes' performances. This is a dilemma faced by many charismatic individuals within the Paralympic movement. Because of its relative youth (Bailey, 2008; Tweedy &

Howe, 2011) charismatic individuals who enter the Paralympic field in one role are often drawn into others, and this was the case with Jimmy. But I fear Jimmy is a dying breed. At the heart of what he does is a philosophy based both upon increasing opportunity for participation and enhancement of performance (Hardman and Jones, 2013a, 2013b).

When Jimmy was asked specifically about his coaching philosophy he referred me to the quote below that was made by Franz Stampfl, the coach of Sir Roger Bannister who was a hero to many of his generation.

> Training is principally an act of faith. The athlete must believe in its efficacy; he must believe that through training he will become fitter and stronger; that by constant repetition of the same movements he will become more skilful and his muscles more relaxed. He must believe that through training his performance will improve and continue to improve indefinitely for as long as he continues to train to a progressively stiffer standard. He must be a fanatic for hard work and enthusiastic enough to enjoy it (Stampfl, 1955: 37).

While the quote above focused upon the athlete, it was Jimmy's belief that the coaching team should work in harmony to achieve the goals of improved performance. This sort of philosophical, faith driven coaching is seen as unfashionable in the modern sporting world, where lay knowledge and high-quality interpersonal skills are being replaced by market-driven coaching programmes, run both by national governing bodies and increasingly the university sector:

> The lineage of the philosopher coaches is in peril, threatened by the march of time and the changing environment of sports. The growing organizational complexity and the commercialization of athletics in pro teams and institutions of higher learning have changed the mix of skills required and sought in coaches (Walton, 1992:157).

While Jimmy may be a dying breed, he still continues to produce national and international standard athletes both in Paralympic and mainstream athletics. He continues to learn from other coaches both old and new and he is keen that his training methods are not outdated, but prefers to communicate personally with other coaches than to attend coaching workshops that are often run in a 'sterile and unpassionate manner'. Jimmy quoted verbatim the simplicity of his role when he said 'training is that process of education of the body which prepares it to meet with safety, exceptional and extreme demands upon its energy' (Abrahams, 1952: 25), and worried that contemporary coaching sciences 'often over-egg the pudding' with the objective of simply looking intelligent to the national governing body and thinking of new ways to re-invent the wheel.

The concerns may be seen by some in the sport of Para-athletics as the ranting of someone on the way out, but the concerns of Jimmy appear, to an extent, to be legitimate. As more money is poured into the sport and a younger generation who have all the qualifications but limited lived experience take senior coaching roles, the long-term future of athletics to someone as seasoned as Jimmy could be seen to be in peril. As a result Jimmy has begun to take a more active role in the last few years in coach mentoring programmes in order to pass on his bountiful knowledge.

> In recent years I have become a mentor to younger coaches, but many of the really young coaches are not eligible for such schemes. It seems ridiculous that getting coaching awards through the sport is open to them but not the mentoring programme. I would like to see mentoring programmes to be open to anyone who has the enthusiasm to coach. It is a passion for pushing people in the training environment while being mindful of various hazards that is the key to producing successful coaches and ultimately athletes. To many people in my sport I am a grumpy old man with nothing to teach the younger generation.

The coach's willingness to mentor others regardless of their experience should be celebrated and it is endemic of the power struggle that seems to be all too common in coaching environments (Denison & Mills, 2014). For me, Jimmy is right to be mindful of the power game, but if he opts out entirely the next generation will not benefit from his considerable knowledge.

The future of coaching Para-athletics

When Jimmy began coaching Para-Athletics in 1984 he started in a world where the International Organisations of Sport for the Disabled (IOSD) namely the Cerebral Palsy International Sports and Recreation Association (CP-ISRA), International Blind Sport Association (IBSA), International Sports Federation for Persons with Intellectual Disability (INAS-FID), and the International Wheelchair and Amputee Sport Association (IWAS) held the power. From 1989 onward the power of these institutions has been in decline and the International Paralympic Committee has grown in stature (Bailey, 2008; Tweedy & Howe, 2011). As such, the coach politicking on behalf of an IOSD was about trying to stop the erosion of power, but as I said earlier this may have had consequences for the athletes under his charge.

Jimmy's ability as a strong political advocate for IBSA as well as an elite coach who through his life has collected knowledge tacitly (Nash & Collins, 2006) will be very hard to replicate in the future, in part because of the professionalisation of both sport coaching and the administration of the International Paralympic Committee. With the push to professionalise coaching at all levels (including disability sport) there is a need to remember that hands-on experience in coaching contexts is arguably more valuable than coaching courses and/or degrees. Such a statement may sit uneasily with the readers of this chapter. Certainly, if you are reading this chapter and you are enrolled on a coaching degree you might be less than best pleased. However, it is important to realise that high-quality coaching knowledge does not come simply from reading books – we need to spend time 'in the trenches' before we have the requisite experience to be the elite level coaches that are required within the contemporary Paralympic sporting context. Coaching, according to Jimmy, is a blend of both science and art, where the variety of experiences, both in training environments and life more generally can lead to enhanced performance (see Bates, 2007).

In our modern desire to make many social practices more scientific, in order to add validity to their pursuit, we have taken away much of what makes us human. The ability of a charismatic coach like Jimmy to pay attention to what a wheelchair racer or visually impaired runner both can and cannot do is fundamentally important to enhancing their performance. By communicating appropriately (see Bowes, 2007) Jimmy listens, learns evaluates and then offers advice that is designed to enhance performance. What is key is that Jimmy does not offer the same advice to everyone under his charge even if they possess the same weakness. Messages need to be tailored to the individual in a manner that will fit with their habitus and disposition, and this will ultimately facilitate a more rapid embodiment of the skill or training activity. Of course, the sport of track and field athletics is appropriate for this one-to-one intervention, whereas for team sports it is much more complex.

We as coaches need to be mindful of blending our knowledge from sport science textbooks as to how the body works both biomechanically and physiologically with tacit knowledge that has been gained from everyday experiences (see Nash & Collins, 2006) and with our own observations of our own bodies and those of others in various stages of movement. In essence, high performance coaching is a magical blend of science and art regardless of whether the body we are coaching has an impairment or not.

Recommendations for coaching, education and practice

The big recommendation I would make to all readers of both this chapter and the book more generally is to forget the distinction between the 'able' and the 'disabled' athlete. The problem(s) of coaching are not that polarised. When you next venture down trackside, do not see your charges as those who can or those that cannot, but rather on a continuum of difference. That is, as any trained group would have a variety of ability – so do not exclude someone from a training session because they have an impairment. Talk to them about what they can and cannot do and make your training sessions more inclusive by adopting the stand of a reflective practitioner (Gilbert and Trudel, 2006). This will allow you to include them in the future – if not right then and there. Remember, as Jimmy says, 'We need to celebrate difference not shy away from it'.

Additional resources and supplementary material

Along with the book you are currently reading I would suggest those who are interested in coaching athletes to become Paralympians get a hold of Vanlandeijck,

Y. and Thompson, W. (eds) (in press). *Training and coaching of the paralympic athlete.* Oxford: Wiley Blackwell. This volume draws upon state-of-the-art knowledge in sport science (loosely defined) to highlight many of the nuances regarding coaching potential Paralympians.

Notes

1   T is for track, the first digit signals visual impairment and the second highlights the class.

References

Abrahams, A. (1952). *Fitness for the average man.* London: Christopher Johnson.

Bailey, S. (2008). *Athlete first: A history of the Paralympic movement.* Chichester, UK: Willey and Sons.

Bates, I. (2007). Coaching experience, coaching performance. In Denison, J. *Coaching knowledges: Understanding the dynamics of sport performance* (pp. 113–137). London: A. & C. Black.

Bourdieu, P. (1977). *Outline of a theory of practice.* Cambridge: Cambridge University Press.

Bourdieu, P. (1984). *Distinction: A social critique of the judgement of taste.* London: Routledge.

Bourdieu, P. (1990a). *The logic of practice.* Cambridge: Polity Press.

Bourdieu, P. (1990b). *In other words: Essays towards a reflective sociology.* Cambridge: Polity Press.

Bowes, I. (2007). Communicating with athletes. In Denison, J. *Coaching knowledges: Understanding the dynamics of sport performance* (pp. 85–112). London: A. & C. Black.

Bowes, I., & Jones, R. (2006). Working at the edge of chaos: Understanding coaching as a complex, interpersonal system. *Sport Psychologist, 20*(2), 235–245.

Crossley, N. (2001). *The social body: Habit, identity and desire.* London: Sage

Csordas, T. (2002). *Body/meaning/healing.* New York: Palgrave Macmillian.

Denison, J. (2010). Planning, practice and performance: the discursive formation of coaches' knowledge. *Sport, Education and Society, 15*(4), 461–478.

Denison, J. & Mills, J. (2014). Planning for distance running: coaching with Foucault. *Sport Coaching Review, 3*(1), 1–16.

Duda, J. & Balaguer, I. (2007). Coach-created motivational climate. In Jowett, S. & Lavallee, D. (eds) *Social Psychology in Sport,* (pp.117–130). Champaign, IL: Human Kinetics.

Gilbert, W. & Trudel, P. (2006). The coach as reflective practitioner. In Jones, R. L. *The sports coach as educator: Reconceptualising sport coaching* (pp.113–127). London: Routledge.

Hardman, A. & Jones, C. (2013a). Philosophy for Coaches. In Jones, R. L. & Kingston, K. *An Introduction to sport coaching: Connecting theory to practice* (2nd Edition) (pp. 99–111). London: Routledge.

Hardman, A. & Jones, C. (2013b). Ethics for Coaches. In Jones, R. L. and Kingston, K. *An Introduction to sport coaching: Connecting theory to practice* (2nd Edition) (pp. 113–130). London: Routledge.

Howe, P.D. (2006). Habitus, barriers and the [ab]use of the science of interval training in the 1950s. *Sport in History, 26*(2), 325–344.

Howe, P.D (2008). The tail is wagging the dog: Body culture, classification and the Paralympic movement. *Ethnography, 9*(4), 499–517.

Howe, P.D. (2011). Cyborg and supercrip: The Paralympics technology and the (dis)empowerment of disabled athletes. *Sociology, 45*(5), 868–882.

Howe, P.D. (in press). Sociology of Sport. In Vanlandeijck, Y. & Thompson, W. (eds) *Training and coaching of the paralympic athlete.* Oxford: Wiley Blackwell.

IPC (2014). *International paralympic committee athletics rules and regulations 2014–2015.* Retrieved from http://www.paralympic.org/sites/default/files/document/1407151625 21888_2014_01%2Bipc%2Bathletics%2Brules%2Band%2Bregulation%2B2014-2015_ final%2B2014-2.pdf

Jones, R., Armour, K. & Potrac, P. (2004). *Sport coaching cultures: From practice to theory.* London: Routledge.

Kimayer, L.J. (2003). Reflections on Embodiment. In J. M. Wilce (ed) *Social cultural lives of immune systems* (pp. 282–302). London: Routledge.

MacAloon, J. (1981). *This great symbol: Pierre de Coubertin and the origins of the modern Olympic Games.* London: University of Chicago Press.

Merleau-Ponty, M. (1962). *Phenomenology of perception.* London: Routledge and Kegan Paul.

Merleau-Ponty, M. (1965). *The structure of behaviour.* London: Methuen.

Nash, C. & Collins, D. (2006). Tacit knowledge in expert coaching: science or art. *Quest, 58,* 465–477.

Purdue, D.E.J. & Howe, P.D. (2013). Who's in and who is out? Legitimate bodies within the Paralympic Games. *Sociology of Sport Journal, 30*(1), 24–40.

Ryle, G. (1949). *The concept of mind.* London: University of Chicago Press.

Stampfl, F. (1955). *On Running.* London: Herbert Jenkins.

Tweedy, S. & Howe, P.D. (2011). Introduction to the Paralympic Movement. In Vanlandewijck, Y. and Thompson, W. *The paralympic athlete* (pp.3–30). Oxford: Wiley-Blackwell.

Walton, G.M. (1992). *Beyond winning: The timeless wisdom of great philosopher coaches.* Leeds, UK: Human Kinetics Press.

Editors' summary reflections

One of the key narratives shared across the case studies has been the experiences of coaches working in sports that have struggled over the last 20–40 years, or thereabouts, to gain recognition and a profile either within the context of disability sport and/or the wider sport landscape. As coaches such as Dantas, Pohlman, and Sawicki evidence, the relatively nascent nature of some sports, and the related struggle to translate participatory/inclusion foundations into high performance strategies, have had implications for the contemporary coaching landscape; in particular, for the sustainability, viability and priorities of coach education frameworks. In Howe's case study, and especially in relation to coach development and career progression, the situation is a little different. Athletics has been a mainstay of the disability and Para-sport movements for a slightly longer period. Thus, in many cases, some of the issues being experienced within other disability realms and Para-sport context (for example, resourcing, talent identification pathways, administrative/political patronage and developing rigorous coach development frameworks, acquiring and implementing interdisciplinary knowledge of disabilities to enhance the coach–athlete dyad), have been borne out earlier within athletics. One particular point of significance Howe raises, however, is the significant notion of embodiment as a means of framing the inherent artfulness required in coaches' pedagogies.

While embodiment/theories of embodiment are not new within the sociology of sport or the analysis of athletes, and practitioners, experiences (Allen-Collinson, 2009; Burroughs & Nauright, 2000; Fitzgerald, 2005; Hunter & Emerald, 2016), Howe reminds us that notions of embodiment have largely been implicit within coaching practices. Coaches, or at least the coach Howe draws upon, have demonstrated that the principles of embodiment (effectively, recognising how the qualities of movement manifest within individual's corporeal performances) lie at the heart of good coaching. Howe's points regarding the way in which coaches utilise an understanding of embodiment to achieve or improve an athlete's abilities, and foster athlete's own attentiveness to their bodies in motion, raises further questions. In what ways, for example, might coaches within disability sport impart their knowledge of physique, physicality and motion to help athletes come to better know their own bodies, and transform this knowledge into better training and performance outcomes? (Such a question becomes particularly pertinent when we consider that many high performance coaches in this book have already noted the limited time able to be spent with their athletes; essentially making such an aim difficult to achieve.) Moreover, can this knowledge ever be genuine or legitimate when there may be a disconnect between the able-ness of the coach and the able-ness of the athlete's bodies?

For Howe, theories of embodiment can help refine and focus coaches' attention on the body *in situ*. However, as Howe's case study, and that of Sawicki, Tromans, Milkins, and Dantas too, attest, the current cultures of high performance sport (and coaching programmes therein) have become inordinately complex; in particular with the over-emphasis on scientific knowledge, involvement of more stakeholders working to improve 'the athlete', increased performance maxims, and resourcing and administrative pressures. Amidst these forces the significance of corporeal cognition in the coach–athlete relationship, and the importance of this to the art of coaching, can be lost. Howe's examination of the Para-athletics coach serves as a good reminder to other practitioners about how easy it can be within the contemporary maelstroms of the high performance world to lose track of the necessity that *knowing* your athlete and the capacities and capabilities of their bodies is, invariably, the start of effective coaching. As such, and what the other case studies in this book underscore, is coaches (and the sporting industries in which they work, writ large), might need to take a closer look at how coaches might gain such knowledge and how it might be nurtured and refined throughout their career. We might also ask, additionally, what opportunities there could be within high performance Para-sport settings to foreground embodiment as part of athlete's overall development and performance objectives? Given that there are clearly advantages of coaches gaining a deeper appreciation and knowledge of athletes' bodies (not unlike Bates, Ferguson, Fivash and Milkins also suggest), how can the lessons of Howe's coach case study be operationalised within other sport settings? The challenge, in the first instance perhaps, may be to simply rethink the ways coach education programmes might, in attending to the art of the profession, educate and develop practitioners' understandings of embodiment.

References

Allen-Collinson, J. (2009). Sporting embodiment: sports studies and the (continuing) promise of phenomenology. *Qualitative Research in Sport and Exercise, 1*(3), 279–296.

Burroughs, A. & Nauright, J. (2000). Women's sports and embodiment in Australia and New Zealand. *The International Journal of the History of Sport*, *17*(2-3),188–205.

Fitzgerald, H. (2005). Still feeling like a spare piece of luggage? Embodied experiences of (dis)ability in physical education. *Physical Education and Sport Pedagogy*, *10*(1), 41–59.

Hunter, L. & Emerald, E. (2016). Sensory narratives: Capturing embodiment in narratives of movement, sport, leisure and health. *Sport, Education and Society*, *21*(1), 28–46.

8

OZZIE SAWICKI – COACHING ALPINE SKIING

The curiosity to be the best

David F. H. Legg and Bradley M. J. McClure

Historical context of Paralympic Alpine skiing

Paralympic sport in Canada traces its roots back to the 1950s, following a similar path to what occurred at Stoke Mandeville Hospital in the United Kingdom. Returning war veterans were encouraged to use sport as therapy and the earliest disability sport teams were wheelchair basketball clubs in Montreal and Vancouver. In the late 1960s wheelchair sport organized itself nationally to effectively host a Pan-American Wheelchair Games in Winnipeg in 1967 and to ensure that a team could compete at the 1968 Paralympic Games in Israel. The Canadian Wheelchair Sports Association was officially formed in 1969 with other disability sport organizations following in the late 1970s after Canada's hosting of the 1976 Paralympic Games in Toronto (Legg, 2000). The Canadian Paralympic Committee was formed thereafter with Canada next hosting the Paralympic Games in 2010 in Vancouver. During this time a number of Canadian icons within the Paralympic movement, including Rick Hansen and Robert Steadward, the first President of the International Paralympic Committee, helped the movement evolve and flourish. A number of Paralympic coaches from Canada have also been recognized as pioneers and trailblazers within their sport and movement. Ozzie Sawicki, profiled here, is one of these outstanding coaches and leaders.

Many within the Paralympic movement, including coaches, athletes and administrators recognize the contributions made by leaders such as Sawicki. The understanding of coaching athletes with a disability, from an academic perspective, however, is relatively limited. Reid & Prupas (1998) analyzed 204 publications in disability sport and found that only five addressed coaching. The reason for this is unknown but the reality continues today with only a few studies available in a North American context to better understand Paralympic coaching.

The need for a better understanding of Paralympic coaching is evidenced by the fact that 3 per cent of Canadians with a disability compared to 30 per cent of able-bodied Canadians are enrolled in sport organizations (Heritage Canada, 2006). In addition, 37 per cent of children and youth with disabilities never take part in organized physical activities compared to just 10 per cent amongst those without disabilities. The lack of specialized coaches is likely one of the key factors resulting in this trend.

We know Paralympic coaches are important but little research exists. Douglas et al. (2015) reported that since 1986 there has been little growth and development relating to coaches in disability sport (Falcao et al., 2015; Robbins et al., 2010; Tawse et al., 2012). Culver et al. (2015) meanwhile reflected on the barriers that para-sport coaches had to overcome in order to build their coaching knowledge, of which there were many. Amongst these were few opportunities for professional development, minimal para-specific coaching materials (Côté & Gilbert, 2009) and few opportunities to work with and meet other para-sport coaches. Sawicki overcame all of these and has made every effort to address each one. Perhaps by understanding how coaches such as Sawicki progressed and ultimately excelled we can address these gaps. To facilitate this we will begin with an understanding of the context that Sawicki entered – para Alpine.

Today, para Alpine is practised worldwide and features six disciplines: downhill, slalom, giant slalom, super-G, super combined, and team events. Para snowboard, initially evolved through an Alpine structure, but has subsequently evolved into an independent snow sport (Sawicki, personal communication, 2016). Competition accommodates male and female athletes with a physical impairment such as spinal injuries, cerebral palsy, amputation, les autres (meaning the others) conditions and blindness/visual impairment (International Paralympic Committee, 2015).

In para Alpine, athletes compete in one of three categories based on their functional ability, and results based on a calculation system that allows athletes with different impairments to compete against each other. Skiers with blindness/visual impairment are guided through the course by sighted guides using signals to indicate the course to follow. Other athletes, depending on their disability, may use equipment that is adapted to their needs including single ski, sit-ski or orthopedic aids (International Paralympic Committee, 2015).

Para Alpine's growth followed a similar pattern to other wheelchair sports after World War II, where the first competitors were primarily ex-servicemen. The earliest competitors were from Austria and Germany, with the first documented Championships for skiers with a disability held in Badgastein, Austria, in 1948 (International Paralympic Committee, 2015).

At this time and until the 1970s, only those athletes with amputations and visual impairments competed in para Alpine events. The first Paralympic Winter Games, meanwhile, did not take place until 1976 in Örnsköldsvik, Sweden. Here, two Alpine disciplines were featured including slalom and giant slalom. Downhill was added to the Paralympic program in 1984 in Innsbruck, Austria, and super-G in 1994 at the Lillehammer, Norway Winter Paralympic Games. Sit-skiing, for those with spinal cord injuries, was introduced as a demonstration sport at the Innsbruck, Austria Paralympic Games in 1984 and became a medal event at the Nagano, Japan 1998 Paralympic Games.

Returning to Canada, skiing for athletes with a disability started in the early 1970s. The Alberta Amputee Ski Association was the first organization catering specifically to athletes with a disability and was created in 1970. Six years later the Canadian Association of Disabled Skiing (CADS) was formed. Jerry Johnston, a mentor to Ozzie later in his career, was instrumental in creating both organizations. Jerry had begun teaching skiing to people with mobility impairments at the Sunshine Village Ski School in Banff, Alberta in the early 1960s (Rhodes, no date). In 1968, Johnston attended the World's Ski Instructors Conference (Interski) in Aspen, Colorado. One of the demonstrations was by US skiers who had disabilities. In 1970, Johnston invited this group to Banff to help him organize a local clinic and a year later Johnston and a colleague began offering similar clinics across Canada. In 1972, Johnston took a number of Alberta-based skiers with disabilities to the US National Races at Winter Park, Colorado. A number of smaller events followed and in 1975 Johnston decided to organize the Canadian International Disabled Ski Meet (later known as the Canadian Association of Disabled Skiers (CADS) Festival) (Rhodes, no date). At this time, athletes with disabilities competed only against racers with similar disabilities. At the Sunshine Race, however, it was decided to have each racer estimate their time. This was a system used by the Japanese Handicapped Skiers Association, which by coincidence had skiers visiting that same weekend. The skier with the actual time closest to the estimated time was declared the winner with the rationale being that everyone would have an equal opportunity to win. This became known as the 'Guesstimation' style (Rhodes, no date).

Following this race, Recreation Canada became involved and organized a meeting for those interested in skiing and water skiing for persons with physical disability. The purpose was to design and organize a national body. Recreation Canada, who was funding the meeting, had a long-term plan for the National Sports Association for the Disabled. Recreation Canada could fund a national body but not individual groups so the proposed formation would provide a collective voice for skiing and water skiing. Several organizations were invited including provincial and local disabled skiing associations, the Canada Ski Association, the Canadian Ski Instructor's Alliance and the Canadian Water Skiing Association, Presidents of agencies for people with disabilities and sport organizations for persons with disabilities such as the Canadian National Institute for the Blind and Canadian Wheelchair Sport Association were also invited. While this meeting did not result in a group originally foreseen by Recreation Canada, it did result in the creation of the Canadian Association of Disabled Skiing, and in 1976 the aforementioned Jerry Johnston was elected as the first President (Rhodes, no date). With Johnston as the lead, CADS took on the responsibility for developing skiing for persons with a disability in Canada and continues today providing grassroots programming. The responsibilities of the elite, high performance Paralympic stream of Alpine skiing, meanwhile, were transferred to Alpine Canada in the early

2000s, and this mirrored a process that occurred with many sports, such as swimming, archery and athletics.

Historical context of Ozzie Sawicki

It is at this point within the development of para Alpine that Ozzie Sawicki first became involved, but it is not just Alpine skiing that Ozzie influenced. Over a 25-year history Sawicki coached in both winter and summer sports, at levels ranging from grassroots to the Paralympic Games. At the Paralympic level he held a variety of roles including Head Coach of Para Alpine and Chef de Mission of the Canadian Paralympic Team.

It was in para Alpine, however, where Sawicki started and where he continues to be a leader as Head of Technical Controls and Officiating for the International Paralympic Committee's (IPC) Alpine Skiing and Snowboard Technical Committee. He is also a leader within the profession of coaching having held such roles as Vice-President, Coaches of Canada, Board member and Chairperson, Coaches Council of the Canadian Paralympic Committee, and Co-Chairperson, Coach Alberta. It is, however, his significant role within the para Alpine skiing community that will be the focus for the remainder of this chapter.

Ozzie was Head Coach and Program Director of the Canadian Para Alpine Ski Team from 2000–2004. In Salt Lake City at the 2002 Winter Paralympic Games, Ozzie's para Alpine team won 12 of the 15 medals earned by Team Canada. This accomplishment was built on a ten-year career as a coach at various levels including a multitude of clubs in Calgary, Banff and Vancouver for able-bodied persons and athletes with a disability. Ozzie's contributions to para Alpine also include administrative leadership responsibilities as evidenced by his work with the Canadian National Coaching Certification Program (NCCP) as a facilitator and evaluator. The NCCP is Canada's national coaching training program and since the 1980s has trained more than one million coaches in 67 sports, with approximately 50,000 coaches trained each year (Culver et al., 2015).

As with many coaches, Sawicki did not start immediately at the international level. Instead, he began as an undergraduate and graduate student in physical geography and geomorphology at the University of Calgary. Like many other Paralympic coaches he started by chance and has built upon his experiences as an able-bodied athlete (Cregan et al., 2007).

For Sawicki it was through Ted Rhodes that he learned about Paralympic sport. Rhodes ran a Learn to Ski program for the Canadian Association of Disabled Skiers (CADS) on Friday nights and he also organized the weather station for the geography department, which is how he came to meet Ozzie. Ted had started the program in 1973 with eight people with disabilities, including persons who had cerebral palsy, visual impairments and amputations. Ted learned that Ozzie had been involved in ski racing as a teenager and asked him to volunteer. This was 1989, a year after the 1988 Calgary Olympic Winter Games where Sawicki had watched with awe the demonstration event for Paralympic Alpine skiers. This was the second and final time that athletes with disabilities would be included in demonstration events during the Winter Olympic Games. Sawicki agreed to Ted's request and was immediately hooked. The following year Sawicki became the Assistant Coach for the Alberta Provincial Para Alpine Team and a year later, and not unusual in disability sport, Sawicki was named Head Coach. A few years following, Sawicki returned to coaching able-bodied athletes ranging from 11-year-olds to high performance level adults. He, nevertheless, remained involved and interested in disability sport, acting as the Chief of Races for the Canadian Championships in 1998 as well as volunteering sporadically with the para Alpine programs in Calgary. In 2000 all that changed when Ozzie was asked to be the Head Coach of the Canadian Para Alpine Team. Two years later Sawicki as the head coach was at the 2002 Salt Lake City Paralympic Games.

Following the Salt Lake Games, the transition of responsibility for para Alpine athletes began moving from CADS to Alpine Canada Alpin, the able-bodied national sport organization (NSO) responsible for Alpine racing. This type of transition had also occurred in a number of other NSOs, including swimming and archery among others, where the previously able-bodied focused organization was now responsible for athletes with a disability. Sawicki continued to manage the para Alpine team and was also now able to learn from the able-bodied system and their coaching network. At this time, Sawicki was also completing his National Coach Certification Program (NCCP) Level 4, for Elite High Performance Coaches at the University of Calgary, and as a result was exposed to a number of other leading sport scientists and coaches.

After the 2002 Winter Paralympic Games, Sawicki turned his attention to other priorities, stepping down as the national para Alpine coach. His commitment to the sport, however, did not wane as he instead focused on system development. He attempted to do this by developing the Carving the Future Introductory Ski Racing Camps program through Alpine Canada Alpin. This program was built, in part, on the Alpine Integration model that was included in the able-bodied Skiing Long-term Athlete Development plan, which he also helped to write, known as Para AIM 2 WIN – Para-alpine Integrated Long-term Athlete Development Model.

Recognizing the need to facilitate athlete development, Sawicki then saw the next step as coach training. As a result, he created the Para-entry Level Alpine Coach Certification Pathway and materials, and most recently assisted in developing Para-development Level Alpine Coach Certification Pathway and materials for the Canadian Ski Coaches Federation. Other publications by Sawicki that continue to be used today include *Alpine Ski Racing: Athletes With a Disability*, and *Alpine Ski Racing: Athletes With a Disability, Technical Considerations*. Alpine Canada Alpin and the Canadian Ski Coaches Federation have continued to build on these initial materials to progress the ability for coaches to understand the para Alpine coaching context.

Amazingly, Ozzie has not confined his coaching interest to para Alpine. While not the focus for this chapter, it is still important to note that Ozzie was named Head Coach of the Canadian Para Athletics team by Athletics Canada from 2009 to 2011, leading the transition from the team competing in Beijing in 2008 to the one preparing to compete in London 2012.

> The rationale for my hiring was that I didn't have an athletics/track and field background, but in Canada track and field at the Paralympic level was in a rebuild framework. There was no coaching rationale, there was nothing in place as a structure, so they wanted somebody to come in that they thought could help develop a new structure for athletics. So my role was to act as that structural lead and bring in athletics expertise as event coaches to lead the programs and oversee how that structure would be built.

Ozzie stepped away from athletics in 2011, and most recently has worked in equestrian as the Canadian Equestrian team's performance advisor leading up to and during the 2012 London Paralympic Games. Today he continues his involvement with equestrian as the Talent Identification Advisor for Equine Canada in the Olympic discipline of eventing, and as the High Performance Advisor for the Canadian Eventing Team preparing for the 2016 Rio de Janeiro Olympic Games.

Beyond the specifics of para Alpine, Ozzie has also been a leader in the Paralympic movement. Sawicki was a Team Canada Mission Staff member and the Coaches of Canada representative at the Beijing 2008 Summer Paralympic Games and was an IPC/FIS official for Alpine skiing for the Vancouver 2010 Winter Paralympic Games. Most recently he was the Chef de Mission for the Canadian Paralympic team competing at the 2014 Sochi Winter Paralympic Games. It was during these Games that Sawicki coined the slogan 'Perform in the moment, take pride in the journey!'. Canada had predicted it would replicate a top three gold medal finish in the final standings, equivalent to what it had accomplished in Vancouver in 2010. Sawicki's vision and leadership helped build a team that accomplished this goal, placing third in the world with seven gold, two silver and seven bronze medals.

Finally, Ozzie has made significant contributions to the avocation and professionalization of coaching for all sports. Ozzie was one of the first to obtain the title of Canadian Chartered Professional Coach and has been involved as an instructor and mentor for a multitude of coaches in Canada. For his efforts, Ozzie has received the 2012 Queen Elizabeth II Diamond Jubilee Medal, 2004 Petro Canada Coaching Excellence Award, 2003 Canadian Ski Coaches Federation Dave Murray Memorial Coach of the Year Award, 2002 Alpine Canada Alpin President's Award for Excellence and the 2002 Petro Canada Coaching Excellence Award.

The case study of Ozzie Sawicki

The genesis of interest and engagement

According to Douglas et al. (2015), a significant portion of coaching science research has focused on understanding how coaches learn to coach (Cushion et al., 2010). Formal learning typically includes coach certification programs while non-formal learning usually involves experiences such as coaching conferences. Informal learning, meanwhile, includes personal experiences and interactions with others. Sawicki used all three of these approaches to learning albeit in different ways throughout his career.

Ozzie's career as a coach began like that of so many others – he was asked. As described earlier, Ozzie was an undergraduate student at the University of Calgary and a faculty member there noted his background in Alpine skiing and encouraged him to volunteer with the local disability Learn to Ski Program at Canada Olympic Park. It was then later as a graduate student, where Ozzie was influenced by his supervisor, Derald Smith, to be curious, organized and to lead. Smith had also been a ski racer, and that bond ignited within Ozzie a desire to remain part of the sport while going through university.

After volunteering for only a short period of time, Ozzie was asked to help out with the Alberta Disabled Ski Team, at the time led by Dan Adams. All Ozzie knew was what he had learned as a skier himself, a situation not unheard of within the coaching literature (e.g. Douglas & Hardin, 2014; Schinke et al., 1995).

To help him become a better coach, Ozzie decided to take a Level 1 Alpine Coaching course. Here again Ozzie was influenced by a strong leader, the course conductor, Nancy Jo O'Neill. Ozzie then took the Level 1 theory course, and again, was significantly influenced by the course conductor, Don McGavern. These names may not mean much to an international audience, but they serve as examples that will likely be echoed in other chapters of the importance of mentorship and personal influence. This also will tie into Ozzie's concern for the future of coaching and recommendations.

Ozzie noted that during the first night of coaching he was terrified. Upon arriving at Canada Olympic Park to volunteer, his mentor Ted Rhodes paired him with three athletes with an intellectual disability. Two had Down's syndrome and the third had a developmental delay that manifested itself with anger management concerns. Ozzie was given his lift ticket and told to teach the three students 'how to ski.' On the first chair lift up the hill the third athlete punched Ozzie. Ozzie without really thinking about it too much punched him back. Both were shocked by the response. The parents, two lifts behind, witnessed the entire episode and were amazed at the interaction and commented that nobody had ever struck their son back. While not advised nor condoned, what this did was challenge the boy and both he and Ozzie become lifelong friends. What Ozzie remembers from that first experience is that he had a choice. He could be afraid or he could meet the challenge head on.

After that first night Ozzie did think that perhaps coaching athletes with a disability was not the right environment for him, and this persisted for another week. But he had made a promise to Ted, someone he admired a great deal, and kept his commitment. By the third week 'he was hooked' and from that point on looked forward to his volunteer coaching duties. Ozzie went from being 'scared silly' to not imagining how he could live without it, and found that after the season ended he missed his athletes and became friends with many, continuing the interactions throughout the summer.

Entrance into elite coaching

In 1993, after completing his graduate degree, Sawicki left Canada for two years to work overseas in Malaysia, and was thus removed from para Alpine coaching. He found himself missing the atmosphere, and so upon returning to Calgary in 1996, he resumed his coaching activities, taking on the leadership of the Sunshine Village Juvenile Ski Racing Program located in Banff, just an hour west of Calgary. He was only coaching able-bodied athletes at this time.

Four years later in 2000, Ozzie was then approached, based on his prior experiences with the Alberta team, to take on the National Team Head Coaching role with the Canadian Para Alpine Ski Team (at the time called the Canadian Disabled Alpine Ski Team). He was approached by Al Matile, Alpine Chair for CADS. Matile thought that Ozzie had an interesting and exciting combination of coaching skills and professional business background with a desire to continue developing and evolving as a leader. At the time, the National Para Alpine Team was transitioning from being administered by CADS to Alpine Canada Alpin. Matile felt that Ozzie had the skills that would benefit the program as it grew, but also that he could be helpful in ensuring a quality transition from CADS to ACA. These challenges when presented to Ozzie were exactly what he was looking for.

Ozzie was also at a point in his life of trying to decide if sport and coaching was a potential career path versus business and industry. Simply put, the sport community enthused and motivated Ozzie far more than the other, and he wanted to see if sport could provide a realistic career option through coaching at a leadership and head coaching level.

From disability to elite sport: the 2002 Winter Paralympic Games

Another hallmark of Sawicki's career was his ability to balance the shift and cultural changes from a disability-focused organization to one that purportedly was centered on elite high performance sport. It was in the early 2000s when Sawicki became the Head Coach of the Canadian Para Alpine Team and this was when …

> Sport Canada was requiring that the disabled national team programs that weren't under the national sport organization umbrella were required to move under the national sport organization umbrella.

Sawicki had the business and coaching backgrounds that thus helped facilitate this merger process and protect the interests of the para team. The transition from CADS to Alpine Canada as discussed earlier resulted in increased funding for the athletes, which then meant a greater financial accountability and increased administrative oversight.

> The expectation was, okay now you're a mainstream national team versus the CADS framework, the expectations grew very quickly in terms of

expectations of athlete performance, expectations of coordination of the World Cup tour, and so on.

What did not happen was a concomitant increase in resources for coaches and this put a significant strain on coaches. At that time the integrated support team was relatively small by today's standards with no sport psychologists, trainers or multiple coaches. The national team had Ozzie and one assistant.

Challenges with the organizational transition was also evident with athletes. Sawicki noted that …

> it was an interesting dynamic of the old guard that said just leave us alone we know what we're doing, and this is how we do it, and the new group that said they were looking for leadership. It was an exercise in how do you create the leadership to get everybody bought into a program.

Sawicki thus saw the para Alpine team as a clean slate that could be built into whatever they wanted. With that, he went to work creating the first program in winter sport to build and implement a testing protocol for Alpine skiers of different disabilities. He also created full measurement structures and feedback loops. It was the first time anyone, as far as they knew in para Alpine, had a written yearly training plan and a quadrennial plan. 'The Paralympic sports had rarely been exposed to that on the winter side.'

All of this culminated with the Winter Paralympic Games in Salt Lake City in 2002. These Games were the most significant event that shaped Sawicki as a coach and his sport, as it was here that para Alpine went from simple to complex. The World Cup program had been in its nascent stage of development, often with volunteer or part-time coaches. In Salt Lake City, the scope of coaching increased, as did the credibility and quality of coaching required. The coaches also took it upon themselves to exert and take ownership of the sport versus the National Paralympic Committees. It was the coaches that sought out leadership roles including positions on the International Paralympic Committee's technical committees. Para Alpine coaches also engaged with the International Ski Federation (FIS), and although they were not able to get para Alpine officially recognized they did have FIS recognized as a patron.

The 2002 Games were also a time when the role and job description of coaches in Alpine skiing for both able-bodied and athletes with a disability were changing. In Canada, financial support for winter sport had increased due to a successful bid to host the 2010 Olympic and Paralympic Games in Vancouver. One such example of this was a new program called Own the Podium, which was designed to ensure exactly what it was called. Canada had hosted the Summer Olympic Games in 1976 in Montreal and Winter Olympic Games in Calgary in 1988, and both times Canada as host country did not win a gold medal. No other host country had ever done that; and Canada did it twice! The Canadian Federal Government was adamant that this would not happen again, and so significant financial resources poured into winter sport at many levels but in particular high performance. Sport Canada was also becoming more equitable with their funding to high performance sport and so opportunities for athletes with a disability and in particular in areas such as exercise physiology was more readily available. Lastly, the creation and adoption of the Canadian Sport for Life's (CS4L) Long-term Athlete Development (LTAD) pathway was also significant as this now argued that the coach should be involved directly in the coordination of athlete development pathways and integrated support teams.

Post 2002

As noted earlier, one of the challenges with the sheer amount of change that occurred in 2002 was that the responsibilities for the organization increased, without a comparable change in funding, and in particular for coaching. This transition then shifted again leading up to the 2006 Paralympic Games in Torino when, according to Sawicki, salaries for coaches for both able-bodied and disabled appeared to increase significantly. What Sawicki noticed is that coaches who perhaps had never shown an interest in working with athletes with a disability were suddenly doing so.

Another change Sawicki observed over this period of time was a change within the athlete. The ones that he coached, particularly in the early 2000s, competed out of sheer will and believed they were good enough to be on the world stage. Ozzie wondered if that changed following Salt Lake City and the increase in funding subsequent to that, and if the athletes that followed were waiting for someone to provide them with the motivation to be elite. He wondered if we had created a more complicated system than was necessary. The increase in funding led to an increase in expectations placed on Paralympic athletes as they were now being asked to train full time and relinquish personal goals related to family, avocation and education. To Sawicki, this might have worked with younger able-bodied athletes because of perceived potential financial benefits once they retired, and simply a broader pool of available athletes. But for Paralympic athletes, they often started older than able-bodied peers due to acquired disabilities, and the money available after retirement was significantly less. As a result, many para athletes may not have been willing to make the necessary sacrifices. Another result of the perceived need to focus 100 per cent on being an athlete was burnout, and thus a lack of those willing to give back to the system once they retired, whether that was as coaches, volunteers or professional administrators.

Mentorship

As has been noted several times, one of the hallmarks of Sawicki's career was the influence and importance of mentors. Derald Smith, Ted Rhodes and Claudio Berto are the three individuals who were at the core of Ozzie becoming a coach, and he remained close to all three. Sadly Derald and Ted have passed away, but remain as significant core influencers. The three individuals made Ozzie appreciate what a mentor could be, the importance of leadership, innovation, creativity, learning, compassion and enjoyment. Sport has always allowed those values to remain front and centre for Ozzie and that is how he evolved in coaching, why he pursued it and why he has remained involved in various capacities and roles. Ozzie is now at a point in his career where mentoring coaches is most important to him. He had people who were exceptional in helping lead his growth as a coach and a person, and he wants that process to continue.

Coaching philosophy

Mentors were thus at the heart of Sawicki's coaching development and were prevalent in the evolution of his coaching philosophy. When asked, Sawicki suggested that his prevailing philosophy is that sport must be coach-managed and directed, but at the same time athlete-driven and focused, with the coach aiding in the delivery of programming. While seemingly perhaps at odds with one another, instead Sawicki was able to combine these two perspectives into one overarching approach. When para Alpine was first transferred to Alpine Canada and funding was being directed from Own the Podium, Ozzie noticed a new focus on athlete testing and sport science. Sawicki was not necessarily against the implementation of science but sceptical where it overshadowed the focus on the coach. This is not to say that the partners such as OTP and Alpine Canada were not important, but Sawicki believed that the coach needed to be the central conductor of these partners while ensuring that they best met the needs of the athlete through an athlete-focused philosophy.

The second element to Sawicki's philosophy was the focus on creativity. In particular, Ozzie found this to be foundational when working with athletes with disability. The able-bodied system had enough athletes to create valid benchmarks and an economy of scale that allow for detailed understanding of equipment. In para sports this was not always the case, and instead as the coach he relied on personal experience, savvy, creativity and an ability to draw from a variety of sources.

Coaching pedagogy

Ozzie's philosophy is a result of both his practical experiences and his educational foundation in coaching. In this section, coaching pedagogy will be reflected in his own education, how he sees his role as a teacher and his views of where teaching intersects with the coaching profession.

Sawicki became a National Elite Coach Level 4 after attending the National Coaching Institute diploma program at both the University of Calgary and University of Victoria from 2004 to 2005. Here, Sawicki studied alongside a number of other coaches from a variety of sports taking a series of modules in a multitude of subjects. Sawicki was also part of the initial group of coaches that created and helped implement the original Competition-Development competency-based coach education process. Much of this was in response to what he perceived as a tremendous need for long-term coaching development, and this was especially true in para sport. Without having coaching resources and related programs, potential development level coaches were not finding places in which to evolve and grow. Sawicki noted the simple reality that without coaches there would be no athletes, and potential athletes would leave sport for other pursuits if no coach was present.

In part, because Sawicki was so grateful for those who trailblazed before him, he is now trying to minimize the barriers for those wanting to coach today. He wonders now if coach education is more complex than necessary with expectations too high for both time required and money spent training, particularly for those at the entry level. The clarity as to what certificates or training opportunities are required is also cloudy, with the possibility that new coaches are being discouraged before they even begin.

A final place where coaching and pedagogy appeared was in the intersection of the two professional practices. Ozzie considers teaching to being a core skill of a grassroots level coach as they are facilitating learning and influencing basic skill development. The grassroots coach focuses on basic skill development, the repetition of these skills, and then consolidating and merging them with the other skills for the purposes of performance. At the elite level, Ozzie sees coaches not necessarily teaching as much, but instead creating an environment to succeed. The focus here is on refinement and creativity to perform basic skills in a variety of circumstances. The key at the initial stage is to not over-challenge. The difficulty inherent within the para sport system is that because there are so few athletes and coaches, ensuring that appropriate programs are being offered for each level of athlete at the appropriate times and stages is almost impossible. What tends to happen as a result is that athletes get mixed together, which can be great as younger or lesser experienced ones can learn from older or more experienced veterans, but the potential negative consequences are that they can be scared or learn bad habits. Within sports psychology this is explained by group efficacy, and specifically the modeling on prior performance and vicarious experiences (e.g. Myers et al., 2004; McCullagh, 1987).

Recommendations for Paralympic Alpine ski coaching, education and practice

Building upon the recognition of how coaching and pedagogy intersect is Ozzie's desire for coaches to take their roles as teachers and mentors very seriously. This has already been addressed, so what follows are further recommendations by Ozzie to improve the coaching profession.

Sawicki's first suggestion is for coach education to become inclusive throughout the entire system.

> Coach education has to become an integrated environment. The para sport coaching context must become part and parcel to the coaching delivery

modules for all levels whether it's an entry level coach, a developmental coach or performance level coach.

Sawicki also believes that there needs to be better mentorship across all levels, moving beyond simply sharing tactical and technical knowledge. Technical and tactical information is available, but typically not the general philosophy of coaching athletes with a disability. Understanding the nuance of psychological, sociological and managerial perspectives between coaching athletes who are able-bodied and disabled is required, and typically this is not available unless through informal interactions with other coaches. McMaster et al. (2012) and Tawse et al. (2012) as reported by Douglas et al. (2015), echoed this concern, suggesting that formal education has failed to provide specific information about disability sport. As reported by Douglas, Bloom and Falcao (2015), while Paralympic coaches have noted that experiences as athletes and other coaches were important sources of knowledge (Duarte & Culver, 2014; McMaster et al., 2012), they emphasized that interactions with specialists, communication with other coaches, as well as athletes with disabilities and their families, were some of the major sources of knowledge acquisition, especially for those coaches who did not have a disability (Banack et al., 2011; Cregan et al., 2007; McMaster et al., 2012).

Sawicki also believes that greater cross-pollination of coaching is needed. When Ozzie attended international competitions in the late 1990s and early 2000s he would typically watch other coaches and consider what best practices they would apply. This happened more frequently when para Alpine was still in its infancy as a shared practice, but it seems that increased competition has created an increasingly protective atmosphere.

A fourth recommendation is trying to find ways to better facilitate and motivate curiosity from both the coach and athlete. The curiosity Ozzie is referring to is about life as a newly disabled person, or curiosity about what life can bring for a person with a congenital disability who has perhaps been protected by parents and society. Sawicki then needs that curiosity to broaden into sport, and whether the athlete wants to be a recreational or high performance athlete. One is not necessarily better than the other, and the differences in the recreational and elite sport approaches may evolve over time so a coach and athlete may need to be patient. Ozzie suggested that 'the physical nature of the disability is secondary without the curiosity to see how they can get better, the rest is irrelevant. Sport gives light and hope against the fear of injury or disability.' What Ozzie further noted is that as he gained experience as a coach he became better at recognizing when to push this curiosity in his athletes and also when to back off. He also learned over time how to interpret that gleam or flicker in the eye that showed latent curiosity. Once you have located curiosity in the athlete, Sawicki suggests it is then the curiosity in the coach that allows the relationship to grow and succeed. The coach needs to be curious in wondering how a person missing an arm and leg on the same side can navigate a slalom course or how a person with a spinal cord injury can adapt their sit-ski for maximum speed.

A fifth recommendation made by Sawicki came from a conversation towards the end of our interview. Here, Sawicki pondered the future of coaching, and commented that there really was not a lot published about Paralympic coaching. In particular, he noted the need for understanding the process of how to become a Paralympic coach.

> There's a lot of science research, there's not a lot of process research in terms of what's the process that makes the coach, what's the process of evolution that allows a coach to become a good coach? What are those experiences that lead to that evolution from a coaching point of view? You don't see much of that anywhere and I do think material like that is out there, that gives people a chance to say I can do this because I see what they went through. Whereas the typical article is on performance indicators based on this, that and everything else. It's over the head of 95 per cent of the coaches that are out there.

A sixth recommendation is that the motivation used by coaches needs to change. When he started, much of what Ozzie used to encourage people with disabilities to try skiing was the lure of the Paralympic Games and being on a world stage. Now, because it is so much harder to reach the high performance level, he says focusing on para Sport from a recreational level and the idea of being active for life is the best approach. Being more than you are now, increasing the duration and quality of life should be good motivators along with aspiring to be a world-class athlete.

A seventh recommendation is that Sawicki believes we need to simplify the language of coaching and engage mentorship at every level of the coaching continuum. To simplify language, we need to clarify the pathway options and identify the component parts that need to be done for coaches at every level without over complicating it. Sport in Canada has accepted the long-term athlete development pathway and transposed a coaching pathway on top of it. The sport system has done this without a critical review of what really is necessary, which might have resulted in needless hurdles, and scaring away potential coaches. In Canada the sport system has also adapted a competency-based coaching model where coaches now have to demonstrate their capability to implement coaching practices versus simply proving the knowledge of coaching through a test. This system may be too expensive and often times, too intensive for the Paralympic context. As a result, sports have had to rely on multi-sport facilitators and learning opportunities that may not always incorporate the Paralympic context.

Perhaps the most important recommendation Ozzie presented for coaches, regardless of whether they are coaching athletes who are able-bodied or disabled, is to get better at asking questions and listening. One might argue that knowledge about disability is relatively unimportant. Others might suggest that detailed knowledge about the social elements of disability including how to approach a person with disability, and the physiological specifics about a disability's etiology, are important. A third perspective is that the disability details are only important once you get to the elite level because of the way in which being creative related to the disability may enable improved performance. What Sawicki suggests is to just follow the general guidelines of asking the individual a question and then listening.

Conclusion

Success to Sawicki is defined as athletes having fun, learning, and getting better. As Chef de Mission for Canada's team at the 2014 Winter Paralympic Games, he wondered if the pressure to perform deterred some athletes from their ultimate goal, while those who focused on the camaraderie, joy of competition, and learning were those that truly succeeded.

As a coach, Ozzie has defined success as self-awareness. As he progressed throughout the coaching ranks he recognized that his experiences had value. Early on in his career, and likely because of his professional training in data and data systems, he questioned the intuition of others and what was described as the art of coaching. He wanted science and evidence to base his decisions. The older he got, the more he understood and appreciated the 'art' of coaching, which arguably may be more challenging and difficult to master.

Sawicki's career has mirrored those from wheelchair rugby, as examined by Tawse et al. (2012). These authors suggested that wheelchair rugby coaches learned to be creative and to adapt to athletes' needs; learned from practical experiences; acquired knowledge from other coaches and relied on veteran athletes, family members, and support staff for knowledge (Douglas et al., 2015).

Sawicki believes that Paralympic coaching may be set to embark on its golden age. Paralympic coaches are just now being recognized by their peers as perhaps better able to adapt, be creative and innovate. They have been raised, albeit perhaps changing, in a more collegial, less intense context so that some of the more successful able-bodied coaches may in fact see this as a viable and attractive option.

The future of Paralympic coaching is thus very bright, but will require the continued leadership, wisdom, and guidance from sage, compassionate, and innovative leaders such as Ozzie Sawicki.

Additional resources and supplementary material

CADS: Canadian Association for Disabled Skiing www.disabledskiing.ca/
CADS Calgary, Canadian Association For Disabled Skiing www.cadscalgary.ca/
Canadian Paralympic Committee www.paralympic.ca/
National Coaching Certification Program www.coach.ca/
Ozzie Sawicki Profiles www.linkedin.com/in/ozzie-sawicki-54191334 and www.coach.ca/ozzie-sawicki-chpc-p156500
Para-alpine | Alpine Canada Alpin www.alpinecanada.org/para-alpine
Para-Alpine Development Programs | Alpine Canada Alpin www.alpinecanada.org/para-alpine/development-para-alpine

References

Banack, H.R., Sabiston, C.M. & Bloom, G.A. (2011). Coach autonomy support, basic need satisfaction, and intrinsic motivation of Paralympic athletes. *Research Quarterly for Exercise Sport, 82*(4), 722–30.

Cregan, K., Bloom, G.A. & Reid, G. (2007). Career evolution and knowledge of elite coaches of swimmers with physical disability. *Research Quarterly for Exercise Science & Sport, 78,* 339–350.

Côté, J. & Gilbert, W. (2009). An integrative definition of coaching effectiveness and expertise. *International Journal of Sports Science & Coaching, 4,* 307–323.

Culver, D., Werthner, P., Taylor, S., Davey, J., Duarte, T. & Trudel, P. (2015). What do we know about coaching disability sports: A Canadian perspective. Presentation at the *2015 VISTA Conference,* Girona, Spain.

Cushion, C., Nelson, L., Armour, K., Lyle, J., Jones, R., Sandford, R. & Callaghan, C. (2010). *Coach learning and development: A review of literature.* Leeds: The National Coaching Foundation.

Douglas, S. & Hardin, B. (2014). Case study of an expert intercollegiate wheelchair basketball coach. *Applied Research in Coaching and Athletics Annual, 29,* 193–212.

Douglas, S., Bloom, G.A. & Falcao, W. (2015). Career development and learning pathways of Paralympic head coaches with a disability. Presentation at the *International Paralympic Committee VISTA Conference,* Girona, Spain.

Duarte, T. & Culver, D. (2014). Becoming a coach in developmental adaptive sailing: A lifelong learning perspective. *Journal of Applied Sport Psychology, 6*(4), 441–456.

Falcão W., Bloom, G. & Loughead, T. (2015). Coaches' perceptions of team cohesion in Paralympic sports. *Adapted Physical Activity Quarterly, 32*(3), 206–222.

Heritage Canada (2006). *Canadian sport policy.* Ottawa: Heritage Canada.

International Paralympic Committee (2015). *Para Alpine,* http://www.paralympic.org/alpine-skiing [accessed 15th October 2015].

Legg, D. (2000). Strategy formation in the canadian wheelchair sports association (1967–1997). Doctoral dissertation. Edmonton, AB: University of Alberta.

McCullagh, P. (1987). Model similarity effects on motor performance. *Journal of Sport Psychology, 9,* 249–260.

McMaster, S., Culver, D. & Werthner, P. (2012). Coaches of athletes with a physical disability: A look at their learning experiences. *Qualitative Research in Sport, Exercise & Health, 4,* 226–243.

Myers, N., Felts, D. & Short, F. (2004). Collective efficacy and team performance: A longitudinal study of collegiate football teams. *Group Dynamics: Theory, Research, and Practice, 8*(2), 126 –138.

Reid, G. & Prupas, A. (1998). A documentary analysis of research priorities in disability sport. *Adapted Physical Activity Quarterly, 24,* 305–316.

Rhodes, T. (date unknown). *Unofficial history of the Canadian association of disabled skiing.* Calgary, unpublished document, Calgary, AB.

Robbins, J., Dummer, G. & Houston, E. (2010). Philosophies and expectations of wheelchair and stand-up collegiate basketball coaches. *Journal of Sport Behavior, 30*(1), 34–45.

Schinke, R.J., Bloom, G.A. & Salmela, J.H. (1995). The career stages of elite Canadian basketball coaches. *Avante 1*(1), 48–62.

Tawse, H., Bloom, G.A., Sabiston, C.M. & Reid, G. (2012). The role of coaches of wheelchair rugby in the development of athletes with a spinal cord injury. *Qualitative Research in Sport, Exercise & Health, 4,* 206–225.

Editors' summary reflections

As many of the case studies have demonstrated thus far, high performance disability sport coaches often take on a number of roles over the course of their careers. Legg's case study of Sawicki demonstrates not only the varied and variable professional roles coaches may assume, but also the useful ways in which a multiplicity of employment experiences can contribute to being a 'better' and/or 'more effective coach'. Sawicki has, for instance, held a number of different key positions within not only the Alpine context, but also in other sporting domains. While some of these role shifts may have been unplanned, in many cases Sawicki (and many of his Alpine coaching peers) have sought to place themselves in more strategic positions within their sports both nationally and internationally. As a consequence, coaches like Sawicki have been well situated to both gain further expertise to enhance their coaching practices, but also to contribute to the development of the sport more generally. It is evident from Sawicki's own coaching journey that the strength of the Canadian Alpine para-sport program has, too, benefited from coaches like Sawicki and his peers actively extending their coaching remits and assuming positions of responsibility and influence within various areas of the sport (for example, as administrators, technical officials, members of officiating panels). While this might not appeal to all coaches, gaining a breadth and depth of understanding of the wider industry has, in Sawicki's experience, helped yield successful coaching results. Yet, encouraging coaches to diversify their expertise, and in particular challenge them to accept leadership positions to advance their own development but also help the advocacy of the sport and its athletes more generally, is difficult.

While Sawicki has proven his ability to regularly perform, and also ensure others he leads and mentors do the same, his experience provokes thought. In particular, it draws out considerations on what high performance disability sport coaching *is* and where it might need to go in the future. For example, the integration of para-Alpine sport within centralized high performance programmes has been beneficial in financial and administrative terms, though it has changed the coaching landscape. As Sawicki identified, with developments within the sport's integration into centralized high performance programmes, increased technical and scientific expertise specialization, more nuanced coach education pathways, and the national performance expectations that come from hosting Winter Paralympics (and the need to sustain successes), coaching para-Alpine sport in Canada has become far more complex and demanding of current and aspirant coaches. We might then ask, in what ways are coaches able to navigate the fine line between developing their own coaching style and meeting the varied demands of the high performance environments in which they work? In what ways, also, might centralized/national governing body coach education and development frameworks need to accommodate the tensions of specificity and appropriateness versus applicability and flexibility? How, in the midst of rapid scientific developments in the sport generally and the emphasis placed upon bio-medical scientific expertise to maximize performance, might the *art* of coaching be maintained and fostered throughout all levels of coach development pathways? In addition, given the increasing encroachment of specialists, stakeholders and support staff in the coaching context, what educational tools, mechanisms and resources might coaches require to work effectively and maintain the value inherent to the coach–athlete relationship?

Sawicki's coaching trajectory, and the issues revealed therein, echo the narratives of many other coaches represented in this book. Like Darling, Bates and Ferguson, and Tromans, Sawicki has evidenced the ethos shared among those who work within the disability and para-sport realms to overcome apprehensions and challenges and just get 'stuck in' and do the very best you can to advance the sport and improve athletes' lives and successes. Given the significant changes in disability and high performance para-sport, and as evidenced with most of the other coach case studies, Sawicki has also highlighted how important adaptability and resilience are as qualities for successful high performance coaches, particularly in times when there are significant shifts in the sport (e.g., centralization of administration and coaching bodies, financial or resource issues, or coach development concerns). Although evident in other professions, specifically for sport coaches these qualities appear important to consolidating their identity and security within their coaching roles, maintaining effective environments for their athletes, and ensuring development and performance pathways that can withstand/cope with external change(s) (Barker et. al. 2014; Cushion, 2007; Ibarra, 1999). Sawicki's adaptability and resilience, and the emphasis he also places on coach mentorship in sustaining the progression of coaches through the sport, and fostering a supportive coaching culture and networks within the sport, provide valuable insights for other coaches in other sports. Not unlike some of the other coach case studies, Sawicki has benefited from his own tenacity and drive, amiable contextual conditions that have afforded him good opportunities, and distinct mentors and networks who have helped advance his career. There is a definite success story here; however, as the likes of Pohlman's, Dantas' and Darling's coaching experiences demonstrate, mirroring this in other high performance sports remains a task.

References

Barker, D., Barker-Ruchti, N., Wals, A. & Tinning, R. (2014). High performance sport and sustainability: A contradiction of terms? *Reflective Practice*, *15*(1), 1–11.

Cushion, C. (2007). Modelling the complexity of the coaching process. *International Journal of Sports Science and Coaching*, *2*(4), 395–401.

Ibarra, H. (1999). Provisional selves: Experimenting with image and identity in professional adaptation. *Administrative Science Quarterly*, *44*(4), 764–791.

9

GLYNN TROMANS

In search of 'fearless' boccia and the 'big hairy audacious goal'

Ian Brittain

Introduction

This chapter outlines the work of Glynn Tromans and his coaching philosophy and pedagogy in relation to his roles as Talent Development Manager and, in particular, Performance Coach for the BC3 squad at GB Boccia. It begins by giving a brief introduction to the sport of boccia and the historical and current status of the Great Britain BC3 squad, before outlining relevant aspects of Glynn's historical background that have a bearing upon his current role. The bulk of the chapter focuses upon Glynn's coaching philosophy and pedagogy and how these shape his work with the BC3 squad. This includes a vision and mission for the squad known amongst themselves as the 'big hairy audacious goal' and underpinned by a drive to play 'fearless' boccia. The chapter then goes on to highlight some of the key current issues that arise for coaches working in boccia, from Glynn's perspective from the international down to the individual national coach level. This includes an outline of how these issues might impact upon the future development of the sport of boccia. The chapter concludes with some recommendations from Glynn for coaching, education or practice within the sport of boccia moving forward.

Historical context of boccia

Boccia is a Paralympic sport introduced in 1984, with no Olympic counterpart, in which athletes throw, kick or use a ramp to propel a ball onto the court with the aim of getting closest to a 'jack' ball. It is designed specifically for athletes with a disability affecting locomotor function and is played indoors on a court similar in size to a badminton court. Players are divided into four classifications depending upon their disability and functional ability. However, all players have impaired functional ability in all four limbs.[1]

- **BC1** – Players with cerebral palsy who are able to use their hands or feet to consistently propel a ball into play. BC1 athletes may have an aide on court to pass them their ball before each shot.
- **BC2** – Players with cerebral palsy who are able to use their hands to consistently propel a ball into play and have greater functional ability than a BC1 athlete.
- **BC3** – Players with cerebral palsy or other disability with locomotor dysfunction in all four limbs who are unable to throw or kick a ball into play and as such are permitted to use an assistive device such as a ramp to propel the ball into play and are supported by an assistant ('ramper').
- **BC4** – Players who do not have cerebral palsy but have another disability with locomotor dysfunction in all four limbs and have similar functional ability to BC2 athletes. Disabilities such as muscular dystrophy and tetraplegia will fall under this classification.

(GB Boccia, 2014)

In terms of Paralympic results up to and including London 2012 the most successful Paralympic boccia nation is Portugal (8 gold, 10 silver, 6 bronze medals) closely followed by South Korea (8 gold, 4 silver, 5 bronze). Great Britain (3 gold, 5 silver, 3 bronze) currently lies fifth behind Spain (5 gold, 7 silver, 7 bronze) and Brazil (5 gold, 0 silver, 2 bronze).

GB Boccia acts as the National Federation for boccia in Britain and is the only route into international boccia competition. However, it is a federation and not a national governing body. Their primary role is the selection and development of the GB Boccia squad. Responsibility for developing the sport of boccia within Britain lies with the home nations (Boccia England, Scottish Disability Sport, Disability Sport Wales and Disability Sport Northern Ireland), who are all represented on the GB Boccia Board. As well as the current five full-time members of staff, GB Boccia supports, through the World Class Performance Plan, 14 athletes and three BC3 Assistants.

Despite the fact that almost half of the sport of boccia is made up of players who have impairments other than cerebral palsy the sport itself within Britain has its roots in the CP Sport organisation. Previously, the coaches were all volunteers and were mainly drawn from the teaching or care professions. They were not qualified coaches and, to a large extent, much of the sport is still like that. Indeed, a Level 1 coaching award for boccia was not introduced by CP Sport/Boccia England until 2012. However, it was very much an 'introduction to coaching' with very little boccia specific content. A Level 2 award, written by the GB Boccia coaches in conjunction with Sportscoach UK was piloted in 2014. There is currently no Level 3 award available in boccia, but the Level 1 award has now been retro-fitted to include more boccia content. GB Boccia is the only organisation in Britain with professional boccia coaches, although none of them have a boccia background. All of their coaching expertise is imported from other sports.

In order to provide some background to this particular case study it is relevant to provide slightly more detail about the BC3 category within boccia. Athletes in the BC3 category are those with the greatest degree of impairment and who use an assistive device such as a ramp to propel the ball.[2] Prior to 2014 the last global medal for Great Britain in the BC3 category was a silver medal at the Atlanta 1996 Paralympic Games by Joyce Carle and Zoe Edge. Since then Great Britain has failed to qualify for the Paralympic Games in the BC3 category until London 2012, where they qualified largely by virtue of automatic entry due to being the host nation. The major championship progression of the BC3 team since Beijing 2008 is as follows:

- 2008 – Beijing Paralympics – did not qualify.
- 2009 – European Championships – lost every match.
- 2010 – World Championships – lost every match.
- 2011 – World Cup – 6th.
- 2012 – Paralympics – 5th.
- 2013 – European Championships – 3rd.
- 2014 – World Championships – 2nd·

The Great Britain BC3 team is currently number one in the official world rankings. The aim of this case study is to look at some of the possible reasons for this turn-around in fortunes and the role that the case-study coach, Glynn Tromans, may have played in it.

Historical context of Glynn Tromans

Date of Birth: 17/03/1969
Current position: Talent Manager and Performance Coach (BC3) with the Great Britain Boccia Federation

Academic qualifications

- 1991 BA (Hons) Business Studies – Coventry University.
- 1992 MSc Sport and Recreation Management – Loughborough University.
- 2009 Elite Coaching Programme Graduate – Ashridge Business School.

Coaching qualifications

- UK Athletics Level 3 Performance Coach in Middle and Long Distance Running.
- Currently enrolled on the UK Sport Elite Coach Apprenticeship Programme (ECAP).

Previous employment

- 1987–1991   Apprentice (with industrial degree sponsorship) at Dunlop Aviation.
- 1993–1998   Lecturer (mainly in economics and marketing) at Tile Hill College, Coventry and Warwick Universities.

- 1998–2000 Full-time athlete.
- 2000–2002 Athletics Development Officer at Greater Warwickshire Sports.
- 2002–2005 Assistant Head of the UK Athletics World Class Potential Programme for Athletes with Disabilities.
- 2006–2007 UK Athletics Performance Manager for Athletes with Disabilities (Ambulant).
- 2007–2009 UK Athletics World Class Talent Manager (non-disabled).
- 2009–2012 Talent Manager for GB Boccia.
- 2012–date Talent Development Manager and Performance Coach (BC3) for GB Boccia.

Other notable achievements

Glynn won 17 UK and National titles on all surfaces including the AAA 10,000m title, three National Cross Country titles, five CAU/World Trial cross country titles and three British Half Marathon Championships. He also represented his country at 17 major events including nine consecutive World Cross Country Championships between 1997 and 2005.

Unpaid coaching roles

When Glynn left UK Athletics in 2009 he went back to voluntary middle- and long-distance coaching at Coventry Godiva Harriers – the club he had been a member of since the age of 12. There he coached a small group of middle- and long-distance and du- and triathletes. Whilst with UK Athletics, where he was working mainly with coach–athlete pairs, he deliberately did not get involved in coaching himself as he perceived that this might lead to potential conflicts of interest. His successes have included getting one athlete to represent England at the 2010 Commonwealth Games in Delhi; another to represent England at cross country; one athlete becoming World and European age group duathlon champion and European age group triathlon champion; and one to be a triathlon medallist at the Beijing 2014 Youth Olympic Games.

Case study of Glynn Tromans

In 2011 the Great Britain BC3 Pair were ranked 23rd in the World. In 2014 they are currently ranked 1st. Having failed to get out of the group stages at London 2012 in the BC3 mixed pairs and no player getting beyond the second round in the singles, the Great Britain BC3 team has the objective of a gold medal in the upcoming Rio de Janeiro 2016 Paralympic Games. This section will, therefore, look at some of the possible reasons for this dramatic turnaround of events. These will include Glynn's own background in elite sport as both an elite performer himself and his roles working in the sport of athletics with both elite performers and coaches. Glynn's own coaching philosophy and pedagogy will be outlined and an overview of the key current issues that arise for coaches working within the sport of boccia and how they might impact upon the future development of the sport of boccia.

Relevance of his previous roles to current position

In addition to having been an international athlete himself, the various roles Glynn had with UK Athletics put him into regular contact with some of the best coaches. A lot of his work in disability athletics involved working with coach–athlete pairs, so he often had contact with other coaches and when he moved to become World Class Talent Manager in non-disabled athletics it brought him into direct contact with professional coaches, again working with coach–athlete pairs. This provided him with excellent opportunities to understand both what makes a good coach and also to clearly understand the importance of the athlete–coach relationship in delivering elite performance.

Development of role at GB Boccia

In 2009 Glynn left UK Athletics to take up a one-year contract as Talent Programme Manager for GB Boccia, with the aim of trying to fill talent gaps for London 2012. As a result of this role he identified a gap at the BC3 level, and in 2010 was offered a contract to manage the BC3 squad in addition to his Talent Programme Manager duties. This involved writing the training programmes for the squad and managing the environment in which they operated, but did not involve any coaching as the squad already had a coach who would take them through to London 2012. Glynn was, therefore, forced to watch the squad perform at London 2012 from the stands as an unaccredited spectator, where they failed to get out of the group stage into the knock-out matches. As part of the post-Games analysis it was decided that there was a need to professionalise boccia, and as part of this Glynn became the coach to the BC3 squad, as well as continuing his role as Talent Programme Manager.

Coaching philosophy and pedagogy

Cassidy et al. (2009) define a person's coaching philosophy as a set of principles that guide the individual's coaching practices and their coaching pedagogy as the 'problematic process that incorporates the interaction between how one learns, how one teaches, what is being taught (Lusted, 1986) and the context in which it is being taught' (p. 7). An individual's coaching philosophy will, therefore, directly impact upon and shape their coaching pedagogy as their coaching principles, and hence their coaching pedagogy, will be guided by their own personal opinions, experiences and values. Glynn agrees with this, stating that everyone is a product of their experiences. In his own case he cites a number of experiences that have shaped his own coaching philosophy and by extension his coaching pedagogy. These include his experiences as a competitive runner up to international level as part of the World Class Performance Plan for athletics, his academic qualifications and delivery experiences in business, marketing, sports management and coaching, his work experience as an Athletics Development Officer, Performance Manager and Talent Manager and finally his experiences as a traveller around the world, both as a tourist and through his work and competitive opportunities as an athlete.

Constructive dissatisfaction

Glynn claims to be a big enthusiast of strategy and in particular constructive dissatisfaction as a strategy for improvement. The term constructive dissatisfaction appears to have been coined by Jim Casey, founder of the United Parcel Service (UPS). Mike Eskew (2006), Chairman and CEO of UPS claims that this means that 'no matter how good a job you're doing, you can always do a little better. It's that ability to transform, to evolve, and to execute on those transformations that has made us successful'. Chopping (2009) claims 'constructive dissatisfaction is different from just being unhappy with results ... it implies an awareness that the way things are is not the way you want them to be ... The real value of constructive dissatisfaction is that it moves us into action mode'. Chopping goes on to claim that if you really want to get better results:

- Look at things you haven't seen.
- Go places you haven't been.
- Do things you haven't done.

Glynn describes himself as fanatical about improving and states that he wants the squad and staff to build something sustainable based upon a clear vision and strategy implemented by world-class people with a consistent message in order to create the best possible environments to operate in. Part of Glynn's philosophy for the BC3 squad came out of sitting in the stands watching the poor performances displayed by them at the London 2012 Paralympic Games and the analysis and self-reflection that occurred within GB Boccia afterwards. There was perceived to be a 'blame culture' in operation at and after London 2012 and Glynn felt that there was a need to build something that everyone involved believes in.

Putting vision and strategy into action

In order to try and put his vision and strategy into action Glynn has set the BC3 squad both a vision for the future and a mission by which to try and achieve the vision. The vision, better known to the BC3 squad and staff as the 'big hairy audacious goal' is to be world leaders in BC3 boccia within the current Paralympic cycle and in achieving this, the Great Britain BC3 squad will not only be the best there is by Rio 2016, but the best there has ever been! In order to achieve this vision Glynn has set the squad the mission of playing 'fearless boccia'. This involves each player being unafraid to play boldly and with courage, to take control of the situation and to be unpredictable in their play. In order to achieve this Glynn believes that the operational environment is actually more important than the results and that how the players behave off the court will make a big difference to the results on the court. Since London 2012, after which Glynn took over coaching responsibilities for the BC3 squad, he has tried to instil in them a set of core values that they all (players and staff) must adhere to. These values are as follows:

- They must respect each other.
- They must be tolerant of each other.
- They must trust each other.
- They must be honest with each other.
- They must support each other.
- They must take collective responsibility for success.
- They must take individual responsibility for their behaviour.

Glynn combines these core values with what he calls the BC3 'Fearless' Charter, designed to empower the players with the belief and trust in themselves and their team mates to play attacking and aggressive boccia. This was not an original idea but a modification of 'Taming Tigers', a philosophy developed by Jim Lawless in his book *Taming tigers: do things you never thought you could* (Lawless, 2012) and delivered as a Key Note Presentation with Glynn in the audience at a UK Sport World Class Performance Conference. The contents of the BC3 'Fearless' Charter are as follows:

- **Act boldly today – time is limited**. Nothing need stop you from acting now – except the whisper that tells you not to. Bold actions will take you towards bold outcomes. It will change you for the better.
- **Challenge your personal rulebook**. Your rulebook tells you what you can and can't do. It's the cage you play boccia and live within. It lets you see the shot but it doesn't let you play it. Challenge your rules and play the shot. Rewrite your rulebook to write your own Paralympic journey.
- **Head in the direction of where you want to arrive, every day**. Know the goal. Don't aim lower – ever. Think about what you have to do to achieve the big hairy audacious goal. Move through the obstacles and gain confidence in what you do. You can move something forward towards this goal every single day.
- **It's all in the mind**. Don't listen to the voices in your head that say 'you can't do it, it's too hard, and there are too many barriers'. Forget the conventional wisdom. It gets conventional results and we want more.
- **The tools for fearless boccia are all around you**. We are connected to six billion people around the world. Connect with the ones who can help you achieve your goal. Don't act alone. Ask for help. Surround yourself with people who will help you. People are the tools. Use the enabling ones to do the thing you want to do.

- **There is no safety in numbers**. Have the courage of your convictions. Say the things you feel strongly about. Have the courage to stand up for what you believe in. Be the one in the spotlight not the one of many in the crowd on the side-lines looking in.
- **Do something scary every day**. Move outside your comfort zone and get in to the zone where you really need to be in order to be the best in the world. Don't put off the difficult conversations until tomorrow.
- **Understand and control your time to create change**. Look at your diary. Does it have everything in it that you need to be doing to be the best in the world? Does it contain 'stuff' that makes no contribution to that at all? Fill your limited time with what helps you to be the best in the world. Get rid of the rest.
- **Create disciplines – do the basics brilliantly**. Every match you win is the product of the training and lifestyle disciplines from your daily life. You will be rewarded in public for what you do in private. You are trying to do something amazing, so break habits and create disciplines. Attitude and energy can be poured into routine!
- **Never, never give up**. Keep the promises you make to yourself. Don't let yourself off the hook. Never lower your standards. Bring excellence to your programme and never, ever give up on that. GB BC3's have made a noble promise to ourselves to be world leaders. Do not accept anything less.

(Tromans, 2014)

Part of the need for everyone connected to the BC3 squad to be fully on board with all of the contents of the 'fearless' charter and the core values is not just so that everyone is 'singing from the same hymn sheet', but also the fact that there are four players in the squad, but Glynn can only take three of them to any particular championship. This means that one player will always be disappointed each time. This effectively makes the players in the squad rivals, which can, of course, help to encourage people to train harder in order to win their place. However, Glynn expects no bitterness if not selected and 'no secrets' as everyone should be focussed on what is best for the Great Britain BC3 boccia team ahead of their own individual ambitions. From the team perspective this does of course give Glynn selection options when approaching a particular championship, but overall he expects everyone involved to 'live the vision, the mission, and the charter'.

Fair and open competition

Glynn believes firmly in fair and open competition and claims that he never studies the 'grey areas' of the sport or the rulebook where others may be tempted to seek a tactical advantage by stretching the boundaries of particular rules or do something on the basis that there currently is no rule covering that issue. In addition, Glynn claims that there is quite a bit of gamesmanship that goes on, but that he will have nothing to do with it. He gave the example of an opposing team manager who tried to unsettle his team whilst they were warming up for the World Championship semi-final by protesting to the umpire about a particular piece of equipment belonging to one of the British BC3 team. However, Glynn made sure that the protest was kept away from the players and was dealt with quickly without upsetting his players' concentration. Glynn would much rather his players use their skill and focus on their own brand of 'fearless' boccia to win games than resort to underhand tactics.

Key current issues that arise for coaches working within the sport of boccia

This section will highlight some of the key current issues that arise for coaches working in boccia from Glynn's perspective. They are separated into the various levels of the sport – international, national, GB Boccia, the BC3 squad level and finally the individual national coach level.

On an International level

Boccia as a sport at Paralympic level was originally designed only for athletes with cerebral palsy, as well as being one of the few sports targeted at including athletes with more severe disabilities. When boccia entered the Paralympic programme in 1984 it only served athletes in the current BC1 and BC2 categories. In 1996 in Atlanta, a category was added for athletes with assistive devices, roughly equivalent to the current BC3 category and the BC4 category was added in Athens in 2004. However, there are still some very disabled people who are not currently classifiable and thus not eligible to play in the Paralympic pathway. As an example, Glynn stated that just a couple of weeks previously on a Talent Assessment Day he had seen a player with spina-bifida whose condition was of cerebral origin putting him into the BC2 classification. He uses a powerchair for daily living and was, therefore, somebody who you might expect would play boccia. However, he did not have quite enough functional spasticity in his shoulder and this may give him an unfair advantage when throwing over other BC2 players. This would make him a high-risk player who may not pass international classification. In the current climate, if this were the case, he would be told he is ineligible to play – leaving few alternatives in sport for him to compete in.

There is, therefore, discussion about the possible introduction of a BC5 classification, firstly at the national level and then, if successful, at the international level. A BC5 classification would be a catch-all category for players who perhaps should be playing boccia but just miss out on the criteria for the BC2 (CP) and BC4 (non-CP) classifications. Glynn believes that it is clearly not good to turn people away from the sport, particularly when they have so few other opportunities, so in this sense a BC5 category makes perfect sense. He sees it as the boccia equivalent of the Les Autres (literally meaning 'the others') classification in track and field competitions for athletes with a disability. However, he still has reservations about the possible implications of this new category both for the sport as a whole and his own BC3 category athletes in particular, as the most disabled group of players in the sport.

Many Paralympic sports have minimal disability classifications, where at first glance it may be difficult to tell exactly what the impairment is. Glynn's personal view (and not necessarily that of the Great Britain Boccia Federation) is that the beauty of boccia is that it provides an opportunity for those with the greatest 'disability' to play competitive sport at elite levels. Moving the sport in the direction of 'less disability' may begin to detract from the more disabled categories (BC1–4) as has been shown in wheelchair rugby by Schreiner & Strohkendl (2006), where the numbers of players in the most disabled categories has declined because the rules and tactics of the game appear to advantage the players in the 'less disabled' categories. Brittain (2009) discusses this issue in more detail in discussing the current tensions within the Paralympic movement of 'trying to move towards an elite sporting model that matches societal perceptions and understanding of what sport should look like, and providing sporting opportunities at the elite level for all their constituent members' (p.119).

Glynn feels it is unlikely that the IPC would give boccia more places in the Paralympic Games as spaces are already highly limited and also sought after by sports not currently on the Paralympic programme. He feels that the logical conclusion is that the introduction of BC5 – a more 'able' class that may more closely match spectator's perceptions of elite sporting performance, would take participation numbers away from and distract attention from the BC1–4 categories, possibly endangering their places at the Games over time. Glynn stated that:

> As I coach the BC3s, who are those with the most severe CP, muscular dystrophy, spinal muscular atrophy, spinal injuries and other conditions that make the act of physically kicking or throwing a ball consistently an impossibility, I would not like to see their place in the Paralympics under threat from players who are more able and have more alternatives.

He also posed the question of where to draw the line at the top of BC5 classification? And what about the people with disabilities who want to play boccia but fall the wrong side of that new line? Will they then introduce a BC6 category? Currently there are options for 'anybody' to play boccia, just not within the Paralympic pathway. Glynn added that if the BC5 category came in to the Paralympic programme and no threat existed to existing numbers, then the GB Boccia Programme would need to be more heavily resourced in terms of funding, care staff, support staff and coaching as the squad size and team size would be bigger. This would place further pressure on players and staff to achieve performance targets in order to maintain funding for the next Paralympic cycle. Overall Glynn is not against change, but feels that the implications and longer-term effects need to be completely understood first. What it also highlights is how issues well beyond the control of an individual coach can impact upon how they might need to plan, think and act moving forward.

Nationally

At this moment in time in the UK there are currently only four professional coaches (all working for GB Boccia) and approximately ten Level 2 qualified coaches (still awaiting certification) to cover the whole of the rest of the country below the GB Boccia level. Glynn claims that there are currently not enough qualified coaches using the same language, techniques, etc. in order to provide a sustainable and consistent supply of players to the top echelons of the sport. In order to achieve this Glynn believes that you not only need more qualified coaches spread around the country using the same terminology and adopting the same high-level coaching techniques, but that the process needs to be top-down in order to ensure an 'end in mind' philosophy as the key goal (i.e. providing top quality, technically advanced players who will train as a unit and aren't afraid to play 'fearless' boccia). Players with Paralympic potential need to be coached with that end in mind, rather than practise to a domestic game.

At the GB Boccia level

The medal target for boccia from the Rio 2016 Paralympic Games stands at 2–5 medals from seven events. There is obviously performance pressure for funding, as funding levels for the sport for the four-year Paralympic cycle after Rio 2016 will be dependent upon how the team performs in Rio and the perceived opportunities in Tokyo 2020. However, overall expense for a particular cycle can vary greatly depending on where events are held. This in turn impacts upon funding needs. So if in one cycle most of the major events are in Europe or North America this may fit within the funding allocation. However, if they perform badly in Rio and UK Sport cut their funding for the next cycle leading up to Tokyo 2020 and it turns out most of the major events are in the Far East, Australia and South America this can then put real financial strain on GB Boccia. This can impact upon what events they can attend and what coaching they can provide, which in turn can impact upon their world rankings and the ability of the players to achieve success at future championships. It is therefore imperative that performance levels are maintained and medal targets achieved.

In addition to this, as outlined in the previous section, there is currently no robust player pathway or supply chain of players within the UK, which actually forms part of Glynn's job in addition to his coaching duties. Glynn feels that Great Britain boccia teams will struggle at the Tokyo 2020 Paralympic Games if this is not put in place now. Work is ongoing with GB Boccia, the home countries and the UK Sport Pathways Team to ensure a robust player pathway exists. This could potentially impact upon financial input from UK Sport into the sport of boccia as outlined above.

Issues specific to the coaching of the GB Boccia BC3 squad athletes

The sport of boccia does not currently operate a centralised system. The four players currently in the GB Boccia BC3 squad currently reside in or near Staines,

Pembrokeshire, Glasgow and Edinburgh. They currently get one full week once a month together to train. The rest of the time the players have to train on their own, which is where the trust and honesty sections of the squad's core values really become vitally important. Glynn writes each player an individual training programme for the time they are apart and each player has to fill in a daily training log, but in essence they all have to trust each other that the training schedule is being followed and that everybody is putting in maximal effort, which can be hard when you are training alone. This is where performance behaviours and trusting that everyone is doing what they are supposed to becomes vitally important.

Although Glynn believes there is not enough coach contact time and that if the sport were fully centralised it might be better, he also believes that the cost implications would be prohibitive due to the care costs of the individual players, as the nature of the disabilities involved would make a centralised system for the BC3 squad unworkable. As a way around this problem, Glynn tries to make at least one visit to each player each month in order to try and maintain a level of personal contact in addition to the training diaries.

Personal/job related issues for Glynn

Like most of us, Glynn feels that there just aren't enough days in the week to allow him to achieve everything within his job in the way he would wish to do, particularly as he has a dual role as Talent Development Manager and BC3 coach. His commitment to his job also impacts heavily on his family life as his regular travelling and training with the squad mean that he often misses key moments in family life such as his kids' birthdays, etc. However, he does concede that the fact that he works from home does actually compensate for this somewhat by both providing an element of flexibility and allowing for him to make up for missing key family moments to a certain degree by being able to take his kids to school and pick them up on each of the days he works from home. This is something that probably wouldn't be possible if he had to commute to his place of work each day.

How these issues might impact upon the future development of the sport

Glynn identified coaching, or more precisely a lack of qualified coaches as possibly the biggest issue for the sport of boccia in the UK at present. Glynn feels that there is a need to contour the sport and the roles and responsibilities of coaches. He felt that more professional coaches would give coaches more time to devote to the actual coaching of the players, especially if the multi-disciplinarity being shown at the top level was to be replicated further down the athlete pathway, with the addition of strength and conditioning coaches, physiotherapists, psychologists and performance lifestyle specialists.

At the moment Glynn feels there is no semblance of quality or consistency of coaching due to the newness of a robust qualifications programme. Indeed many 'coaches' remain unqualified, which means the quality of the coaching and the playing techniques taught to new and up-and-coming players can vary wildly, making the job of the current professional coaches at GB Boccia and Glynn's job as Talent Manager even more testing, as in some cases they may have to completely re-train potentially talented players in order to remove bad technical or tactical habits they may have picked up from unqualified coaches. This situation will improve as more coaches become qualified.

Recommendations for boccia coaching, education and practice

After reflecting for a while on the question regarding whether he had any recommendations for coaching, education or practice within the sport of boccia Glynn came up with the following inter-connected issues.

Integrating knowledge from other sports into boccia

The idea of integrating knowledge from other sports into boccia is a very recent thing and probably came about largely due to the fact that all of the four professional coaches now working at GB Boccia came from other sports that were much further down the professionalisation pathway. As an example of this, Glynn stated that when he joined the sport in late 2009 the concept of periodisation didn't exist in boccia coaching. This allows players to peak at the correct time in order that their maximal performance can coincide with the major tournaments in order to optimise their opportunities of winning medals.

Multi-disciplinarity of boccia

As part of the integration of knowledge from other sports, boccia as a sport, has become much more multi-disciplinary and this should increase nationally with the addition of performance analysts, physiotherapists, conditioning coaches, etc. all playing an increasing part. This has been in place for some time at GB and international levels. As the sporting standards in boccia increase worldwide, the addition of all of these new layers to the coaching process will become increasingly important in making the difference between winning a medal and not winning a medal at major championships. Glynn also maintains that a multi-disciplinary approach further down the player pathway would be a great improvement, particularly as it would get away from the current situation of the coach having to do everything. This would also give the coaches time to improve their own coaching skills and to focus more effectively on the coaching part of the process.

International versus national competition structure

Glynn feels that the international competition structure is definitely improving with the addition of World Open ranking events to the major championships, which he feels can only improve the sport. In addition, he also feels that the international ranking system is significantly improved and will be truly representative by the end of the 2015 season. However, on the downside he feels that domestic competition and the current domestic ranking structure is quite poor. If the domestic situation is to improve and operate effectively, Glynn asserts that it has to involve the whole sport from grassroots to international level, which requires a strong working relationship between GB Boccia, as the national federation, and the home nations as the national governing bodies for the sport. Developing players simply need more competitive opportunities.

Federation versus national governing body

Currently GB Boccia is the only route into championship level boccia competitions such as the World and European Championships or the Paralympic Games. However, GB Boccia is only a federation. It is not the national governing body for the sport of boccia in the UK. This function is carried out by the home nations (Boccia England, Scottish Disability Sport, Disability Sport Wales and Disability Sport Northern Ireland). Therefore, for the sport of boccia to really make progress in the UK it will be necessary for the links between GB Boccia and the home nations to be very strong and for them to work closely together to put in place a player and support-staff pathway that is well co-ordinated and planned out. Glynn claims that when GB Boccia spots a player through a talent initiative, they often have to start from scratch in terms of the technical coaching and development, whereas if the pathway were in place from the grassroots level up, when GB Boccia spotted a talented player they could simply concentrate on taking them from talented to world class. Glynn does, however, admit that even at the GB level they do not know it all and are constantly learning, but he does feel that they are getting closer to coaching excellence.

Presentation of boccia at major competitions

Although Glynn thought that the London 2012 Paralympic Games were fantastic for disability sport generally he actually felt that the boccia presentation could have been better. Glynn highlighted some of the issues that he felt could have been better handled:

- There was no effective live feed, even of scores, never mind the matches themselves.
- There was limited commentary at the venue to explain to spectators what was going on and there was very little TV coverage of boccia.
- There were too many matches on at the same time, which made it hard for spectators to follow the action or know what was going on.
- Time clocks, officials' tables, scoreboards, etc. were placed in such a way that the scores and even parts of the court could not be seen by some spectators.

- The finals were not properly showcased. Glynn feels that the medal matches should be one at a time – big matches holding everyone's attention with commentary and live camera work, which are showcased in the same way as at the National Paralympic Day that has been held each subsequent year where the crowds have been able to get really involved in the action.
- There was not enough opportunity for the crowds to really understand and engage with the sport.

Overall Glynn felt London 2012 was an amazing event. In fact he felt it was probably the best boccia experience that anybody had ever had, with fantastic crowds and a great venue. However, overall he felt it was an opportunity missed. He did admit that he might possibly be overstating things, but he did believe it could have been better both in the Arena and on the Channel 4 television coverage.

It would appear, if the National Paralympic Day presentation of boccia is as good as Glynn says it is, that lessons may well have been learned from London 2012 and that the presentation issues, in the UK at least, may be a thing of the past. Hopefully these lessons will form part of the transfer of knowledge process to the Rio 2016 Paralympic boccia organisers in order to inspire future generations of players, coaches and spectators to become involved in the sport of boccia. It may also be a reflection of sports growing popularity and media coverage that those involved in the sport now feel able to highlight such issues, where previously they may have simply been happy to be on the Games' programme.

Additional resources and supplementary material

Boccia International Sports Federation (BISFed): http://www.bisfed.com/

GB Boccia: http://www.gb-boccia.org/

Boccia England website: https://bocciaengland.org.uk/

Disability Sport Northern Ireland: http://dsni.co.uk/performance-sport/performance-pathways/boccia

Disability Sport Scotland: http://www.scottishdisabilitysport.com/sds/index.cfm/learning-coaching-and-education/

Disability Sport Wales: http://www.disabilitysportwales.com/what-sports-can-i-do/boccia/

Notes

1   For a description of the rules and how the sport of boccia is played please visit http://www.gb-boccia.org/ and click on 'About Boccia' under the Main Menu tab.
2   For a short video of these assistive devices in use please go to https://www.youtube.com/watch?v=F1W77kY-0c8

References

Brittain, I. (2009). *The paralympic games explained*. London: Routledge.

Cassidy, T., Jones, R. & Potrac, P. (2009). *Understanding sports coaching: The social, cultural and pedagogical foundations of coaching practice* (2nd Ed.). London: Routledge.

Chopping, W. (2009). *Constructive dissatisfaction* (https://confusionmanagement.wordpress.com/2009/03/18/constructive-dissatisfaction/) [accessed 21st December 2014].

Eskew, M. (2006). Practice *'constructive dissatisfaction'* (http://money.cnn.com/popups/2006/biz2/howtosucceed/34.html) [accessed 21st December 2014].

Lawless, J. (2012). *Taming tigers: Do things you never thought you could.* London: Ebury Publishing.

Schreiner, P. & Strohkendl, H. (2006). The disappearance of athletes with severe disabilities in wheelchair rugby. Paper presented at the *Vista 2006 Conference,* entitled 'Classification: Solutions for the Future', held in Bonn, Germany, 6th–7th May.

Tromans, G. (2014). *BC3 'fearless' charter.* Personal communication.

Editors' summary reflections

Some of the case studies thus far have emphasised the important role coaches' particular pedagogical styles have in the successful personal and professional development of their athletes. Brittain's case study foregrounds, for example, how particular coaches' strategies and philosophies of learning, and their wider understanding of education within the high performance context, have implications for the day-to-practice, the coach–athlete dyad, and the coach's identity and place within the organisation's performance programmes. Like other coaches, Tromans draws on his previous experiences as an international athlete, his networks with coaches, and his knowledge from working within the sporting industry to shape his coaching practice and philosophy. Tromans has, Brittain highlights, benefited from having good connections with a range of different coaches and coaching styles upon which he can adapt and model his own coaching style. Comparable to other coaches in this book (e.g., Fivash, Darling, Bates, Drew), Troman's ability to navigate the issues and adversities of the high performance terrain and be a successful coach start with also having a strong work ethic and personal drive (Barker et al., 2014a). Troman's motivation and reflective attitude has manifested itself in his particular coaching philosophy; specifically, the emphasis he places on constructive dissatisfaction and the development of a collective team culture framed around core values. The 'fearless' charter Tromans has created, in this regard, has invariably offered a means by which athletes can not only be inducted into the team and familiarised with the coach and their expectations, but also develop a sense of collective identity, team unity and accountability. This, invariably, takes on particular importance when athletes may be at times distanced geographically from each other and their coach. As Tromans identifies, the development of a team vision has also been useful in managing expectations; for example, with regards to the frequent issues of selection and deselection that are a natural part of high performance sport.

Tromans' experiences in high performance sport generally, particularly the time as Athletics Development Manager and Talent Identification Manager, too, have afforded him valuable expertise in being able to refine his strategies for identifying, assessing, and developing athlete talent. After witnessing boccia athletes' difficult entry into the high performance environment, Tromans emerges (again, in a similar way to his peers in other sports) at the 'right' time to take the professionalisation of the sport and its coaching to the next level. In particular, to help develop sustainable development and coaching programmes underpinned by sound performance objectives and clear long-term strategies. Tromans' effort to develop his athletes and improve the quality of boccia in high performance settings has, as Brittain reveals, not been easy. Persistent classification issues, competing domestic and international demands, management of decentralised training regimes, geographic distance, limited resourcing, and negotiating professional and personal life all contour Tromans' work. While these are significant (and will be discussed further in the concluding chapter of this book), there are other fundamental concerns and questions that emerge from Tromans' experience.

Boccia is, Brittain asserts, in the nascent phase of its development as a high performance sport. As such, there are lessons that can perhaps be learnt from outside of the sport about how to strengthen the professionalisation of boccia, and in so doing create better security and clearer pathways for coaches and athletes. While fortifying the sport may be desirable, professionalisation is ultimately contingent upon developing synergies between the agendas and imperatives of local, national, transnational and international governing bodies. It is clear that boccia, not unlike other disability sports covered in this book and elsewhere, still has some way to go before the various tiers of the organisation are working together effectively and there is greater accord between participatory, development and high performance priorities. Within these ambitions there are further issues too. For example, the necessity of more robust and sport-specific coaching pathways (again, a call shared among other contributing coaches to this book). Moreover, even when educational programmes are developed for current and aspiring boccia coaches there remains the need to ensure that these adequately reflect the complexities and realities of coaches' work; in particular, by adopting multi-disciplinary approaches that better equip coaches to address their athletes' physical, bio-medical, physiological, psychological, and social needs both in and beyond the immediate sport setting. Yet in so doing, to rehearse Sawicki here, we must be mindful not to lose the art of coaching.

These issues may take some time to resolve, but as Brittain notes there are more immediate considerations that could be addressed that would improve coaches' work, such as the environment in which athletes compete, and/or the development of the high performance profile of the sport more generally (e.g., competition scheduling, practical and logistic arrangements within competitions, education and engagement with fans, and enhanced media coverage). The outlook for boccia as a high performance sport may appear to be going in a positive direction. However, not unlike other high performance sports (Barker et al., 2014b) the development of its athletes and, importantly, the sustainability of its coaching programmes, and the success of coaches too, cannot be left to chance. Addressing some of these concerns may, hopefully, better enable coaches such as Tromans to drive the sport and its constituents forward.

References

Barker, D., Barker-Ruchti, N., Rynne, S. & Lee, J. (2014a). 'Just do a little more': Examining expertise in high performance sport from a sociocultural learning perspective. *Reflective Practice*, *15*(1), 92–105.

Barker, D., Barker-Ruchti, N., Wals, A. & Tinning, R. (2014b). High performance sport and sustainability: A contradiction of terms? *Reflective Practice*, *15*(1), 1–11.

10

FROM MELKSHAM TO RIO

A coach's 20-year journey in para-swimming

Anthony J. Bush

Introduction

This chapter is a response to the calls for there to be more focused empirical sports coaching research (Taylor & Garratt, 2010; North, 2013). Sports coaching research provides the impetus for the development of the profession, thus, it is important that the research undertaken addresses the methodological concerns that have restricted the field in the last couple of decades (see Gilbert & Trudel, 2004; Bush et al., 2013). These concerns relate to a methodological fundamentalism that privileges quantitative ways of knowing and a predominance of college/university team sports as the medium for focus. This chapter addresses both of these concerns, locating the work within a qualitative methodological orientation and foregrounding [high performance, disability] swimming as the empirical context. Additionally, despite the increase in sporting events and opportunities for athletes with a disability, there is a paucity of empirical research on coaches of athletes with a disability (Cregan et al., 2007). According to North (2013), layer on layer of theoretical and conceptual developments have been based on limited evidence and what we are witnessing is the emergence of a pervasive and ominous theoretical base for the field of [disability] sports coaching as the empirical evidence strains underneath. Emphasising this pervasive and ominous nature of the theoretical base of [disability] sports coaching is that only a minority of the in excess of the 1000 published sports coaching papers are grounded in empirical evidence, of which some are cited ad mortem (North, 2013). It is also worth emphasising here that the empirical papers on coaching athletes with a disability can be counted on one hand (for example Bush & Silk, 2012; Tawse et al., 2012; Cregan et al., 2007). In addition to being empirically driven and addressing the scarcity of enquiry into coaching athletes with a disability, this chapter also speaks to the call from Rynne et al. (2010) of the need for the coaching 'workplace' to be examined, as to date it has been a site that has been largely overlooked.

Historical context of para-swimming

For people with or without a long-term limiting illness or disability, swimming is a popular way of keeping physically active. Consistently, over 2.5 million people are swimming once a week, making it the top participation sport by a significant margin. The latest Active People Survey data (Sport England, 2015a) highlights that during the interim period from April 2014 to March 2015, 13.93 million people aged 16 years and over without a long-term limiting illness or disability (39.3 per cent) played sport once a week for at least 30 minutes at a moderate intensity at least once a week. During the same time period, 1.56 million people aged 16 years and over with a long term-limiting illness or disability (17.2 per cent) played sport once a week. These data highlight the significant – and worrying – difference between the participation in sport of those aged 16 years and over who have a long-term limiting illness or disability. This difference is also mirrored in young people, with individuals with long-term limiting illness or disability less likely to participate in sport than their peers. There are also important differences in participation in sport of young people who have a long-term limiting illness or disability between participation in school compared with out-of-school participation. It is important to recognise that for young disabled people the most popular physical education activity area is swimming (Fitzgerald & Kay, 2004) and it is also the most popular sport that disabled people of all ages participate in out of the school context (Sport England, 2015b).

The importance of swimming is also emphasised by the degree to which elite swimming is supported with funding from UK Sport. UK Sport make investment decisions on a four-year basis to cover a complete Olympic or Paralympic cycle based on an eight-year performance development model and allocate funding on the basis of their 'no compromise' strategy, with the resources directed at sports and athletes with medal winning potential. In the current funding cycle (Rio 2013–2017) the total funding from National Lottery and Exchequer income to UK Sport is £543m, and from this the Olympic sport of swimming has been awarded £20.8m (fifth highest allocation behind rowing at £32.6m, cycling at £30.5m, athletics at £26.8m and sailing at £25.5m) and the Paralympic sport of para-swimming has been awarded £11.7m, which is the highest allocation to any Paralympic sport (UK Sport, 2015a). This support for para-swimming, representing an increase of £1.2m from the London 2012 cycle and a £8.2m increase from Sydney 2000, highlights the consistent high performance of the para-swimmers over the last four Paralympic cycles (UK Sport, 2015b).

The International Paralympic Committee (IPC) is the global governing body of the Paralympic Movement. In addition to organising the summer and winter Paralympic Games, the IPC also acts as the International Federation for nine sports (including para-swimming), supervising and co-ordinating World and European Championships and other competitions. The IPC has approximately 170 National Paralympic Committees (NPCs), each NPC is responsible for a team's preparation and management for the Paralympic Games and other IPC-sanctioned events. In

Great Britain, the NPC is the British Paralympic Association (BPA). The BPA will work closely with the national governing body for swimming, British Swimming, which comprises the three home countries' national governing bodies of England (Amateur Swimming Association (ASA)), Scotland (Scottish Swimming) and Wales (Swim Wales).[1] British Swimming has responsibility for the high performance representation of the sport and aims to 'create a world class environment centred around the athlete and coach which is supported by the programme enabling performance at the highest standard to maximise gold medal opportunities' (British Swimming, 2013, p.2).

Para-swimming's development has been symbiotic with the evolution of the Paralympic movement. Tracing the genealogy of para-swimming reveals that since its inclusion as one of eight sports at the first official Paralympiad in Rome 1960, through to and beyond the first summer Paralympic Games in Toronto 1976, it has undeniably become one of the biggest sports at the Paralympic Games in terms of both the numbers of competitors and the number of events. In the Paralympic Games in London 2012, athletics accounted for more competitors than any other discipline with over 1000 athletes, swimming was second with around 600 competitors in 148 medal events. In these 148 events, Team GB was represented by 44 athletes who won a total of 39 medals (seven of which were gold). In 2015 Glasgow hosted the seventh IPC Swimming World Championships with 67 countries represented in 152 medal events, in which GB won 32 medals (ten gold, 12 silver and ten bronze). For the Paralympic Games in Rio de Janeiro 2016 the respective targets are 40 medals with ten gold, and 50 medals with 15 gold (British Swimming, 2013).

Para-swimming comprises medal events in freestyle, backstroke, butterfly, breaststroke and medley events across distances that range from 50m to 400m. The events take place in a standard 50m pool, with swimmers starting from a variety of positons dependant on the degree of functionality the athlete has. Athletes can have a physical, visual or intellectual impairment and are subject to classification into one of now 14 classes. It is important to note that in swimming, simply having the impairment is not sufficient information for classification, it is the impact on the sport that must be proved. The IPC swimming integrated functional classification system includes an assessment of the swimmers' range of motion and co-ordination determined by medical experts (bench test) and a swimming test. In order to classify the swimmer for competition, points are awarded for both tests depending on the event in which they wish to compete. The sport-class names in swimming consist of a prefix 'S', 'SM', or 'SB' and a number. Freestyle, backstroke and butterfly have the prefix 'S', breaststroke 'SB' and individual medley 'SM'. Swimmers with physical impairments are classified from 1 to 10 with the aforementioned prefix. Within categories labelled 1–10, athletes with the lower classification numbers have the more severe activity limitation than a higher number. Swimmers who have visual impairments compete in the sport classes 11 to 13, with sport class 11 swimmers having complete or nearly complete loss of sight, while sport class 13 swimmers will have a greater degree of vision than sport class 11 or 12 athletes. Introduced in London 2012 was the sport class 14 for athletes with an intellectual impairment.

Through the classification of an athlete's impairment, it is envisaged that an equitable and fair sporting environment is created. Thus, the overarching goal of the classification system is that 'winning or losing an event depends on talent, training, skill, fitness, and motivation rather than unevenness among competitors on disability related variables' (Sherrill, 1999, p. 210), which according to the IPC (2015) are the same factors that account for success in sport for able-bodied athletes. However, it should be noted that the classification system within Paralympic sport has been a site of critique by scholars who perceive the very process of classification of athletes by the IPC as a pernicious vehicle through which athletes – and others in the Paralympic 'practice community' such as coaches, officials and spectators – have become marginalised (Howe & Jones, 2006).[2] It is interesting to note that advocates of the IPC swimming integrated functional classification system see the impact of rationalising competitive categories has resulted in the sport having fair, viable and vibrant competition that also have the additional benefits of reducing confusion for spectators and sponsors alike. However, Howe (2008) suggests that this predominantly serves the IPC in improving the efficiency and speed of events, and that the reduction of over 21 classes does not attend to the requirements of the 'practice community'.

There is no question that British Swimming sees the development of coaches as one of their priority areas in achieving their performance objectives at an elite level. Coach development is identified as a specific key area of strategic focus in their 2013–2017 strategy with the implementation of a framework for quadrennial coach development, aiming to enhance the expertise, innovation and best practice of not only current elite coaches, but also the next generation of elite coaches. UK Sport also run three schemes that also aim to develop world-class coaches in the Olympic and Paralympic sports. Working in collaboration with these sports, these three schemes are the 'Elite Programme' (developing established coaches to become world leading coaches), 'Elite Coaching Apprenticeship Programme (ECAP)' (designed to accelerate the development of emerging coaches already in the high performance system), and the 'Athlete to Coach Programme' (transitioning and supporting athletes towards being a world-class coach). Underpinning this is a substantial coach development programme for coaches at all stages of their coaching journey. Each of the home countries run a similar suite of programmes that have been developed in line with the United Kingdom Coaching Certificate (UKCC) criteria which have been guided by the requirements of the Qualifications and Credits Framework (QCF). For swimming, all home countries 'provide' the UKCC Levels 1, 2 and 3 in coaching swimming.[3] Additionally, all of the home countries have similar auditing and accountability checks and measures to ensure the quality of the provision. For example, in England, the ASA is the leading 'provider' of aquatic qualifications. It should be noted that the ASA is an Awarding Organisation (AO) and is regulated by the Office of Qualifications and Examinations Regulator (Ofqual). It is the responsibility of training providers to deliver the course specifications to participants that have been prescribed by the AOs. The

Institute of Swimming (IoS) is the largest trainer of swimming teachers and coaches in England and provides the ASA's suite of training courses and continuing professional development (CPD) seminars.[4]

Historical context of Steve Fivash

Steve Fivash has been involved with both able-bodied (AB) swimming and para-swimming for over 20 years, helping athletes achieve their goals at the Olympic Games in Athens 2004, the Paralympic Games in Beijing 2008 and the Paralympic Games in London 2012. As part of his role as GB Development Coach for British Para-Swimming, Steve developed, implemented, led and managed the British Para-Swimming Diamond – now termed 'Fast Track' – Programme. Every two years, this programme takes a select group of talented athletes from the World Class Podium Potential (WCPP) Programme and sets out to facilitate their transition to the World Class Programme (WCP), place new and better prepared athletes on the Senior National Team and expose the athletes to camps and competitions with tailored support to enhance their podium potential. Nine swimmers were selected for the programme 18 months before London 2012. Steve was involved with coaching and mentoring the swimmers and home coaches. Seven of the nine swimmers were selected for London 2012, with three of the swimmers winning 1 x gold, 2 x silver and 3 x bronze medals. In addition to the athletes on the Fast Track Programme, Steve also supported 15 athletes who achieved 20 podium finishes (including five gold medals).

Prior to entering elite sports as a career move, Steve was in business management (including project management and change management) and manufacturing planning for 24 years.

Employment history

Currently, Steve is the GB Development Coach for British Para-Swimming, a role that he has held for eight years focusing on activities that aim to maximise the podium potential of talented para-swimmers. Prior to this, from 2006–2007, he was the Regional Talent Development Coach for the South East and South West regions. Within this role he was responsible for the delivery of the Advanced Apprenticeship in Sports Excellence (AASE), working with both coaches and athletes. He also led the ASA English Talent Programme which encompassed a range of swimmer and coach development activities. The year prior to this (2005–2006) he was the Regional Development Officer for the South East and South West regions. Steve had responsibilty for the delivery of a number of projects. These projects included the Swim21 NGB Club Accreditation Programme, Physical Education School Sport and Club Links (PESSCL), recruitment of Community Sports Coaches and the CPD of existing coaches, developing swimmer development pathways based on Long-Term Athlete Development (LTAD), and volunteer education. From 2001–2005, Steve was the Assistant Swimming Coach at the University of Bath. Whilst in this role, he assisted and led the University swim programme at all levels from age group to elite performance. Steve undertook the Active Sports Swimming Co-ordinator role for the county of Wiltshire between 2002 and 2004 in which he implemented the Active Sport programme. For seven years (1994–2001) Steve undertook the role of Head Coach at Melksham Swimming Club. It was within this role that he developed and led the swimmers and club programme. Whilst in this role, Steve produced medallists at Age Group National, District and County Championships.

Overlapping Steve's work as Head Coach at Melksham Swimming Club, was his work in business management (1990–2001) which included many roles (Senior Planner, Operations Manager, Logistics Manager, Planning Manager) at a number of companies (Avon Technical Products, KAM Engineering and Sykes-Pickavant). Prior to this, he was involved in manufacturing planning for 13 years (1977–1990).

Qualifications

Steve has acquired a range of professional and formal qualifications on his career journey. His professional qualifications specific to swimming include the Amateur Swimming Association (ASA) Coach (Level 4) and ASA Club Coach (Level 3). More generically, he has also acquired an England Basketball, Assistant Coach (Level 1) and British Weight Lifters Association (Leaders Award). Steve's formal qualifications include the Institute of Leadership & Management (ILM) Coaching & Mentoring (NVQ Level 5) in 2015 and a Neuro-Linguistic Programming Sports Practitioner award in 2013. Steve also graduated from the University of Bath in 2005 with a first-class honours degree in Coach Education and Sports Development and prior to this, in 2003, acquired a Higher National Diploma in Coach Education and Sports Performance from the University of Bath and was awarded the programme's top academic student prize. In 1991, Steve graduated with a Higher National Certificate in Business Studies from the City of Bath College.

Case study of Steve Fivash

Getting into coaching

In the United Kingdom, there are in excess of 1.1 million people involved in the practice of sport coaching, delivering coaching sessions to approximately 10 million participants every year (Bush, 2012). 80 per cent of sport coaches contribute their time on a voluntary basis, with it estimated that there are 240,000 paid sports coaches, of which 80,000 of these are employed in a full-time capacity (Skills Active, 2011). Steve's coaching journey has taken him circuitously through all employment permutations. Through his childhood years, Steve describes himself as someone that had a passion for sport but was not a particularly gifted athlete. After leaving school, college and then working in manufacturing, Steve arrived at coaching swimming quite by chance:

> Basically it was taking my children to swimming lessons when they were probably about 5, 6, or 7 and a friend of mine who I knew inside the sport said 'we desperately need volunteers … can you come and help?'. I said I don't know anything about swimming and he said 'don't worry about that! Just stand there and look good and I will do the rest'.

Starting off by coaching once a week on a Saturday morning for half an hour, things progressed rapidly:

> Somewhere along the line after a few years the head coach, which I didn't appreciate at the time, knew he was leaving as his job was taking him elsewhere and I had started to get a bit interested in coaching … and when he left he said 'Steve, I want you to be the new head coach of the local swimming club in Melksham'. I was really taken aback with this but he obviously saw a lot about me that I didn't. I think at this time I only had my assistant teacher's qualification. But I took on the job, the other coaches there were quite happy for me to do it … or probably they didn't want to do it and I was the mug that said yes!

Over the next five years, Steve transformed the club from having the weakest team in the county to one of the top clubs. However, the coaching was unpaid:

> I was doing all the coaching and I was in a full-time job. I was doing 40 to 50 hours a week and then I was coaching as well which with all the admin was another 20 hours a week and sometimes with competitions an additional 30 to 40 hours a week. I got to a point in my late 30s when I was thinking with my work that I didn't really want to continue doing what I'm doing at the moment for another 25 or 30 years until I retire … or do I want to give sport a go? So, I decided at that point in time that sport was more attractive and that I wanted to challenge myself to see how far or how good a coach I was.

This desire to continue to improve is characteristic of the findings of Rynne et al. (2010), with coaches fuelled by personal factors such as wanting to be the best that they can and the love of the sport, as well as external factors such as a desire to assist their athletes to be successful. There is no question that during his time as Head Coach – and all of his subsequent coaching appointments – Steve put the needs of his athletes before his own by facilitating the departure of his most talented athletes to a performance swim programme:

> I was fortunate because at the same time I was coaching the group in Melksham a number of very talented swimmers came through … and there were a couple of very capable swimmers that won medals at age group nationals. At the same time in the late 1990s, the University of Bath set up a performance swim group programme and a spin-off of this was an age group

program. The way that that was set up is that they invited swimmers into the programme that had achieved district and regional qualifying times or reached regional finals, and then they could offer them a lot more pool time and professional coaching than I could do (or any club coach) as we only had 12 hours of water at this time.

Coach knowledge, learning and coach education

During his time as Head Coach at his club in Melksham, Steve had acquired his ASA Level 3 club coach award. It is important to note that Steve – like the majority of Paralympic coaches – has completed coach education programmes that focus exclusively on working with able-bodied athletes (Cregan et al., 2007; Tawse et al., 2012). A number of studies have problematised the impact of coach education qualifications on coaching practice positing that the formal coach education process is rarely considered important or valued by the coaches undertaking them (Nelson et al., 2013; Nash & Sproule, 2012; Piggott, 2012). Coaches tend to utilise a blend of critical self-reflection and the experiences of other coaches for their professional development rather than formal coach education programmes (Jacobs et al., 2014). Thus, it can be argued that formal coach education programmes are not effective in achieving the desired outcome of improving coaching practice. Nash & Sproule (2012) suggest that it is not the sport-specific components of the formal coach education process that are perceived by coaches as an issue, it is the inadequacy of the process to take account of fulfilling the coach's requirements in relation to wider aspects of coaching such as psychology or pedagogy. This is highlighted by Steve, who describes the benefit of having studied for his honours degree:

> There are things from a sports science point of view where I can sit down and talk a little bit with coaches about what the results of a step test means and areas of nutrition or strength and conditioning because we did that a lot on the university programme and there's lots of theory to back this up within the course. You do not get the detail in the NGB qualifications. Yes, they do cover it but it would be a very small module as opposed to four years of in-depth study. And there is a rigorous filtering on the university course to ensure that what you are learning is contemporary and up to date … and that you have the knowledge and skills to meet the demands of the learning outcomes to be awarded your degree.

Steve also intimates that it is accepted within NGBs that a degree is an essential part of an elite coach's profile and that the element of self-study and critical reflection (reinforced by degree-level study) cannot be underestimated in the development of coaching expertise. Indeed, as previously mentioned, Jacobs et al. (2014) identify constant critical reflection as a tool that enables coaches to move closer to their individual idea of a 'good coach':

When I was at the University of Bath I did the ASA coach qualification I think it was titled, which is the senior qualification. At the moment, I think the highest qualification is club coach because it's considered that if you want to be an elite coach you probably need a degree to go with it because there is recognition in sports they cannot go into the detail of – in my case four years of study. And it is challenging because of the very nature of doing a degree course, it does challenge you to keep challenging your assumptions (through study and self-study) and from that you get a lot deeper level of understanding.

Steve talks about how far he progressed during his four years of study and that he had to make sacrifices along the way:

I definitely moved a long way from when I was 40 to when I was 44, and I learned so much not only through the course and learning off the other people in my cohorts ... and to be honest I probably learned more off the people around me as I did anywhere else. So I was really lucky, but I had to make a lot of tough choices and sacrifice and there have been times when family came second (which I don't necessarily agree with), but the need was there and I made a decision to do it with my wife and I have made it work and I think because of that it has allowed me to be where I am today.

Importantly, not only did Steve study for his degree, he attributes his development as a coach to a number of contributory factors. Firstly, he was mentored by three World Class coaches in his role as assistant coach with the University of Bath programme:

At the same time [as studying for my HND/Degree] I was then taken on as an assistant coach with the University of Bath programme, mainly supporting Dave Lyles who headed up the student programme. Also in the swimming programme at the same time was a great guy called Ian Turner, who was the GB Head Coach at the time and very well respected in the sport. Another coach there was Andre Varontsov, who eventually went on to become the Head Coach of the Russian national swimming team, taking them to London 2012. Dave Lyles later left the University and became the first European on the Chinese swim team, again in 2012 ... so I had the opportunity to work with some really great, great coaches and I learned a tremendous amount not only about swim coaching but about what coaching is all about and the softer skills you need to coach ...

Ian Turner's background was as a school teacher and he is probably one of the best communicators I've seen ... just the way he got the message across to the athletes. And from my point of view, if you were here to learn I couldn't fail to learn in this environment and from these people. Andre was quite a shy coach and again when I spoke to him about principles of training and planning – he effectively wrote LTAD with the Russians – his knowledge was incredible ... my challenge was getting it out of him, which was the difficulty.

> David was technically one of the best breaststroke coaches in the world ...
> you only need to look at his success both here and elsewhere ... I couldn't fail
> to learn. I just threw myself into every opportunity and was challenged.

Secondly, he was able to work with a number of world-class swimmers:

> Because the University of Bath was a high performance centre (HPC) we
> had some great swimmers in the pool. These swimmers were mainly coached
> by Andre and Ian, but within David's group we had Olympic swimmers,
> World Championship swimmers and Commonwealth Games swimmers so
> the standard throughout the whole setup was extremely high. I can remember
> coming on poolside in August 2001 thinking I knew a little bit about
> swimming, and, within about ten minutes I knew that I knew absolutely
> nothing ... but what I did know really didn't add up to much but these guys
> were really great as I think I must have convinced them that I was passionate
> about the sport and wanted to learn. I wanted to learn – not only in the
> water – but I coached as much as I could and got really sucked into the
> education from the degree course ...
>
> Andre gave me the opportunity to work with an athlete at technically my
> first GB training camp (with a GB open water swimmer). The open water
> swimmer came back with our first ever medal at the World Championships
> six weeks after the training camp. I know I hadn't made a massive contribution
> but Andre's comment was that 'you put the edging on the medal' and to me
> to get that recognition from some of the coaches ... and Ian would trust me
> enough when he was away to coach his swimmers, and that was a fantastic
> experience ... I mean I have got Olympic and World Championship
> swimmers in a lane and I was coaching them ... how can you not fail to get
> something from that.

Thirdly, Steve always attempted to put theory into practice in the pool:

> For me I just focused on the coach education side of my degree and that was
> great because I could then have all the theory in the classroom and lectures
> and attempt to put it into practice ten minutes later in the pool. Sometimes
> it was great and sometimes I had to go away and think again, and this was all
> part of the learning process and it certainly helped my reflective practice. I
> continually talked to the other coaches and sometimes they were quite
> complimentary but other times they were critical ... but again that was great
> for my coaching education.

Steve signposts UK Sport's attempts to develop elite coaches through their elite
programme and elite coaching apprenticeship programme and highlights that the
experience that he manufactured for himself at least mirrored the experiences of
the few identified coaches that undertake the programme:

And I think at the moment UK Sport have got their elite coaching programmes for a small cohort to go through to be active in their NGBs. So it is being addressed within the UK Sport areas across all sports ... but each year there's only one, possibly two, swimming coaches that are accepted onto that particular course. So the route I decided to take actually put me in a good place because I finished the degree in 2005 and had gained four years elite coaching experience –that at the beginning was a baptism of fire – that was a wonderful experience and I had come through both so that I had academic knowledge and practical technical knowledge and I could apply both, and I still apply both today.

Steve's transition into disability swimming following the completion of his degree course in 2005 was again as accidental and forced as his evolution into coaching in the first place:

In 2005 my degree course came to the end and there were no coaching opportunities to continue on at the University of Bath ... so unfortunately I had to leave and my coaching at this point in time took a back seat for about 18 months. During this time, I was employed by the Amateur Swimming Association (ASA) as a Regional Development Officer (RDO) but that was more to do with the management of participation swimming. Making sure that the swimming clubs had enough pool time, led by people with the correct qualifications, that the clubs were inclusive ... and this was my first contact with people who were swimming with disabilities. Those contracts came to an end – because I was basically maternity cover – and I ended up cutting the story short about working with British Disability Swimming as it was called then (late 2006 early 2007), and to be honest it was the best thing that ever happened to me. A guy called Lars Humer, who was the head coach at the time, asked me if I would like to come and work for disability swimming and offered me the job and I haven't looked back since.

Disability sport coach as 'bricoleur'

I begin this section through recourse to the concept of the bricolage. The term is derived from Claude Levi-Strauss' (1966) discussion of it in *The savage mind*. He deployed the French word bricoleur, which describes a handyman or handywoman who makes use of the tools available to complete a task (Denzin & Lincoln, 2000; Harper, 1987). Although the term bricoleur has been appropriated and articulated in relation to sports coaching research (see Bush et al., 2013), it seems appropriate to deploy this term to describe the multiplicity of demands placed on Steve in his coaching role. The central argument for appropriating this nomenclature in the context of disability sport coaching is the need for the profession of sport coaching to be seen as something far more complex than the reductionist 'elite' performance discourse allows. Currently, success in sport is simply characterised by the winning of medals, and therefore the function and concomitantly the roles of a coach have been defined as those solely focused on the activities relating to improving the sporting performance of an individual or a team. What we see with Steve's role is a need for the coach to literally utilise all 'tools' available, akin to that of a handyman or handywoman, and thus we can consider him as a bricoleur in action.

Linked to this articulation, the dominant – and as a consequence rarely challenged –discourse on coach education programmes is that there exists a taken-for-granted assumption of what constitutes a good coach leading to coach education programmes serving to homogenise or normalise coaching practice and transform it into a 'professionalised' activity, with a coach's competence being certified against clearly benchmarked standards (Taylor & Garratt, 2010; Nelson et al., 2006). Thus, there is a real disconnect with what providers of coach education programmes are delivering and the requirements of those undertaking the coach education qualifications. It could be argued that until the reality of what coaches actually do and the understanding of why they are doing it –moving beyond the behaviours, actions and roles undertaken in making an individual or team better at a specific sport – is translated into coach education programmes, then they will continue to be perceived by many of the recipients as not contributing positively to what they are doing in the 'real world' of coaching. In the 'real world' of disability coaching, Steve found himself being challenged in his role:

> So really for the last eight years now I've been working with what we now call 'para' swimmers mainly looking at swimmers with a physical disability, visual impairment or more recently swimmers with learning difficulties, and it challenged my coaching to the point where I've been used to dealing with people that had, putting it crudely, two arms, two legs and could see and could listen. And so the challenge for me as a coach was how I adapt what I want to tell them, the messages you want to give them, so that they can get on and do it … Because it's working to their ability, and as a coach I find that I have become a better coach because I had to think more about what I wanted to do … what the set comprised of, the volume of the set, what they were physically capable of doing, how can I deliver the message … because if you're dealing with somebody who is visually impaired lots of visual demonstrations are a bit of a waste of time! I had to change the way that I delivered messages.

Steve really focuses his coaching on what he describes as 'process goals':

> It's more about looking at process goals … we don't talk too much about the outcome. We talk about the process of how we can move from where we are today, what steps we are going to take, what technical improvements do we need to put in place, what sports science support skills we need to bring in … so to some extent my role has morphed from coach to a one-stop shop … I am a filter to see where the athlete is and see what they need at that

period in time and I'll make a call whether I need to talk to other people to come in and help.

In our neoliberal present, where sports funding is inexorably linked to medal success, Steve's focus on process goals is an attempt to reduce the pressure on the athlete:

> Our sport is funded through UK Sport and they base a lot of their funding decisions on gold medals, either achieved or forecast. So at a senior level, at an NPD level, they focus on winning those gold medals at the major championships, either at a Paralympic Games or World Championships or whatever the benchmark competition is for that year. As a programme we make a conscious decision not to burden the athlete with that level of expectation because it's going to put the heck of a lot of pressure on the athlete. The athletes that are very elite, they know where they are in the world rankings, they know if they're world number one, number two or number 20 ... so from that point of view they have enough expectation on themselves. As it is they have their own expectations and the expectations of the coach that they are working with ... and then there's their community ... their parents, friends and acquaintances, Facebook, Twitter ... you name it.

In addition to reducing the pressure on the athlete, Steve is adamant that a focus on process goals facilitates the management of the athlete:

> The more popular you become, the more interest to generate and in sport that's all about being on the podium. So from my point of view I work with the athletes about the process of how we're going to move from where we are today to achieve whatever goal that they set themselves. Because it's very hard if you've only got one thing in mind (i.e. delivering a podium finish) and for whatever reason – you know you could've done everything right, your preparations gone great, the sport science support has been fine ... everything has gone spot on – but on that particular day three people are better than you (because that's the nature of sport) and you end up fourth. It's far easier to manage –it's never easy! – working with the athletes, the coach and other people if it's about the process goals.

Thinking of the athletes and putting their needs first is something that Steve identifies as an important dynamic of being a coach in para-sport:

> I think that any coach that comes into a para-sport needs to be more involved with simple things, because one or two of our athletes in the past, for example, haven't been able to feed themselves because of their impairment. So you need to think about other people and carry a second plate around and say 'what is it that you want?' and then you have to cut the food up. I just did it ... if this person can't do that then I must do it. Initially it is unexpected

because you have not absorbed yourself in their environment or culture ...
Unloading the bus is another good example. Normally when a team goes
away we have 30 or 40 bags on the bus, and some guys can't carry the
suitcase ... and so you get your own bag and then you collect somebody
else's. Now that is what we do. I know of certain AB situations that they will
get their suitcase and walk off ... well that's fine but it's almost selfish, so you
have to park all that and become more aware of other people's needs and I
think as a coach in para-sport you just do it.

Steve also describes other situations where he has had to ensure that he puts others'
needs to the forefront of his practice:

The first time you pick up someone's leg and arm and walk around poolside
that's what it is ... you do feel a bit self-conscious the first time, but when
you have done it a couple of times, you just get on with it. The same as
when you're standing by the block they need a hand to get on the block or
to steady them, you do feel quite self-conscious with helping them the first
time. Then you think that you are there to help them perform ... so you just
get on and do it. It is part and parcel of what you do because the athletes see
you absorbed into their way of doing things then they accept you.

In putting his athletes first, Steve creates a strong bond with the athletes that he is
working with. Previous research has highlighted a conscious attempt by coaches
to *create* an idealised image (Goffman, 1959) of themselves for their athletes (Potrac
et al., 2002), however, the data consistently yielded that Steve has core values that
shaped his practice:

I don't know what I do, I know I'm honest, committed and engaged and I
am consistent with these, and so for people who don't like or conform to
what my values are then there will be a much harder relationship. But,
through the consistency and honesty and trust and with these real core values,
it works ... I'm sometimes challenging but fair, so if the athlete knows they've
done it wrong, I challenge them a bit more and always give them a couple of
chances before it gets more heated shall we say. If you do it wrong once, you
get another few chances to get it right. Because I am consistent all the way
through, that element of trust is always there. So that's me.

Reflecting on whether this high degree of trust and consistency has forced his
coaching role to evolve into something that takes him to places that typically a
coach wouldn't need to deal with:

Yes, and that's some of the problem because there is a high churn rate in staff
within the EIS. If you look at the staff that we have today on the sport
science side none of those were involved in London three years ago apart

from the science manager. So I have only one person out of the half a dozen that were there three years ago. So I have been there seven years and I have seen three nutritionists in that time ... so, you just build up a level of trust and understanding and they are just beginning to open up and they have gone. Because these people are ambitious, they know that if the sport doesn't get the funding then they are out of the job themselves so they are looking – and quite rightly too – they are looking after themselves and look to get into another sport or into industry that is more secure doing what they're doing, then why shouldn't they? But it means that at that time of crisis just after the Paralympic Games is probably the most vulnerable time for everybody involved because we don't know what funding we can get, we don't know if we've got a job, and we are looking out for ourselves, and the athlete to whom we have been saying 'you're the centre of everything' is almost left fending for themselves ... they are not, but that is the perception that they see. And yes, I do get involved with things that are far beyond what the coach should be doing, and I do get some of the sports science team asking me 'why are you dealing with this' and I'm perfectly blunt and say that they [the athletes] trust me and by the time that they have built up the relationship with you, you will be gone. So, the athletes would always talk with me and I will have a conversation with the support staff, but only with their permission, and you are going to tell me and I will feed it back in. They know that I am a constant. So it is really difficult and I do find myself having these difficult conversations.

Steve described that career transition and especially termination is something that he finds particularly worrying and emotionally draining. After London, he was surprised by how few of the para-swimming athletes retired, however, he foresees a number of issues as we move forwards:

After Rio there definitely will be [more retirements] and I think for those guys it's going to be very, very difficult because when I did have the original conversations before London and they didn't want to talk about it because they were so focused on performing in London – they didn't want to talk about what was going to happen on the 1st October as I termed it. They didn't even want to contemplate it ... and I know that the EIS/UK Sport do provide transition services ... there is up to three months of transitional funding if you meet the criteria ... but three months isn't a very long time. You talk of able-bodied people being made redundant sometimes being out of work for six months and they are perceived to have a profession ... what we got here are elite athletes and they are great at being elite athletes, but what other professional skills have they got? They have got some key skills such as discipline, timekeeping, they are very motivated so if you can catch their imagination they will be great at what you want them to do ... but it's getting through the door and I perceive some of our athletes didn't retire because they suddenly realised this and they could carry on ... but age eventually catches up with everybody.

... so there will be more of a challenge after Rio... and I do really worry about all the athletes, about what they are going to do when they finish ... how are they going to maintain a good standard of living? Yes, there are disability benefits but that is nowhere near to the level of funding they have been receiving. Some of these guys have mortgages, loans ... how are they going to live? One or two I can think of have got families, how are they going to manage going forwards? Especially in the time of austerity when, and I know unemployment is dropping but what are they going to do ... but they won't talk about it before they get there, that's the biggest stumbling block.

Steve sees the future of Paralympic swimming in the hands of society and also the parents. The future of the sport is based on the need to engage individuals with disabilities into physical activity, and to grow those grassroots numbers in order to facilitate more to come through into competitive swimming.

The biggest challenge we face is with society accepting people in at grassroots level – accepting that they have skills and can do as well as an able-bodied person – they might swim slower with a disability but it is all about opportunity at that level.

So, it is about society deciding that they can access these opportunities and it's about the parents being brave enough to allow their child to experience that opportunity, because I don't know how the parents feel because I've never felt confident to ask them, but I can only guess that they blame themselves for whatever impairments the child has because it might be from birth. There is a huge amount of blame I believe and because of that there is a huge amount of protection. They do it from a love point of view, not because of a selfish thing, there's a huge amount of love there ... and the parents' biggest concern or worry in all this emotional mix is that they are going to expose their child to something that they're not going to be very successful or good at, and them being stigmatised as not very good or different from the norm. And some of the biggest challenges we have in para-swimming is getting the parents to let go because they have been for a period of time the only person in their child's life and are quite possessive – not in a nasty way – but they really want their son or daughter to be successful in what they do.

And then they come to me and I say, 'oh yes we will go off and do this that and the other'. 'You can't do that', they say and I say, 'yes we can and you'll be surprised'. And in a nice way - we work with such small numbers – we challenge the athletes in social skills as well as being an athlete, or just in day-to-day living and the way that they live and they suddenly realise they can be as good as anybody else.

One issue that Steve identifies as impacting access is that once the initial barriers are overcome and an athlete is identified as having a talent:

> all the athletes are based in able-bodied clubs. There is probably only one coach and setup where there is dedicated para-swimming with para-swimmers … in Manchester … where the coach will just work with para-swimmers … everywhere else is a combination of the two.

So, although Howe (2008) suggests that for Paralympic events – that are not reliant on technology – it is easier across the board to be selected for the Paralympic than the Olympic Games (due to the lower number of competitors), it can be seen that a far greater challenge for individuals with an impairment might be overcoming the access issues initially, parental concerns, fear of failure and then being lucky in the geographical lottery in relation to a club that has a coach with the skills to provide the facilitative coaching environment to nurture and develop their talent. Bloomfield (2003) suggests that it is imperative for sporting organisations to value and integrate programmes for athletes with a disability within mainstream sporting environments, something that will need to be assimilated into sport plans. As a result of increased integration, the awareness of working with athletes with a disability amongst the coaching workforce will be increased and thus reduce the impact of the geographical lottery currently dominating provision. Concurrent with this would therefore be a reduction in the necessity for training groups to be differentiated by able-bodied or para-swimmers. Additionally, facilities need to follow these advancements, with priority investment into leisure provision for disabled people. Enterprises such as the nationwide Inclusive Fitness Initiative (IFI) that aims to have facilities accredited and also instructors specifically trained in marketing and managing exercise for disabled customers need to be supported by sporting organisations. Unfortunately, statistics, such as four out of five leisure venues not providing proper access for disabled participants and only 39 per cent having a useable toilet (Collins & Kay, 2014) are simply not acceptable. There are comprehensive guidance notes available for providing swimming facilities – and other leisure facilities – for disabled participants (see Sport England, 2010) and so this requires strategic investment in the infrastructure alongside the need for coaches to embrace participants with a disability into their coaching sessions.

Recommendations for Paralympic swimming coaching, education and practice

This chapter is written from an understanding of sports coaching as a complex, social, dynamic and relational activity, and that sports coaches should be considered primarily as educators – pedagogues – who facilitate participant learning in a wide range of pedagogic settings (Jones, 2006; Bush, 2007; Bush et al., 2013). The pedagogic setting in this chapter is elite para-swimming, and in order for coaches to operate effectively in this challenging context, this has necessitated a theorising of multiple roles of a coach in order to attempt to capture the reality of coaching. This means moving beyond the roles articulated through formal coach education processes - motivator, leader, systematic methods instructor – that reduce coaching to a simplistic and unproblematic activity. Recent work has tried to theorise the multiple roles of a coach (Jones, 2006; Bush & Silk, 2010; Morgan & Bush, 2014; Bush et al., 2013) – however, from this case study, empirical evidence can signpost to additional key roles relating to placing your para-swimming athletes needs to the front of your practice. Pseudo-parent, social worker, counsellor, transformative leader, careers officer, caregiver, and cook are roles that can be clearly articulated from Steve's story. Deploying the concept of 'coach as bricoleur' seems to be a good starting point in attempting to capture the reality of the coaching context. Understanding a coaching episode to be akin to a handyman or handywoman who makes use of a multiplicity of tools available to complete a task presents an image of coaching that moves away from the simplistic portrayal of a coach undertaking limited roles and functions to simply make an individual better at sport.

It was intimated earlier in the chapter that the formal coach education process is rarely considered important or valued by the coaches undertaking them (Nelson et al., 2013; Nash & Sproule, 2012; Piggott, 2012). The challenge for all in the formal coach education chain is to recognise the complexity inherent in the profession of sports coaching and attempt to develop a suite of programmes that the consumers – the coaches – attach a value to. Steve – like most coaches – perceives the formal aspect of coach education (coach certification) to be something that must be acquired to meet the requirements of employers … but intimates that the real learning about their profession comes from, and here I am borrowing from Nelson et al. (2006), formal opportunities afforded by degree studies, non-formal activities afforded by workshops and training camps, and the informal learning opportunities afforded by daily experiences, interaction with mentors and peers and exposure to the environment. As found in the study by Tawse et al. (2012), this information must be utilised by NGBs to supplement – perhaps replace components of – their formal training requirements. Steve's development as a coach has taken place over decades (and is still ongoing) and has been a journey full of twists and turns. Although talking about 'bricoleur' in a completely different context, Kincheloe (2001, p.690) states that 'learning to become a bricoleur is a lifelong process', which again should be seen as analogous with developing as a coach. Indeed, Gallimore et al. (2014, p.268) go as far as to say that a 'commitment to ongoing learning is a hallmark of effective sport coaches'. The outcome for British Para-Swimming is that they ended up – by complete accident – with the ideal coach running their Diamond Programme. The challenge for British Para-Swimming – and other sporting organisations – is how to be more systematic in the way that a talented individual's passion for a sport can be harnessed, nurtured and developed. Perhaps working with higher education institutions, those responsible for developing the programme specifications of formal coaching qualifications, can look to integrate or embed learning outcomes into appropriate degree programmes enabling a fast-track to acquiring specific UKCC qualifications. An additional consideration for all NGBs is the transitory nature of the support staff that work in para-sport. All athletes require stability – especially at high transition points, such as following an Olympic or Paralympic Games – and more should be done to prevent the burden of expectation to fall on the shoulders of the coaches that remain a constant in the athlete's existence.

Steve is passionate about attracting more individuals with a disability into swimming, not only for the possibility of identifying talent for the future, but also for the well-documented benefits of lifelong sporting participation and a healthy lifestyle. Steve emphasises empowerment, independence and developing a high degree of self-responsibility in his swimmers, and by locating the athlete at the centre of everything he does he can be seen to practise a humanistic approach to sport coaching which is accepted as the benchmark in coaching practice (Bush, 2012; Lyle, 2002). This is captured by Cregan et al. (2007) who state that coaches working with Paralympic athletes not only improve the athletic performance of their athletes, but also the quality of their life outside of sport. Although, Howe (2008) intimates that empowerment for most impaired athletes is still a dream, there is no question that Steve provides the pedagogic environment to give his athletes the best opportunity to flourish both in and out of the pool.

Additional resources and supplementary material

ASA Awarding Body qualifications and their specifications: http://awardingbodyasa.co.uk/asa-awarding-body-qualifications/

British swimming strategy 2013–2017: http://www.youblisher.com/p/564821-British-Swimming-Strategy-2013-2017/

Sport England disability infographics: http://www.sportengland.org/our-work/disability-sport/

Sport England once a week participation in sport: http://www.sportengland.org/research/who-plays-sport/

The Qualifications and Credits Framework (QCF) explained: http://awardingbodyasa.co.uk/qualification-and-credits-framework-explained/

Example qualification specification: ASA level 3 Certificate in Coaching Swimming (QCF): http://www.swimming.org/assets/uploads/library/Qualification_Spec_-_L3CS_-_RW_Signed_Off.pdf

Institute of Swimming: http://www.swimming.org/ios/about-us/the-institute-of-swimming/

UK Sport Coaching: elite programme, elite coaching apprenticeship programme, athlete to coach programme: http://www.uksport.gov.uk/our-work/coaching

Sports Coach UK: Using critical reflection to become a 'good coach': http://www.sportscoachuk.org/sites/default/files/no11%20Using%20critical%20reflectoin%20to%20become%20a%20good%20coach.pdf

Notes

1   In addition to swimming, British Swimming is also the NGB for diving, synchronised swimming, water polo and open water in Great Britain.

2   Howe & Jones (2006) utilise the conceptualisation of the 'practice community' as articulated by Morgan (1994, 2002) which includes primary agents (the athletes) and also secondary agents (for example, coaches, officials, sponsors, spectators and the media), all of whom benefit from the sustainable pursuit of the sport.

3 In addition to the UKCC coaching swimming qualifications, all home countries also provide UKCC endorsed (Level 1 and 2) qualifications in teaching aquatics, coaching water polo, coaching synchronised swimming and coaching diving.
4 In order to be ASA licenced you must attend regular CPD seminars.

References

Bloomfield, J. (2003). *Australia's sporting success: The inside story.* Sydney: University of New South Wales Press.

British Swimming. (2013). *British swimming strategy 2013–2017* [online]. Retrieved from: http://www.youblisher.com/p/564821-British-Swimming-Strategy-2013-2017/

Bush, A.J. (2007). What is coaching? In J. Denison. (ed). *Coaching knowledges: Understanding the dynamics of sport performance* (pp.3–23). London: A & C Black.

Bush, A.J. (2012). Introduction to sports coaching. In A. J. Bush et al. *Foundations in sports coaching* (pp. 1–13). London: Pearson.

Bush, A.J. & Silk, M.L. (2010). Towards an evolving critical consciousness in coaching research: The physical pedagogic bricolage. *International Journal of Sports Science and Coaching, 5*(4), 551–565.

Bush, A.J. & Silk, M.L. (2012). Politics, power and the podium: Coaching for Paralympic performance. *Reflective Practice, 13*(3), 471–482.

Bush, A.J., Silk, M.L., Andrews, D. & Lauder, H. (2013). *Sports coaching research: Context, consequences and consciousness.* London: Routledge.

Collins, M. & Kay, T. (2014). *Sport and social exclusion* (2nd ed.). London: Routledge.

Cregan, K., Bloom, G.A. & Reid, G. (2007). Career evolution and knowledge of elite coaches of swimmers with a physical disability. *Research Quarterly for Exercise and Sport, 78*(4), 339–350.

Denzin, N.K. & Lincoln, Y.S. (2000). Introduction: The discipline and practice of qualitative research. In: N. K. Denzin & Y. S. Lincoln (eds). *Handbook of qualitative research* (2nd ed.) (pp.1–28). Thousand Oaks, CA: Sage.

Fitzgerald, H. & Kay, T. (2004). *Sports participation by disabled young people in Derbyshire* [online]. Retrieved from: http://www.efds.co.uk/assets/0000/1676/OOO11.pdf

Gallimore, R., Gilbert, W. & Nater, S. (2014). Reflective practice and ongoing learning: A coach's 10-year journey. *Reflective Practice, 15*(2), 268–288.

Gilbert, W. & Trudel, P. (2004). Analysis of coaching science published from 1970–2001. *Research Quarterly for Exercise and Sport, 75*(4), 388–399.

Goffman, E. (1959). *The presentation of self in everyday life.* Garden City: Doubleday.

Harper, D. (1987). *Working knowledge: Skill and community in a small shop.* Chicago: Chicago University Press.

Howe, P.D. (2008). *The cultural politics of the Paralympic movement: Through an anthropological lens.* London: Routledge.

Howe, P.D. & Jones, C. (2006). Classification of disabled athletes: (Dis)empowering the Paralympic practice community. *Sociology of Sport Journal, 23*, 29–46.

International Paralympic Committee. (2015). *Swimming classification* [online]. Retrieved from: http://www.paralympic.org/swimming/classification

Jacobs, F., Claringbould, I. & Knoppers, A. (2014). Becoming a 'good coach'. *Sport, Education and Society, 19*(8), 1–20.

Jones, R.L. (2006). Dilemmas, maintaining 'face' and paranoia: An average coaching life. *Qualitative Inquiry, 12*(5), 1012–1021.

Kincheloe, J.L. (2001). Describing the bricolage: Conceptualizing a new rigor in qualitative research. *Qualitative Inquiry, 7*(6), 679–692.

Levi-Strauss, C. (1966). *The savage mind.* Chicago: University of Chicago Press.

Lyle, J. (2002). *Sports coaching concepts: A framework for coaches' behaviour.* London: Routledge.

Morgan, H.J. & Bush, A.J. (2014). Sports coach as transformative leader: Arresting school disengagement through community sport-based initiatives. *Sport, Education and Society.* DOI: 10.1080/13573322.2014.935319

Morgan, W.J. (1994). *Leftist theories of sport: A critique and reconstruction.* Urbana: University of Illinois Press.

Morgan, W.J. (2002). Social criticism as moral criticism: A Habermasian take on sport. *Journal of Sport and Social Issues, 26,* 281–299.

Nash, C. & Sproule, J. (2012). Coaches' perceptions of their coach education experiences. *International Journal of Sport Psychology, 43,* 33–52.

Nelson, L., Cushion, C. & Potrac, P. (2006). Formal, nonformal and informal coach learning: A holistic approach. *International Journal of Sports Science and Coaching, 1*(3), 247–259.

Nelson, L., Cushion, C. & Potrac, P. (2013). Enhancing the provision of coach education: The recommendations of UK coaching practitioners. *Physical Education and Sport Pedagogy, 18*(2), 204–218.

North, J. (2013). Philosophical underpinnings of coaching practice research. *Quest, 65*(3), 278–299.

Piggott, D. (2012). Coaches' experiences of formal coach education: A critical sociological investigation. *Sport, Education and Society, 4,* 535–554.

Potrac, P., Jones, R. & Armour, K. (2002). 'It's all about getting respect': The coaching behaviours of an expert English soccer coach. *Sport, Education and Society, 7*(2), 183–202.

Rynne, S.B., Mallett, C.J. & Tinning, R. (2010). Workplace learning of high performance sports coaches. *Sport, Education and Society, 15*(3), 315–330.

Sherrill, C. (1999). Disability sport and classification theory: A new era. *Adapted Physical Activity Quarterly, 16,* 206–215.

Skills Active. (2011). Sport and recreation [online]. Available from: http://www.skillsactive.com/news/major-investment-to-enhance-the-sporting-workforce or www.skillsactive.com/PDF/Sector_Skills_Assessment_Summary.pdf

Sport England. (2010). *Accessible sports facilities* [updated 2010]. Retrieved from: https://www.sportengland.org/facilities-planning/tools-guidance/design-and-cost-guidance/accessible-facilities/

Sport England. (2015a). *Once a week participation in sport* [online]. Retrieved from: http://www.sportengland.org/research/who-plays-sport/

Sport England. (2015b). *Disability infographics* [2015]. Retrieved from: http://www.sportengland.org/our-work/disability/

Tawse, H., Bloom, G.A., Sabiston, C.M. & Reid, G. (2012). The role of coaches of wheelchair rugby in the development of athletes with a spinal cord injury. *Qualitative Research in Sport, Exercise and Health, 4*(2), 206–225.

Taylor, B. & Garratt, D. (2010). The professionalisation of sports coaching: Relations of power, resistance and compliance. *Sport, Education and Society, 15*(1), 121–139.

UK Sport. (2015a). *Current funding figures for Rio (2013–2017)* [online]. Retrieved from: http://www.uksport.gov.uk/our-work/investing-in-sport/current-funding-figures

UK Sport. (2015b). *Historical funding figures* [online]. Retrieved from: http://www.uksport.gov.uk/our-work/investing-in-sport/historical-funding-figures

Editors' summary reflections

The effectiveness of coaching programmes within high performance sport environments relies, often, upon the establishment and sustainability of quality coach education and development structures and pathways (preferably and adequately resourced by national and international governing bodies). Such a framework, at least in an ideal world, would produce 'successful' coaches who might in turn develop 'successful' athletes across the mass-participation to elite sport spectrum. Bush's examination of Fivash highlights that while effective coaching education and development frameworks might exist 'in-house' these are often incongruent, or at least distinct from, formal coaching qualifications provided by the tertiary sector, and/or informal coaching experience, knowledge and expertise. Bush's stance here reflects the work of many other scholars who have highlighted some of the tensions with regards to the quality and content of coach education programmes and their ability to reflect the realities of the coaching experience (McMahon, 2013; Nelson et al., 2013; Piggott, 2012; Stodter & Cushion, 2014). Moreover, regardless of the educational/coaching pathway, there are a range of aspects of the coach's identity, role and work that go beyond our conventional description of a coach, our understanding of what working with disability sport athletes, and/or what we understand the demands of working in a high performance environment might be.

Within the context of para-swimming in the United Kingdom (contoured by increasing participation at the grassroots level and improved funding opportunities at the elite level post-London 2012 Olympic games), these issues carry added weight. As Bush explains, para-swimming, not unlike some other sports, sits under the auspices of the national swimming association and thus must adhere to its funding maxims and related high performance directives. This is, of course, an accepted part of the high performance sporting context. However, for Fivash (and rehearsing the experiences of Ferguson, Tromans, Dantas, and Milkins) the environment is further complicated by issues arguably bespoke to disability sport (for example, classification debates, developing coaches with appropriate expertise to meet athletes' specific physical, physiological, and medical needs, closer athlete–coach relationships, geographic inequalities in talent identification and a lack of practical support coupled with high coach turnover). There is, thus, considerable substance to Bush's assertions about recognising the multiplicity of coach's roles with formal coach education, *and* providing better support to alleviate the potential burden that some coaches may feel as a result of these compounded and overlapping identities within high performance disability sport settings.

For Bush, but also for Cregan et al. (2007) and others, it may not be enough for coaches within a para-sport context to improve performance; rather, if we acknowledge coaches' wider roles, they must also try to improve the quality of their athletes' lives beyond the sport. We could easily accept such assertions. As far as Fivash's experiences attest, it is evident that high performance disability sport coaches assume roles, duties and obligations that extend well beyond the conventional role of a coach and/or their educational dimensions of the coach as a pedagogue. However, Bush's discussion raises a few questions that might warrant pause for thought among aspiring and current coaches. What, for instance, is the coach and disability coach's role(s)? How might they differ? Need they differ? How do our assumptions about disability shape how we might coach (and work more generally) in high performance? How might assumptions about high performance shape the pedagogical and non-pedagogical aspects of the coach–athlete relationship within high performance disability sport? In what ways might the characteristics of 'good' and 'effective' high performance disability sport coaching be acknowledged, supported, fostered and celebrated?

Although not exhaustive, and reflecting ongoing disciplinary debates (addressed throughout this book), such questions might hopefully open needed dialogue among coach educators and coaches within the high performance disability context. What is clear is that Fivash can be considered an exceptional coach. Yet, perhaps more importantly, his experiences remind us that while the world and journey of a high performance disability sport coach might be unplanned, challenging, uncertain, complicated, nuanced, political, stressful and demanding, there is a characteristic passion among those who work in the sector and something innately rewarding in coaches' experience when working with these particular athletes that transcends the job description and its associated woes.

References

Cregan, K., Bloom, G.A. & Reid, G. (2007). Career evolution and knowledge of elite coaches of swimmers with a physical disability. *Research Quarterly for Exercise and Sport*, 78(4), 339–350.

McMahon, J. (2013). The use of narrative in coach education: The effect on short- and long-term practice. *Sport Coaching Review*, 2(1), 33–48.

Nelson, L., Cushion, C. & Potrac, P. (2013). Enhancing the provision of coach education: The recommendations of UK coaching practitioners. *Physical Education and Sport Pedagogy*, 18(2), 204–218.

Piggott, D. (2012). Coaches' experience of formal coach education: A critical sociological investigation. *Sport, Education and Society*, 17(4), 535–554.

Stodter, A. & Cushion, C.J. (2014). Coaches' learning and education: A case study of cultures in conflict. *Sport Coaching Review*, 3(1), 63–79.

11

BEYOND HIGH PERFORMANCE DISABILITY SPORT COACHING?

Geoffery Z. Kohe and Derek M. Peters

Introduction

The lives and experiences of the various coaches examined within this book have revealed some of the complexities and issues of the high performance disability sport coaching landscape. Through critical discourse analysis of the coaches' stories (guided by the work of Cherney et al., 2015; Fairclough, 1995, 2003; Titscher et al., 2000; Wodak & Meyer, 2015), we have identified a number of prevalent themes and points of congruence in the case studies. While each coach's story may have been unique with regards to geographic context, the sport/s they focused on, or their career pathways, it is evident that there are shared concerns, experiences and beliefs coaches have about their working contexts and professional identity. As we discuss below, many coaches, for example, spoke in unison about their inherent passion to work with disabled athletes and/or within disability sport. There was also considerable accord with regards to the resource struggles and the utility of employing a wide array of formal and informal support networks. A number of coaches also spoke in harmony about the organisational and broader structural forces (e.g. high performance funding maxims) that were increasingly influencing their working lives and career trajectories. In what follows we analyse some of these key themes in the hope that it might bring us closer to understanding coaches' work and its significance. Our examination of the case studies also enables us to raise a number of considerations about the current state of this specific coaching setting and its future challenges. Subsequently, we also consider the collective impact these case studies might have on inspiring change within the industry and improvements in the way other coaches may be better developed and supported.

Themes

Dedicated and enthusiastic individuals

Many of the coaches had varied backgrounds and starting points with regards to commencing work in the high performance and/or disability setting. For the most part, however, the genesis of their involvement stemmed from a mix of personal conviction and motivation, an innate (com)passion for helping develop people, an inherent love of sport, and an affectation for coaching/education as a means to help others recognise and achieve their sporting (and at times broader life) goals and aspirations (Cregan et al., 2007; DePauw & Gavron, 2005). While the eventual roles and career pathways varied, and were shaped by various external factors over the course of their careers, coaches' initial sparks of interest seemed to be ignited from within; and thus, as the empirical data from the case studies reveals, were deeply personal. Essentially, the identity and role of the coach appears predicated first by just being a good person, and after that, being a good person who tries to do good work and inspire goodness in others. Moreover, and what becomes clear when looking at coaches' perseverance and adaptability, their emotional investment and attachment drives their enthusiasm and commitment to their work, fuels their motivation and, importantly, provides considerable resilience and fortitude in times of adversity. Echoing Raylene Bates' assertions here, this intrinsic drive becomes especially important when it comes time for coaches to just get on with it and/or get whatever needs to be done for athletes done. Although it might be possible to see this sort of personal conviction and commitment to a wider cause as rather altruistic, many of the coaches expressed considerable humility about themselves and the selflessness evidently imbedded in their work (DePauw & Gavron, 2005; Banack et al., 2011; McMaster et al., 2012). This said, a highly individualised and intrinsically nuanced set of emotions was, for many coaches, an important part of starting out and also continuing to work in the area.

Personal dedication to others, to sport, to coaching, and/or to disability mattered. However, having the 'right' personal attributes and qualities provides only part of the story with regards to an individual's entry into coaching. As evidenced within their biographies, employment histories and personal reflections, the coaches all came to work in the disability sport context having had prior interest in sport(s); either in a general sense or with regards to a specific sport. For the majority of the coaches a love of sport (and for physical activity and leisure, in some cases) was a key part of their personal and professional identity. Exhibiting a passion for sport, or a particular sport, was evidently entrenched in the coaches' understandings of themselves, their work and their underlying motivations (Potrac et al., 2013; Potrac & Marshall, 2011). While it may not appear as part of formal coaching job descriptions, an inherent conviction to (the) sport and its participants in this setting may be considered a clear coaching prerequisite. That sporting interest appears as an influential factor for coaches is, to a degree, unsurprising. Coaches may come into the occupation having had either significant experience as an athlete within the professional setting, a substantial stint of playing and competing in sport(s) at lower levels, and/or a more general lifelong commitment to competitive sport and recreational physical activity (McMaster et al., 2012). Although the coaches' pathways into high performance disability sport examined here have differences, moving into coaching was clearly seen as an extension of existing sporting commitment.

Prior interest and serendipity

A coach's personal affection for their sport (and the inherent commitment they exhibit to the social values associated with sport) may translate into a number of different coaching, and invariably wider employment contexts. The progression from player to coach may seemingly appear natural, or seamless, yet the majority of coaches did not start out with an initial interest in disability sport or with the expectation of developing rewarding careers working with athletes with disabilities. Though the coaches may not have originally started out with a love or passion for disability sport *per se*, the general and genuine emotional affiliation to sport appears to be advantageous in the transition into working in the disability sport context. Although in some cases (for example, with Pohlman and Bates) an affinity to the lives, needs and aspirations of athletes with disabilities and disability sports can be a driving factor influencing their coaching pathways, it is not necessarily a precursor to the coach's decision to get involved. As the case studies reveal, involvement in disability sport and/or high performance disability sport offered timely, valuable and, in some cases, unforeseen opportunities to maintain the important connections to the sporting world and the athletic communities to which they had been a part, and the chance to fuel their personal sporting passions.

The coaches' internal commitment to sport also appears to have effectively translated into external motivation with regards to developing their particular disability sport(s), supporting the athletes under their charge, driving, and indeed in many cases changing and challenging both participation and performance agendas. Irrespective of commencing their careers in different countries, at different times, in different sports and at different professional levels, the majority of the coaches all seemed to emerge at the '*right*' time. Yet, as many of the coaches themselves point out, their entry into disability sport was somewhat fortuitous. That is, largely a serendipitous confluence of circumstances involving quite random social connections and opportunities; for example, coaches having the available time and space, a willingness to shift or adapt their coaching pathway and career ambitions, exploring an opportunity to pursue a new personal challenge or professional opportunity, or the chance to help develop and improve the lives of others. Having embarked upon a career in high performance disability sport coaching, the coaches identified a range of support networks, teams, and organisational infrastructure that enabled them to successfully, or otherwise, go about their work. Yet, it is evident that each coach has borne a significant amount of responsibility for the development of their sport at local, national and often international levels over the course of their career. In particular, they have each been fairly instrumental in raising the profile of their chosen sports, maximising player recruitment and development, improving organisational, administrative and financial structures (or at least advocating for their improvement), and assisting the transition, and public and political recognition of their sport from participation to high performance.

From the coaches' self-reflections, and the emphasis they place on improving athletes' personal and professional capabilities, it is evident that they do not always see how their day-to-day work contributes to advancing the wider profile of disability, and specifically disability sport. Irrespective of whether they envisioned a future working in high performance disability sport, the coaches have carved out not only a space for themselves and left an, invariably, indelible impression on the athletes and the sport in their respective countries, but also helped add meaning, value, respect, recognition and professional identity their roles. These coaches have, however, collectively been part of a vanguard that have begun to establish high performance disability sport coaching as a distinct, credible and legitimate professional career pathway.

In/formal coaching backgrounds

As beneficial as various fortuitous entrances into high performance disability sport coaching have been, depending on chance and circumstance is not necessarily the most reliable, appropriate or strategic way in which to embark upon a coaching career; certainly if the ultimate intention is to work within high performance settings. Accordingly, what emerged within coaches' experiences were tensions between the value of personal involvement in, and passion for, the sport, informal coaching experience (within and beyond disability sport), and formal coaching qualifications. While some coaches had gained formal tertiary or sport-specific qualifications en route to their current occupation, the strength of many coaches' CVs lay instead in their significant professional/semi-professional sporting participation and coaching experience that occasionally spanned across more than one sport. Whilst many of the coaches recognised the profession as having pedagogical, learning, and developmental theory underpinning it, the need for well-established and hard-earned practical knowledge and experience was paramount. The general belief among coaches was that their work requires a rather bespoke combination of both formal and informal education, and experience and development, which moulds their wider skill set. Herein lies the issue. For the most part, current and aspiring coaches have a range of tertiary degree programmes and organisational, sport or level-specific formal coaching programmes, qualifications and development pathways available to them. These, invariably, aid in preparing coaches to take up a number of coaching positions in the field and work at a number of performance levels. As many coaches in this book lament however, there is a significant void in both formal and relevant coaching pathways to develop current and aspiring coaches in the area of disability sport, especially towards high performance disability sport levels.

The programmes on coaching disability sport that are available, such as courses within national sport governing bodies, coaches here suggest are not always the most useful or appropriate to the specificities of their particular sport, or needs and abilities of its athletes. What is needed, coaches suggest, are efforts led essentially by national governing bodies to establish clearer and more specific pathways for particular disability sports. Moreover, in addition to bespoke pathways, coaches spoke in unison regarding the need for greater congruence between formal generic coaching programmes, formal disability coaching programmes (of which there are relatively few), and practical opportunities for coaching experience in the field. Whilst some countries (e.g., the United Kingdom and the United States of America) have made progress with regards to universities offering specific disability sport or disability sport coaching modules and similarly named degrees, there are still considerable opportunities for these programmes to develop greater synergy with national governing bodies' professional pathways and qualifications. Collectively, all formal routes into coaching athletes with disabilities could perhaps, better reflect upon and more effectively incorporate the lessons to be learnt from the lived experiences of the high performance coaches in our book in order to make formal qualifications more meaningful, ecologically valid and therefore more valued across the full range of disability sports and in all performance contexts.

Resourcing and support

The state of high performance disability sport coaching as articulated in the case studies, and in particular its challenges with regards to formal coaching provision and opportunities, is understandable. Unlike able-bodied sports, high performance Paralympic sport(s) have only experienced considerable growth in the last 30–40 years, largely as a result of political, socio-cultural, legal, and education shifts that have altered perceptions and possibilities with regards to disability writ large (Hums et al., 2003). Concomitantly, disability sport has, generally speaking, not been as fortunate with regards to public and political recognition, economic support, or infrastructure (Braye et al., 2013). As many of the coaches reveal, and although the situation appears to be slowly changing, a number of disability sport organisations began independently of an overarching national governing body, or still remain separated in some organisational, administrative or financial way from centralised sporting governance. In effect, this has afforded opportunities for some disability sports, and some coaches for that matter, to operate with relative autonomy. However, as participation in disability sport at the highest levels has increased and the sports have strengthened their national and international profiles, the need for improved and more sustainable resourcing is recognised by coaches as an increasingly prevalent issue, with a rather unanimous focus on Paralympic success.

Even though coaches noted a number of specific resourcing issues pertinent to their sports or national contexts, there was considerable consensus for greater organisational support across the board and, in particular, improved parity in resourcing to help progress the sports in the manner and rate afforded to able-bodied sports. As the coaches variously attest, the perennial issues over the lack of resourcing are, by and large, an accepted part of the contexts in which they operate. Moreover, as in the cases of individuals like Bates, Ferguson, Pohlman and Fivash, coaches work irrespective of these constraints to 'just get on with it' and ensure the continuity of the sport and their athletes' performances at the highest levels; in many cases by drawing upon pre-existing sport networks within and beyond sport to help maintain and drive their programmes. Given the differences in participation, popularity, performance platforms, and commercial leverage between disability, para- and able-bodied sport (and even the evident disparity between disability participation and para-high performance sport), the issue must still be considered contentious. However, it was evident that coaches genuinely felt the need for substantial shifts in the organisational cultures they were a part of to better meet their needs and working lives as coaches and improve the opportunities for future athletes and coaches coming through the system; however formal or organic.

Geography

Support networks may enable some coaches to work more effectively and efficiently. However, the success of these networks has, at times, been borne out of necessity as coaches seek to overcome the adversities of geography and distance that frequently can separate them from their athletes and make many of the day-to-day practicalities of their work difficult. The coaches highlighted how establishing, maintaining and developing high performance programmes (on limited budgets and resources, too, remember) is compounded by having to traverse long distances. For example, by either coaches themselves travelling to scouting and training camps, domestic and international competitions, or organisational meetings, or, irregularly bringing in athletes from far-flung areas to central locations for training, development and competition. Although in larger countries, such as Canada, the United States of America or Australia, geographic difficulties may appear a relatively obvious limitation to facilitating a national high performance programme (particularly where time differences and vast distance can naturally be prohibitive), issues of distance appear evident in smaller countries too (for example, New Zealand) where athletes and coaches (and at times also their families) must travel to train and compete. As such, and although geography may affect coaches of other high performance sports, for the coaches examined in this book it is a prevalent issue entwined with, and exacerbated by, concerns over limited resourcing and the increasing desires (in some cases) for greater organisational support. Coaches working in able-bodied sporting contexts often have a number of athletes spread across the country, and thus holding multiple 'regional' training camps, selection events and competitions to support athlete development is far more pragmatic and realistic. Disability sport coaches, it seems, often work with only a select handful of talent identified and selected athletes who are often dispersed individually across the country or even further afield, rendering regional and mass talent identification and selection events implausible.

In many cases, travelling is a necessity predicated on the need to be in a single yet not necessarily central location where coaches and athletes can access appropriate high performance facilities and support. For some coaches, the location, availability and cost of using facilities, having spaces to host training and selection camps, and the sites of national and international competitions have a discernible impact on the pressures of the job, their management of athletes, and the promotion and development of the sport more generally. While the coach may work to provide a maximal training and performance environment where possible, occasionally their efforts are not always met with positive consequences. As Bates identified, athletes can face difficulties in being physically relocated to centralised programmes (if albeit temporarily) that remove them from their familiar routines, support and the comfort and familiarity of their local/home environments. There are also potentially many more pragmatic, and disability- and indeed athlete-unique travel and relocation issues to be overcome for disabled athletes and their support networks as identified clearly by both Bates and Ferguson. While a coach may not be able to always ensure how well athletes respond to such shifts, developing a far greater sensitivity toward athletes' adaptability, resilience and wellbeing does appear critical for promoting a positive and supportive coaching environment and optimal performance culture.

Specialised knowledge and expertise

The potential negative effects of 'geography' on the coach–athlete relationship within high performance disability sport, are further complicated by the fact that athletes within these sports often have particular, highly individualised, and complex physical, physiological, medical and psychological characteristics and needs that require specialised knowledge and support. Not only must the individual athlete be aware of their own bio-medical and health concerns, so must their families, carers, support workers, potentially their peers, medical professionals and of course their coach. Given the closeness of the coach–athlete relationship within any high performance context, for the case-study coaches working with athletes with disabilities, an acquisition and intimate understanding of each athlete's bio-medical history, specificities and competencies is paramount. In order to achieve maximal performance with their athletes, most coaches require some sort of an appreciation of each athlete's unique biological, physical and psychological capacities and competencies. For coaches within disability sport however, given the potentially wide-ranging body and health issues their athletes may have to deal with, this bio-medical knowledge takes on even greater significance (Dieffenbach & Statler, 2012; Goosey-Tolfrey et al., 2008; Price, 2006). The coach, for example, must consider what counts as peak performance for each individual athlete and how it might be achieved in relation to their specific abilities (Goosey-Tolfrey et al., 2008).

Yet, concern about their athletes' bio-medical capacities carries weight not just in terms of the immediate coaching context (e.g. in relation to training, performance, or classification concerns), but also in their more routine day-to-day interactions beyond the sport. Particularly where coaches are taking on multiple roles such as carer, support worker, parent, friend, nurse, etc., as many coaches in this book seem to do, possessing a breadth and depth of medical and technical expertise relevant to each athlete's often unique condition appears salient to not only being an effective coach, but also to being an empathetic one capable of offering personalised care, attention and appropriate support that extends beyond their conventional work as a coach (Tawse et al., 2012). The development of specialised bio-medical expertise may, potentially, be included in some formal and informal coach education opportunities (some disability coaching modules/ programmes include coverage of select bio-medical issues pertinent to aspects of some disabilities) yet, as far as coaches here indicate, such knowledge appears to be largely gained 'on the job' and after considerable time being faced with the realities of athletes' varied experiences. This said, while having a basic appreciation of athletes' physiology is helpful for all coaches, providing further formal and informal opportunities for coaches to gain more intimate interdisciplinary, holistic, scientific and bio-medical knowledge is crucial for the future development of disability sport coaches at all levels.

Classification

The need for high performance disability sport coaches to be evermore cogniscent of the bio-medical idiosyncrasies is particularly pronounced when it comes to issues around classification (Beckman & Tweedy, 2009; Tweedy et al., 2014). In high performance sport environments all coaches need to be aware of their athletes' eligibilities to play, train, be recruited, and/or eventually selected for national and international competition. For the most part, coaches (or specifically the administrative team supporting them) must regularly ensure players' eligibility in the legal and technical sense of meeting organisational or governing body requirements (e.g., with regards to age, professional status, visa compliance, national affiliation/genealogy, and/or relevant legal obligations and constraints) (Howe, 2008; Hums et al., 2003; Tweedy et al., 2014). Whilst some of these issues clearly affect coaches of high performance disability sport, a further and primary concern is ensuring the eligibility of the respective players as regards the specific, nuanced, and often frequently changing demands of the disability classification system under which the sport operates at each performance level. These classification systems, often developed by researchers and scientists working in collaboration with international federations, are constantly evolving across the sporting spectrum.

In the main, classification systems have been designed and enforced primarily to ensure parity in competition and equity in play where athletes' disabilities are varied and variable (Tweedy et al., 2014). As the science of high performance sport and of specific disability conditions has improved, this knowledge has infiltrated competition sport and, in particular, the desire of sport organisations to provide more robust participation and performance regulations. Having classification systems does, as some of our coaches concur, enable fairness in participation and improve the transparency and accountability in selection and competition. As such they appear to be a largely accepted component of the framework of disability sport, particularly at high performance levels. Yet, classification systems are not flawless or infallible. In some cases, while the existence of the classification system is meant to assist coaches in ensuring they and their athletes have clearer expectations about the competitive standard, rules and regulations, there remain ambiguities and inconsistencies across and within many sports both at the high performance and lower-league levels that compound coaches' daily work and the long-term management of their programmes (Tweedy, 2003; Tweedy et al., 2014).

A consequence of having highly bespoke classification systems (in which the definition and characteristics of individual disabilities are fragmented into separate, and arguably more easily identifiable, categories) is that coaches are required to not only have an in depth knowledge of their athletes' bio-medical capacities and qualities, but also keep themselves abreast of shifting classification policies. Coaches, therefore, must not only be able to regularly field full and physically fit teams, they must do so in accordance with strict classification regulations, for instance by fielding teams that include only athletes with permitted individual classifications and who, as a collective, do not exceed the permitted team total classification. Notwithstanding the additional demands on the coach of this continual exercise in computational mathematics during competition, athletes can also be classified and certified for participation in one event or tournament then be de- or re-classified for the next depending on standards changing or alternations in the classification mechanism being employed (Tweedy et al., 2014), or even changes in the classification of the athlete themselves based on changes in individual circumstances. This might seem straightforward and merely an accepted part of the demands of high performance disability sport work. Yet, with classification systems often changing, international and national inconsistencies in classification structures, and the ever-present reality of qualified/qualifiable athletes getting injured, ill, or removing themselves from the team (even during competition), coaches can face perpetual conundrums that add to their daily stress and ability to work effectively; particularly in terms of achieving consistent success with a permanent fixture of athletes. As a result, a coach must become particularly calculating not only on the court/pool/field-side, but at all stages of the player identification, selection, development and progression through to elite level competition. In high performance disability team sport, therefore, the coach's role is not just to develop the team to 'gel' and perform maximally, it is a case of developing the team to gel and perform under the additional constraints of the prevailing classification system. For example, in Paralympic wheelchair basketball, players are classified by a points system ranging from 1 to 4.5, where the higher points represent those with the least physical impairment, and during a match the cumulative team classification total must not exceed 14. Rapid player substitutions through tactical decision making, injury or in response to changes made by the opposition means the coach has to not only consider the best player/s to field, but the impact this will have on the eligibility of the team's overall classification total. Whilst clearly a requirement to coach team sports such as wheelchair basketball, none of the case-study coaches identified mathematical ability as an essential part of their role. Interestingly, and as an aside, but clearly within the remit of this book in trying to make a difference to how people think and to change pre-conceptions and perceptions about disability sport and athletes with disabilities, the wheelchair basketball classification system seems at odds with many of the others. The highest numerical classification is the player with the least impairment and the team total cannot go above a threshold. Surely this emphasises the greater importance or rating of the least disabled athlete as an individual and as a greater sub-component of the team. Why is the least impairment not the lowest classification category, and the greatest physical impairment the highest classification category and why is the required team total not a minimum threshold? Surely reversing the classification categories and requiring a minimum threshold to be met would send a far more powerful disability-supportive, and athlete-empowered message across and beyond what is one of the world's most prominent disability team sports?

Although it might be in the best interests of the overall development of the sport for coaches to recruit more and more players, the end point is that the selection of players for national teams and international competition is highly restrictive and depends substantially on the prevailing classification systems. The inevitable limitation within these systems is that classification regulations enforce coaches to make tough decisions about who can eventually 'make the cut'. What complicates classification matters further is that there is, at present, still limited scientific expertise as to the performance potential and limits to performance in and across the varied categories; which, of course, is one of the reasons why such systems frequently change. Given the presence that classification issues have on coaches, at least those examined here, what might be required going forward is for greater integration of disability-specific sport performance science to inform classification. Whilst classification may still continue to hold relevance, in order to help coaches to do their job, there appears an urgent need to more closely align any and all classification frameworks with sport-specific and scientifically underpinned sport performance capacities rather than rather more subjective perceptions and presumptions about what disabled bodies are and what they might or might not be able to do (Wu & Williams, 1999).

Adaptability

Irrespective of the individual differences in the approaches the coaches take, there are evidently synergies in the issues that shape their working lives and the distinct characteristics of high performance sport. In many cases, these issues and the overall environments of high performance disability sport coaching bear similarities within able-bodied high performance sport (Cushion, 2007); indeed, some of the coaches did not readily, or immediately, distinguish their particular work or roles as all that unique (McMaster et al., 2012). The emphasis in coaches' narratives, for the most part, was first and foremost on enabling, through effective coaching, athletes' personal and professional development and performance potential to be realised. This may, of course, seem understandable; indeed, this imperative to assist athlete performance is the bedrock of the profession. Yet, as the case studies demonstrate, because the conditions of high performance disability sport *are* different in many respects (e.g., resourcing, support structures, networks, geography, expertise and classification, etc.), coaches in these settings are, to a degree, a unique collective. Moreover, the above issues, which are varied within and across coaches' individual experiences, provide evidence that there are shared themes that might frame a deeper understanding of high performance disability sport coaching. These themes have, for instance, necessitated that all of the coaches acquire a level of adaptability and resilience that enables them to navigate the shifting terrain of their working environment while simultaneously maximising their athletes' performances, long-term performance programmes and their own personal and professional development and job security. This adaptability is not merely a consequence of their years of experience and natural career progression, it is clearly influenced by the complex external conditions and circumstances that emerge in the confluence of disability and high performance sport settings. In order to *be* and *perform* as a coach in this environment having the capacity to adapt is, thus, an essential trait.

Across their sports, the coaches have demonstrated an adaptability that has enabled them to work, or at least try to work, effectively when faced with the many adversities, issues and challenges that come as part of high performance and/ or disability environments. An ability to adapt can be clearly seen in many of the coaches' experiences when they assume additional roles, responsibilities within their daily lives and careers that transcend conventional coaching remits or job descriptions. In many cases, these roles develop as the coach reacts (often instinctively) to external factors (for example, limited resourcing and support networks, or the inability to hire a broader range of appropriate staff). As such, while taking on additional roles may not be expected, for many of the coaches accepting a multiplicity of roles is merely an extension to the regular expectations placed upon them.

The job is, some of the coaches exemplify, by nature highly varied. As such, accepting multiple roles becomes normalised within their coaching context and entrenched within coaches' respective identity construction (this is particularly so where there is a discernible blurring of home, work and personal life). That coaches accept the multifarious nature of the work is, perhaps, not surprising. Indeed, to return to one of the initial themes, coaches working in high performance disability sport exhibit incredible passion, commitment and personal conviction in their work. Subsequently, coaches appear not to think twice about 'getting stuck in' with whatever needs to be done to help their athletes develop and perform to the best of their abilities. Approaching the job with this sort of ethos, an ethic of care so to speak, is invariably advantageous when it comes to accepting the breadth of roles that this sort of coaching can, and does, entail. Many of the roles that coaches here have regularly assumed may, understandably, potentially push other coaches out of their comfort zone or challenge them beyond the limits of their training and expertise. For the coaches however, any sense of trepidation, anxiety or concern about extending themselves appears subsidiary or even non-existent. While such an ethos may be found among other high performance or able-sport contexts, it is especially pronounced among our coaches with regards to who they are, who they are as coaches, and their ability to support and develop the performance of the athletes, not just identified as being in their squad, but being *'under their care'*!

Sustainability

Notwithstanding the individual and collective magnanimity of their work, the coaches here are not infallible. While they have worked for decades to advance their respective sports and better the lives and performances of their athletes, they have been constantly limited in what they have been able to do and achieve, largely as a result of some of the factors we have already identified. However, what is also apparent in reviewing coaches' journeys is that many of the high performance programmes are effectively driven by either a small team and/or the agency of the coach. While this can get results, it calls into question how sustainable high performance disability sport coaching can be if so much of the daily work and development of the athletes resides with the coach. Given some of the perennial uncertainties of maintaining high performance sports generally (e.g., funding streams, talent identification and recruitment, organisational and coaching infrastructure), and the exacerbation of these concerns across disability sport, and in our case the reliance on key individuals to drive high performance disability sport programmes, the issue of sustainability warrants consideration. Many of the coaches in this book have been working in their sports for a considerable time and/ or consider continuing in the present role/s for the foreseeable future. As laudable as such commitment and dedication is, it does beg the questions of what, or who, comes next, when will they emerge, and from where will they come and how will they be supported to develop?

Eventually coaches leave or transition into other positions within the sport. Ideally, there are suitably equipped, qualified and willing coaches to replace them in the ranks. However, this may not always be the case. Some of the coaches specifically identified concerns over the development of clear coaching pathways that might lead talented individuals to take up positions in the upper echelons of disability sport coaching. From mass participation levels through to high performance, maintaining a healthy stock of coaches who are capable of ensuring the continuity of performance programmes is vital. While some national and international federations may be addressing this, it is evident that some of these coaches feel more work needs to be done at the organisational level. A coaching programme cannot, clearly, rest on the shoulders of one coach (or a small committed group of individuals). Rather, what is needed is for more strategic approaches to coach recruitment, education and development pathways to better ensure that the current trajectories of peak performance and success at the national and international levels can successfully be maintained. In some instances, the incorporation of para-sport within centralised high performance programmes appears to yield benefits in this regard. However, this is not always an option for some coaches (for example, in countries like the Czech Republic and elsewhere) where ideological, political, financial and historical differences currently work against such integration. For the time being, and not withstanding current levels of organisational support, it seems to remain a necessity for coaches to 'go the extra mile' to ensure the immediate, medium- and long-term viability and success of their programmes.

The coach case studies have demonstrated the varied career trajectories individuals have taken to eventually work at the highest level in their chosen sports. Their experiences demonstrate that coaches' career trajectories are rarely ever set in stone, but, like in many other forms of employment, shift according to individual agency and external market forces. Their respective careers have been mapped out upon the changing socio-cultural and political landscapes of disability and inclusion, and, the persistent economic shifts within modern capitalist sport that have contoured and redefined high performance working environments. Dedication, empathy, adaptability and resourcefulness have proven invaluable in helping these coaches navigate their careers successfully. Yet, what lies ahead for them, and for aspiring future coaches?

Career trajectories

As the coaches and/or authors of the chapters have identified, disability sports have moved (at varying paces) from mass participatory agendas (and a focus of general talent identification and selection) to rigorous high performance models underpinned by strict, measurable, accountable objectives. Within these models, athletes with disabilities are, more often, being strategically targeted on the basis of their development and performance potential at the elite level. In some cases there is synergy between mass participatory programmes and the imperatives of high performance programmes, particularly in regards to affording aspiring athletes clear, well-supported, development pathways to participation at the highest level (Fitzgerald, 2013). However, in some cases, certainly in the United Kingdom, there is an incongruence in the ability of the mass participation-based disability sport context to effectively, and regularly, feed into their high performance counterparts. As some of the coaches have identified, often their pathways through the sport are stymied by unclear, inconsistent, varied or ambiguous development opportunities, or the availability of appropriate educational frameworks at key points in their development. For coaches, such difficulties can complicate their efforts to successfully advance their careers and be in the best position to recruit athletes onto programmes who will achieve and fulfil the organisation's performance maxims.

Moreover, what seems to matter even more is for coaches to ensure the continual achievement and progression of their athletes and teams in measurable terms; essentially goals scored, matches and competitions won, league rankings, and medals won. Such material objectives are part and parcel of high performance sport, and are closely scrutinised by national federations and central sport authorities. As a result, what we are witnessing at the elite levels of disability sport is a distinct replication (and acceptance) of high performance sport cultures elsewhere. Specifically, routine change in funding regimes whereby 'successful' elite sports and athletes secure funding and thus 'survive', while others 'suffer' funding cuts that become self-perpetuating in terms of supporting continued athlete development and performance. In terms of coaches working, or wishing to work, in this environment this split may have significant implications in terms of both their short-term career prospects and working conditions (though, we acknowledge this is an accepted characteristic of operating in the high performance environment), but also longer-term employability, general career development and relationship between coaches, their athletes and parent organisations (Cregan et al., 2007).

Over the course of the last three decades or so, we have witnessed considerable development in the high performance settings for disability sport affecting coaches' work (e.g., the growth of the Paralympic movement, improved integration of disability sport within sport mega-events like the Olympic Games, and the return of specialised events such as the Invictus Games). These new spaces are affording current and aspiring coaches not only new performance settings and new expectations of athletes under their charge, but also creating new employment opportunities (Cregan et al., 2007; Cruickshank & Collins, 2012). New events, new sports, new specialist categories of competition at the national and international level all, for example, offer fertile ground where high performance coaches could ply their expertise. While the coaches covered here have worked across the development and performance spectrum, mass participation and high performance disability sport contexts (and the nature of coaching therein) have become increasingly divergent and diversified. While it may still be possible to transition across and within the spectrum, given the differences in focus of the two pathways and the varied nature of demands they place on individuals, coaches considering their career trajectories may need to think about who they are and what they want out of the sport.

Conceptualisation and terminologies of disability and high performance coaching

Returning to the discussion in the introduction, one theme remains to be discussed; specifically – the broader conceptualisation and terminologies of 'disability' and their place within the high performance setting. Interestingly, before the more obvious discussion around 'disability', there is first the necessity to reflect on the potential impact and interpretation of the term ' high performance' in both our initial call for contributions and the resultant case-study coaches and sports that have been included. Although clearly not our intention from the outset, all of the case-study authors have identified coaches and sports that are clearly Paralympic in their motivation and self-attributed definition of high performance.

As far as the chapters attest however, the coaches did not challenge the nomenclature of disability as a term of reference or raise it as a point of concern or relevance in their experiences. Though it might feature in the nature of the work that coaches do, and their considerations within the coach–athlete relationship, the association with the term disability does not appear to exclusively, or discernibly, define their job title. Coaches in this book talked more frequently about coaching high performance sport or high performance athletes, and/or, fluctuated between references to para-sport/para-athletes and disability sport/disabled athletes/athletes with disabilities. Coaches' acceptance, or ambivalence, toward considering the appropriateness of the term is, perhaps, unsurprising. Indeed, within some sports, teams, clubs and national organisations, the terms are used indiscriminately and often interchangeably; inclusive sport, para-sport, Paralympic sport, or just the specifics of the disability (e.g., cerebral palsy/blind/wheelchair, etc.). While the use of the term may be highly politicised in academic literature, public policy and organisational rhetoric (DePauw, 1997; Braye et al., 2013; Brittain, 2004), and notwithstanding the points of differentiation within which high performance disability sport coaches work, the conceptualisation of the term appears of less concern to the coaches here. To this end, as the very people coaching at the high performance level seem to use the terms interchangeably and in reference to and in communication with their athletes, teams, support networks, organisations and federations, why can we not take the arguably most inclusive approach of accepting the use of any and all of these terms? Why do we need to undermine this by continually engaging in, apparently in this context at least, irrelevant academic debate around the most appropriate terminology. Whose identity is it that matters? In any sporting context the identity of the athlete is the singularly most important identity to acknowledge. In the contexts of these high performance coaches we are confident in suggesting that terminology is not an issue as they have adopted an athlete-centred approach and included athletes in their discussion of how they would like their identities to be portrayed. Drawing on the work of Richard et al. (2015) and others, essentially what we are arguing for here is a move *toward* greater appreciation, recognition and power being afforded to the athlete in the construction and articulation of their own identity, both within and beyond the coach–athlete relationship and context.

The individuals examined here seem to establish their career identity as a coach first and foremost, then as a high performance coach (which, admittedly, for some is just the context in which they ply their trade). Irrespective of any formal training or qualifications in disability, they appear not to consider themselves primarily or exclusively as disability sport coaches, or even, coaches of athletes with disabilities. The distinction is important here as it provides a small insight into the relevance of the perpetual tensions raised over terminologies and meanings, and the consequences for coaches' identities, daily work and organisational and athlete relationships. At the institutional, government and academic levels continued consideration has been given to breaking down bio-medical and socio-cultural models of disability that have long-served to disempower, alienate, disenfranchise, stereotype and marginalise individuals with disabilities and the groups to which they belong (Misener & Darcy, 2014). While these efforts remain important however, it appears that at least within high performance sport contexts coaches have already made significant inroads into challenging conceptions and reconfiguring perceptions of their work and the communities of athletes they represent (Purdue & Howe, 2012).

Future considerations

The thematic analysis of the case studies has revealed a number of issues and unresolved questions regarding coaches and their work. We cannot hope to answer these issues with this book or in this conclusion alone. Our desire here is that the case studies, along with our observations and suggestions below, might provoke thought and sustain ongoing debate in the field. To return to the book's original premise, we sought to provide socio-culturally focused case studies from a range of high performance disability sport coaches working across varied sports. While the authors of these case studies have provided richly detailed accounts of some of the complexities that shape coaches' experiences in this domain, it is evident that the narratives have also raised further questions about coaches' lives, identities, relationships and working contexts. The themes have invariably uncovered some primary concerns and focal points for further research in this regard. Yet, greater exploration of the distinct political, social and organisational context in which high performance disability sport coaches work is certainly warranted (Rynne et al., 2009). Irrespective of the work done by our various authors here to illuminate the collective issues and individual exceptionalism of the coaches, there is still scope to better understand the conditions that contour this particular coaching world and its constituents. We believe, more specifically, the case studies underpin the need for more recognition of the multiplicity, fluidity, dynamic, ambiguous, shifting roles, identities and spaces coaches may occupy throughout their careers and in their varied day-to-day roles. To this end, although this book has provided one mechanism to enable high performance disability sport coaches' voices to be heard and shared in an effort to collectively improve their practices, work remains to be done.

The selection of case studies provided in this book has evidenced the exemplary work being done by particular individuals (and their support teams) to advance their respective sports and develop athletes' performances therein. Yet, it is clear in many cases that their time in the sports is limited, and moreover, the organisations that support them cannot carry on relying on the somewhat unplanned, serendipitous, trajectory of coaches entering disability and para-sport. As many of the coaches themselves identified, the lack of discernible and/or appropriate development pathways for interested coaches is a barrier, and there is a distinct need for more sport organisations to seriously consider their current formal coach development opportunities and educational support infrastructure (Cregan et al., 2007; Fitzgerald, 2013; Martin & Whalen, 2015). Relatedly, and recognising the increased complexities of high performance coaching, there appears to be specific calls for tailored coaching accreditations that might better provide coaches' interdisciplinary knowledge and expertise that seems to be a more substantive feature of their work.

The development of formal coach qualifications, and of disability-sport/ coaching-specific degree programmes (such as those available at the University of Worcester and elsewhere) is laudable, yet given the issues our coaches have raised about the necessity of knowing the athlete and the breadth of their needs and abilities first and foremost, particular care needs to be taken when badging formal disability sport coach education programmes. Although we recognise that disability sports require specific knowledge with regards to players' physical conditions, abilities and classification, we believe a paradigm shift may be required; essentially, a turn from coaching disability sport toward coaching the person first, then the sport, then optimising performance (Penney & Kidman, 2014). This is not to say, however, that knowledge of the pragmatic and technical aspects of the sport is unimportant – far from it. Rather, and as many of our coaches detailed, this expertise can be better utilised when coaches have a far greater understanding of their athletes' highly individualised, and at times complex conditions (beyond merely the direct training or performance contexts). Many coaches, of course, may already adopt this approach. Given this need, and the paucity of research on disability within sport science, what we suggest is also for the establishment in recognised courses in sport medicine, physiology and performance analysis for athletes with disabilities (Webborn & Van De Vliet, 2012). What future coaches interested in disability sport may need to consider is matching technical competencies within disability with the development of a wider athlete-centred and non-sport specific skill set (which some of the select disability coaching courses are beginning to do). Such courses, integrated within current university medicine or sport science programmes, could go a considerable way to placing a more substantial emphasis on developing coaches' wider scientific expertise on disability and the implications of disability on the limits of peak performance in all sport and coach development settings.

High performance disability sport coaches are knowledgeable, passionate, highly intrinsically motivated individuals first and foremost, on whom the future of disability sport depends. As such, there is an evident need for academics to help their voices be heard by not only aspiring or current coaches and athletes but, importantly, also by the organisations they are a part of and other stakeholders in the industry. Within this remit there is also a need to explore the many variant types of coach–athlete relationship and the ways that this affects coaches' respective identities and practices. For example, within this particular collection of case studies, the majority of coaches were able-bodied individuals working with athletes with disabilities. Only in one instance, that we are aware of, was there a coach with a disability (Rostislav) who was coaching athletes in a sport with the same condition. While Rostislav did not deliberate on this as a feature of his particular coaching, he did recognise it as a factor in his motivations to get into the sport and work to improve the lives of other individuals. Rostislav's experience notwithstanding, there is still a future need to explore perceived identities and assumptions about coach–athlete relationships where the disability is not shared (e.g. able-bodied coach – disability athletes) and to better understand athletes with disabilities' conceptualisation and interactions with disabled coaches and vice versa. Moreover, there remains space for others to augment emerging research exploring identities within reverse-integration sport settings whereby able-bodied players are permitted to compete in the same disability sport up to, generally, the sub-elite level.

Conclusion

The critical analysis and thematic discussion above has been framed around the contents of this book's case studies; essentially, traversing ten sports in a number of high performance contexts. Each case study illuminated the lives, experiences and identities of individual coaches who have been involved in the field for some time, and have held key roles in developing high performance programmes. While reflecting the general remit of sport coaches elsewhere, their roles have been multiple and varied, not only complicated by external forces (e.g., resourcing, organisational support, geography), but also by unique specificities of the athletes with whom they work. The case studies here demonstrate that while coaches' roles may be challenging, their intrinsic desires to work in the industry and to better the lives and opportunities of their athletes, coupled with tenacity, determination, adaptability and resilience, provides substantial impetus to help overcome the adversities they face in successfully delivering their high performance programmes. Such narratives are revealing in the attention they draw toward the realities of some coaches' lives and work and the implications their work has on the sustainability and future of their sports at the highest levels.

We are cognisant, of course, that these are only a small select sample of disability sports, but what they do reveal is that the terrain of high performance disability sport coaching is diverse and the nature of coaching practice within wide-ranging. While not designed to be generalisable, many of the conclusions and points raised may be relatable, transferable and identifiable in many other coaching contexts. Indeed, many readers may find familiarity in, and take comfort and reassurance from the coaches' narratives and find echoes of their stories in their own working lives and practices. Moreover, it is evident that these case studies also demonstrate the career possibilities that lay within high performance disability sport for current and aspiring coaches. Irrespective of coaches' potential aspirations with regards to high performance disability sport coaching, there appear to be many pathways within and across sports available to interested, committed and enthusiastic individuals (who may or may not possess/obtain formal coaching qualifications). In the majority of cases, our coaches did not necessarily aspire or potentially intend to work in the high performance context, though arrived there via a combination of hard work, dedication, progression through the organisation, or longevity in the sport. Regardless of the sports, what is clear is that some coaches (certainly those featured within this book) build their careers within participatory settings. As such, in the interests of strengthening the educational and development opportunities within the industry, and providing clearer pathways for aspirant coaches interested in working with high performance athletes with disability, there is, we believe, a need to consider the relevance of current coaching provision for such individuals and how new coaching recruits are targeted. Recent research, as part of the Supporting & Promoting Inclusive Coach Education (SPICE) project (Vinson et al., 2015), for example, clearly identified the need for further enhancement of national governing body provision to promote sport coaching opportunities to people with disability.

The future of high performance disability sport coaching may still face challenges, yet there is considerable evidence in these case studies of a vibrant climate for coaching and some invaluable advantages of undertaking this particular career pathway (DePauw & Gavron, 2005; Fitzgerald, 2013; Martin & Whalen, 2015). In order to ensure the sustainability of coaching programmes and to fortify career pathways of current and future workers in the area, we need to move beyond a focus on the immediate coaching environment and appreciate, and build upon, the wider milieus in which coaches ply their trade. There is a clear need, in this regard, for an appreciation of a wider multi-sport coaching pedagogy (as evidenced in the likes of Bates), organisational recognition of non-specialist routes into coaching and the entrenchment of interdisciplinary knowledge within coaching programmes. Again, asserting the emphasis coaches within the case studies placed on the diversity of their work, we argue for the increased integration and involvement of specialists and significant others that impact upon the lives of athletes with a disability (e.g., doctors, bio-medical support workers, families and/or carers, educators, and professional support workers, governing organisation representatives) to be better accounted for in coach development and education. This might begin, perhaps, with more rigorous examination of the personal/individual motivations with regards to coaching and disability to better understand and accommodate individuals' career trajectories, whether those be toward high performance, sub-elite, and/or mass participation. Such an approach might, we believe, provide aspiring coaches with a more holistic framework to underpin their understanding of the coaching landscape and further inform their subsequent decision making to pursue a coaching career within disability sport.

The establishment of specific qualification pathways and accreditations and the alignment of these with professionally recognised degree programmes within disability sport would, also, be a considerable starting point. Reflecting our points above, the course content might include multi-sport coaching pedagogies, *plus* sport science (e.g. performance analysis, biomechanical analysis, sports nutrition), medical, physical, biomechanical, psychological and socio-cultural intricacies applicable to both the athlete and their sport, ranging from activities of daily living to the pinnacles of performance potential. To remind readers in the United Kingdom, for example, there is currently no national coaching certificate for disability sport. What might help the development in this regard is for greater coordination and advocacy among the international community of disability sport practitioners to target qualification providers and national governing bodies to support coach development and the progression of relevant qualification frameworks.

This book, we believe, provides robust empirical research evidence that there is an increased demand for national governing bodies to adapt to the changing context of high performance disability sport and coaches' needs and desires vis-à-vis professional recognition and institutional career pathways. Part of this advocacy may, too, focus on obtaining greater representation and participation of high performance disability sport coaches within the upper echelons of sport organisations, increased resource and knowledge sharing among current coaches within and across disability, improved collaborations with the diversity of stakeholders and significant others affecting high performance athletes and coaches at the point of practice, and, in particular, within the education and professional development programmes of coaches and coach educators. As such, their experiences, particularly with regards to their entrance into disability and/or high performance settings, should, we hope, light a path for others. Regardless of the eventual mechanisms, and in addition to the ongoing need for research to foreground the lives of coaches working in the area, our ultimate imperative here is to call for multi-agency and interdisciplinary discussion and collaboration between coaches, educationalists, exercise and sport scientists, medical professionals, national governing bodies, disability advocates, to secure the future of disability and para-sport at all levels.

As you have now clearly made it to the end of our book, we hope that you have enjoyed reading it. We also hope that it has made a difference – to you, your thoughts about disability sport and athletes with disabilities, your practise, maybe the people around you, the athletes you coach, your coach, your research, your degree programme, your aspirations for a career in disability sports coaching, your lobbying for and participation in more formal and informal disability sports coach learning opportunities, your continuation and hopefully enhancement and greater empowerment as a coach in disability sport, your local, regional, national and international sports organisations and federations, and maybe even national and international policies regarding disability sport and broader disability relevant issues *per se*.

If reading this book has had a benefit of any kind, made a difference to you or someone else, or if you have enhanced anything relating to disability, disability sport and/or coaching or in any other context by using something gleaned from our book, please let us know! We would love to find out if our research has made an impact, so please do not hesitate to email your story to us at *HPDSC@worc.ac.uk*

References

Banack, H.R., Sabiston, C.M. & Bloom, G.A. (2011). Coach autonomy support, basic needs satisfaction, and intrinsic motivation of Paralympic athletes. *Research Quarterly for Exercise and Sport, 82*(4), 722–730.

Beckman E. M. & Tweedy, S. M. (2009). Towards evidence-based classification in Paralympic athletics: Evaluating the validity of activity limitation tests for use in classification of Paralympic running events. *British Journal of Sports Medicine, 43*, 1067–102.

Braye, S., Gibbons, T. & Dixon, K. (2013). Disability 'rights' or 'wrongs'? The claims of the International Paralympic Committee, the London 2012 Paralympics and Disability Rights in the UK. *Sociological Research Online, 18*(3), 16.

Brittain, I. (2004). Perceptions of disability and their impact upon involvement in sport for people with disabilities at all levels. *Journal of Sport and Social Issues, 28*(4), 429–452.

Cherney, J.L., Lindemann, K. & Hardin, M. (2015). Research in communication in disability and sport. *Communication & Sport, 3*(1), DOI: 10.1 177/2167479513514847

Cregan, K., Bloom, G.A. & Reid, G. (2007). Career evolution and knowledge of elite coaches of swimmers with a physical disability. *Research Quarterly for Exercise and Sport, 78*(4), 339–350.

Cruickshank, A. & Collins, D. (2012). Culture change in elite sport performance teams: Examining and advancing effectiveness in the new era. *Journal of Applied Sport Psychology, 24*(3), 338–355.

Cushion, C. (2007). Modelling the complexity of the coaching process. *International Journal of Sports Sciences, 2*(4), 395–401

DePauw, K. (1997). The (in)visibility of DisAbility: Cultural context and 'sporting bodies'. *Quest, 49*(4), 416–436.

DePauw, K.P. & Gavron, S.J. (2005). Coaches of athletes with disabilities. *The Physical Educator, 48*, 33–40.

Dieffenbach, K.D. & Statler, T.A. (2012). More similar than different: The psychological environment of Paralympic sport. *Journal of Sport Psychology in Action, 3*(2), 109–118.

Fairclough, N. (1995). *Critical discourse analysis.* New York, NY: Longman.

Fairclough, N. (2003). *Analysing discourse: Textual analysis for social research.* London: Routledge.

Fitzgerald, H. (2013). *The coaching chain: Reflections of disabled athletes and coaches. A report for sports coach UK.* Research Institute for Sport, Physical Activity and Leisure. Leeds Metropolitan University. Retrieved from: http://www.sportscoachuk.org/sites/default/files/Reflections%20of%20disabled%20atheltes_0.pdf

Goosey-Tolfrey, V.L., Diaper, N.J., Crosland, J. & Tolfrey, K. (2008). Fluid intake during wheelchair exercise in the heat: Effects of localized cooling garments. *International Journal of Sports Physiology and Performance, 3*(2), 145.

Howe, P.D. (2008). The tail is wagging the dog: Body culture, classification and the Paralympic movement. *Ethnography, 9*(4), 499–517.

Hums, M.A., Moorman, A.M. & Wolff, E.A. (2003). The Inclusion of the Paralympics in the Olympic and Amateur Sports Act: Legal and policy implications for integration of athletes with disabilities into the United States Olympic Committee and national governing bodies. *Journal of Sport & Social Issues, 27*(3), 261–275.

Martin, J.J. & Whalen, L. (2015). Effective practices of coaching disability sport. *European Journal of Adapted Physical Activity, 7*(2),13–23.

McMaster, S., Culver, D. & Werthner, P. (2012). Coaches of athletes with a physical disability: A look at their learning experiences. *Qualitative Research in Sport, Exercise and Health, 4*, 226–243.

Misener, L. & Darcy, S. (2014). Managing disability sport: From athletes with disabilities to inclusive organisational perspectives. *Sport Management Review, 17*(1), 1–7.

Penney, D. & Kidman, L. (2014). Athlete centred coaching: A time for reflection on meanings, value and practice. *Journal of Athlete Centered* Coaching, *1*(1), 2–5.

Potrac, P. & Marshall, P. (2011). Arlie Russell Hochschild: The managed heart, feeling rules, and emotional labour: Coaching as an emotional endeavour. In R. Jones, P. Potrac, C. Cushion & L. T. Ronglan (eds), *The sociology of sports coaching.* London: Routledge.

Potrac, P., Jones, R., Purdy, L., Nelson, L. & Marshall, P. (2013). Towards an emotional understanding of coaching: A suggested research agenda. In P. Potrac, W. Gilbert & J. Denison (eds), *Routledge handbook of sports coaching.* London: Routledge.

Price, M. J. (2006). Thermoregulation during exercise in individuals with spinal cord injuries. *Sports Medicine, 36*(10), 863–879.

Purdue, D. & Howe, P.D. (2012). See the sport, not the disability: Exploring the Paralympic paradox. *Qualitative Research in Sport, Exercise and Health, 4*(2), 189–205.

Richard, R., Joncheray, H. & Dugas, E. (2015). Disabled sportswomen and gender construction in powerchair football. *International Review for the Sociology of Sport*, DOI: 10.1177/1012690215577398

Rynne, S. B., Mallett, C. J. & Tinning, R. (2009). A review of published coach education research 2007–2008. *International Journal of Physical Education, XLVI* (1), 9–16.

Tawse, H., Bloom, G.A., Sabiston, C.M. & Reid, G. (2012). The role of coaches of wheelchair rugby in the development of athletes with a spinal cord injury. *Qualitative Research in Sport, Exercise and Health, 4*(2), 206–225.

Titscher, S., Meyer, M., Wodak, R. & Vetter, E. (2000). *Methods of text and discourse analysis.* London: Sage.

Tweedy, S. (2003). Biomechanical consequences of impairment: A taxonomically valid basis for classification in a unified disability athletics system. *Research Quarterly for Exercise and Sport, 74*(1), 9–16.

Tweedy S.M., Beckman E.M. & Connick M.J. (2014). Paralympic classification: Conceptual basis, current methods, and research. *American Academy of Physical Medicine and Rehabilitation, 6*(8), 11–17.

Vinson, D., Christian, P., Jones, V., Matthews, J., Williams, C. & Peters, D.M. (2015). *Investigating the culture of coach education in the UK: The Supporting and Promoting Inclusive Coach Education (SPICE) project.* Sports Coach UK. Predominantly available at http://www.sportscoachuk.org/resource/supporting-and-promoting-inclusive-coach-education-spice

Webborn, N. & Van de Vliet, P. (2012). Paralympic medicine. *The Lancet, 380*(9836) 65–71.

Wodak, R. & Meyer, M. (2015). *Methods of critical discourse studies* (3rd ed.). London: Sage.

Wu, S.K. & Williams, T. (1999). Paralympic swimming performance, impairment and the functional classification system. *Adapted Physical Activity Quarterly. 16*(3), 251–270.

INDEX

able-bodied coaches 35, 202
Abrahams, A. 120
access to facilities 179
accreditation programmes 58, 201, 204
acoustic devices 114
acquired disability 55, 136
Active People Survey 164
Adams, Dan 133
Adams, Valerie 68, 69
adaptability 195–7
adapted sport 2, 3, 15–17, 87
adaptive rowing *see* Para-rowing
Adopt an Athlete 40
Advanced Apprenticeship in Sports
    Excellence (AASE) 167
Ainscow, M. 64
Alberta Amputee Ski Association 129
Albrecht, G. 89
Allen-Collinson, J. 124
Allen, J. 8
Alpine Canada Alpin 129, 131, 134, 137, 141
Alpine skiing 127–44; case study of Ozzie
    Sawicki 132–8; conclusions 141; editors'
    summary reflections 143–4; historical
    context 127–30; historical context of
    Ozzie Sawicki 130–2; recommendations
    138–41; resources 141
Alpine Ski Racing: Athletes With a Disability
    (Sawicki) 131
Amateur Swimming Association (ASA)
    165, 166, 167, 168, 171, 173, 181, 182
amputees 33, 61, 88, 105, 114, 128, 129
Andrews, D.L. 31, 40, 43

Annerstedt, C. 43
archery 61
armed forces 25, 30–1
Armour, K. 66
Arnberg, Debbie 28, 36
ASA *see* Amateur Swimming Association
assistive devices 113–14, 146, 153
Association of Invalid Sports 98
ataxia 8, 20
athetosis 8, 20
athletes' village 69, 70
athlete testing 137
'Athlete to Coach Programme' 166, 181
athletics 60–76, 113–26; background of
    case-study coach 115–16; case-study
    coach reflections 116–21; case-study
    narratives of Raylene Bates 64–71;
    editors' summary reflections 75–6,
    124–5; funding 164; future of coaching
    Para-athletics 121–2; historical context of
    Paralympic athletics 61–2, 113–15;
    historical context of Raylene Bates 62–4;
    international context 61; national context
    61–2; overview 60; recommendations
    71–2, 122; resources 72, 122–3;
    strength-based approach 60–76
Athletics Canada 131
Athletics New Zealand 61, 62, 67, 71–2
Australia 42, 191
awareness 14–15

Bailey, S. 119, 121
Balaguer, I. 116

Balduck, A-L. 22
Balish, S. 68
Ballard, K. 64
Banack, H.R. 139, 187
Bannister, Sir Roger 120
Barker, D. 144, 160, 161
Barker, R. 65
basketball 88, 102, 104 *see also* wheelchair basketball
Bates, I. 122
Bates, Raylene: case study 64–71; editors' summary reflections 75–6, 187, 188, 191, 192; historical context 62–4; narratives 64–9; recommendations 71–2; strength-based approach 60
Batts, C. 31, 40, 43
Beckman, E.M. 16, 193
Beijing 2008 Paralympic Games 26, 70
Bell Athletes Connect programme 8
Berliner, D.C. 53
Berto, Claudio 136
bio-medical knowledge 111, 192–3, 204
bio-medical model of disability 200
birth disability 55
Bizub, A. 45
Black, Ken 72
blame 150, 178
blindness 25, 128, 200
Bloom, G. 139
Bloomfield, J. 179
boccia 145–62; case study of Glynn Tromans 148–57; editors' summary reflections 160–1; historical context 145–7; historical context of Glynn Tromans 147–8; overview 145; recommendations 157–9; resources 159
Boccia England 146, 158, 159
Bourdieu, P. 116, 117
Bowes, I. 77, 119, 122
brain injury 40, 54
Braye, S. 37, 190, 200
Brazil 7, 77, 79–82, 84, 85, 88, 90, 92, 95, 146
bricoleur, coach as 173–4, 180
British Disability Swimming 173
British Dressage 46, 47, 56
British Equestrian Federation 46, 55
British Horse Society 46, 48
British Paralympic Association (BPA) 16, 165
British Para-Swimming 167, 180
British Swimming 165, 166, 181
Brittain, I. 1, 14, 31, 72, 154, 200
Bruening, J. 60

Buckley, J. 16
buddy systems 33, 41
burnout 38, 136
Burroughs, A. 124
Bush, A.J. 163, 168, 173, 179, 180, 181

Caddick, N. 31
CADS *see* Canadian Association of Disabled Skiing
'callers' 114
Canada: Alpine skiing 127–9, 131–2, 134–5, 141, 143; geographical distance 191; Para soccer 7–10, 11–17, 18–20, 22, 23; rural communities 68
Canada Soccer 10, 11
Canadian Association of Disabled Skiing (CADS) 129, 134, 141
Canadian Cerebral Palsy Sports Association (CCPSA) 8, 10
Canadian Soccer Association 8, 9, 10, 14, 18
Canadian Sport for Life (CS4L) 136
Canadian Wheelchair Sports Association 127, 129
carded athletes 62, 63, 73
career pathways 198–9, 200, 201, 203–5
caring 60, 70–1, 75, 76
Carle, Joyce 147
case studies: Alpine skiing (Ozzie Sawicki) 132–8; athletics (Raylene Bates/unnamed) 64–71, 116–21; boccia (Glynn Tromans) 148–57; overview 1, 2, 5–6; para-equestrian dressage (Clive Milkins) 48–54; Para-rowing (Tom Darling) 28–39; Para soccer (Drew Ferguson) 10–17; para-swimming (Steve Fivash) 168–79; sitting volleyball (José Antônio Guedes Dantas) 81–90; wheelchair basketball (Rostislav Pohlman) 102–7
Casey, Jim 150
Cassidy, T. 60, 65, 66, 72, 81, 149
categorical approach 105
categorical imperative 70
CCPSA *see* Canadian Cerebral Palsy Sports Association
centralised programmes 31, 67–8, 155–6, 192
cerebral palsy 7–8, 14, 22, 114, 146, 153, 200
Cerebral Palsy International Sport and Recreation Association (CPISRA) 7, 8, 9, 10, 19, 20, 121
Charlton, Jackie 9

Cherney, J.L. 186
Chopping, W. 150
Christensen, M.K. 96
Christiansen, Sophie 47, 51, 52, 53, 55
classification systems: athletics 62; boccia
  153–4; overview 193–5; para-equestrian
  dressage 46, 55–6; Para-rowing 25, 26,
  33, 35; Para soccer 16, 20, 23; para-
  swimming 165–6
coach–athlete relationship 33–4, 53, 57, 58,
  89, 149, 192, 202
coach development 166, 184, 197, 198–9,
  201, 204
coach education: Alpine skiing 132–3,
  137–9; athletics 121–2; boccia 149–53,
  156–7, 160; overview 189–90, 193, 197,
  201–2, 204, 205; para-equestrian dressage
  55, 58–9; Para-rowing 36–7; Para soccer
  17–18; para-swimming 170–3, 174, 179,
  180, 183–4; sitting volleyball 79, 84–6,
  96; wheelchair basketball 105
coaching background 189–90
coaching pedagogy 71, 137–8, 149–50,
  170, 179, 204
coaching philosophy 37–9, 51–4, 75, 120,
  137, 149–53
coach recruitment 197, 204
Collins, D. 38, 48, 121, 122, 199
Collins, M. 179
Commonwealth Games 61, 62, 63, 69
communication skills 43, 53, 89, 90, 91
communities of practice 86
community engagement 37, 43
Concept 2 system 32, 40
conceptualisation and terminologies
  199–201
constructive dissatisfaction 150, 160
continuing professional development
  (CPD) 167, 182
continuity of coaching 197
Convention on the Rights of People with
  Disabilities 90
Cooper, R.A. 31
Copa Brazil 85
corporeal schema 117
Côté, J. 68, 84, 88, 128
Cottingham, M. 28
CP (cerebral palsy) football see Para soccer
CPD (continuing professional
  development) 167, 182
CPISRA see Cerebral Palsy International
  Sport and Recreation Association
CP Sport 146
Craven, Sir Philip 2

creativity 137
Cregan, K. 15, 86, 130, 139, 163, 170,
  181, 184, 187, 199, 201
critical self-reflection 170
Crossley, N. 117
Cruickshank, A. 38, 199
Csordas, T. 116
cultural capital 117
Culver, D. 86, 128, 130, 139
Cushion, C. 44, 72, 75, 132, 144, 184, 195
cycling 67, 164
Czech Republic 98–101, 103, 104, 108,
  111, 198

Dantas, José Antônio Guedes: case study
  81–90; coaching trajectory and
  experience 81–6; coach's knowledge
  and skill 86–90; editors' summary
  reflections 95–7; historical context 80–1;
  recommendations 90–2
Darcy, S. 28, 200
Darling, Tom: case study 28–39; editors'
  summary reflections 42–4; historical
  context 26–7; Para-rowing 24;
  recommendations 40
Davies, E. 45
Davis, L. 82, 107
Davis, P.A. 107
Deaflympics 61, 72
de Bosscher, V. 12
decentralisation of programmes 12–14, 23
de Coubertin, Pierre 113
dedication 187–8, 198
degree programmes 121, 170, 171, 180,
  189, 190, 204
De Haan, Jouke 77, 78, 79
Denison, J. 81, 116, 117, 117, 121
Denzin, N.K. 173
DePauw, K. 1, 15, 60, 64, 65, 66, 82, 86,
  87, 92, 187, 200, 204
dependence 89
diaphoresis (sweating) 33
Dieffenbach, K.D. 192
difference 87, 91, 122
diplegia 8, 20
dipsia (thirst) 33
disability: conceptualisation and
  terminologies 199–201; 'disability' or
  'para' 2, 3–4; disabled coaches 54,
  202–3; models 200; as otherness 82, 92,
  96; public perceptions 4
disability benefits 178
disability classification see classification
  systems

disability rights 90, 100
disability sport: conceptualisation and
    terminologies 199–201; 'disability sport
    paradox' 81–3, 90; overview 1–6; prior
    interest and serendipity 188–9
Disability Sport Northern Ireland 146, 158,
    159
Disability Sport Wales 146, 158, 159
disabled coaches 54, 202–3
dispositions 117–18, 119
distance 31–2, 34, 42, 191–2
Douglas, S. 128, 132, 133, 139, 141
Downs, Peter 72
Down's syndrome 133
dressage see para-equestrian dressage
Duarte, T. 139
Duda, J. 116

Edge, Zoe 147
education see coach education
Egypt 79
eligibility 193, 194
Elite Coaching Apprenticeship Programme
    (ECAP) 55, 58, 166, 172, 181
Elite Coaching Programme 172, 173
Elite Programme 166, 172, 173, 181
elite sport: Alpine skiing 134; boccia 154;
    para-equestrian dressage 50, 55;
    Para-rowing 33, 38, 39, 40; para-
    swimming 164, 177; sitting volleyball
    88–9, 90
embodiment 116–17, 124–5
Emerald, E. 124
emotional aspect of coaching 60
emotional labour 69
empathy 43, 91, 198
empowerment 37, 87, 181
English Talent Programme 167
enthusiasm 187–8
equal rights 88, 90, 100
equestrian sport 55–6, 132 see also
    para-equestrian dressage
equipment 25, 36, 51, 93, 100, 106–8,
    113–14, 128
Erickson, K. 88
Eskew, Mike 150
'ethical caring' 70, 71
ethic of care 69, 70, 196
exclusion 64, 88
expectations, managing 37
expertise 53, 192–3, 201, 202

facilities 179
Fairclough, N. 186

Fairhall, Neroli 61
Falcao, W. 128, 139
family life 69, 106, 156, 171
'fearless' boccia 145, 150, 152, 155, 160
female coaches 60, 69–71, 76
Ferguson, Drew: case study 10–17;
    conclusions 18–19; editors' summary
    reflections 22–3; historical context 8–10;
    overview 7, 191; recommendations 18
Fér, O. 99
FISA (Fédération Internationale des
    Sociétés d'Aviron) (World Rowing
    Federation) 25, 26
fistball 77
Fitzgerald, H. 35, 64, 66, 124, 198, 204
Fitzgerald, K. 164
Fivash, Steve: case study 168–79; coach
    education 170–3; editors' summary
    reflections 184–5; getting into coaching
    168–70; historical context 167–8;
    recommendations 180–1
Flemr, L. 111
football see Para soccer
Foucault, M. 116
Fraser-Thomas, J. 88
French, D. 92
Fristensky, Gustav 101, 102
Frogley, M. 105
Frontiera, J. 38
funding: Alpine skiing 135–6; athletics 65;
    boccia 155; overview 190, 197, 199;
    para-equestrian dressage 58; Para-rowing
    28–9, 39, 40, 42; para-swimming 164,
    175, 177, 178, 184; sitting volleyball 79,
    82, 95

Gallimore, R. 180
gamesmanship 152
Garratt, D. 72, 163, 174
Gateway to Gold 30, 40
Gavron. S. 1, 15, 82, 86, 92, 187, 204
GB Boccia 145, 146, 149, 152, 154, 155,
    157, 158, 159
GB Wheelchair Basketball 29
gender politics 76
geographical distance 31–2, 34, 42, 191–2
Gifford, P. 68
Gilbert, W. 18, 84, 122, 128, 163
Goffman, E. 19, 19, 176
Goodman, Scott 62
Goosey-Tolfrey, V.L. 192
grants 32, 82
Great Britain 78, 79, 100, 145–7, 165
Great Britain Boccia Federation 154

Green, S. 31, 72
guides 114, 128
Gustafsson, H. 38
Guttmann, Dr. Ludwig 61

habit 118
habitus 117
Hainsworth, J. 92
Hall, E.T. 108
Hamill, Jessica 69
Hanrahan, S.J. 38
Hansen, Rick 127
Hardin, B. 133
Hardman, A. 120
Hargreaves, A. 62
Harper, D. 173
Hartels, Lis 45
Hassanin, R. 112
Hawkins, B. 31
head injuries 8, 48, 49
Hellenic Olympic Committee 40
Hellier, Kirsten 68
hemiplegia 8, 20
Heritage Canada 128
Higgins, N. 64
high performance disability sport coaching:
    Alpine skiing 127–44; athletics 60–76,
    113–26; beyond high performance
    disability sport coaching? 186–207;
    boccia 145–62; conceptualisation and
    terminologies 199–201; conclusions
    203–5; dedicated and enthusiastic
    individuals 187–201; future
    considerations 201–3; overview 1–6,
    186; para-equestrian dressage 45–59;
    Para-rowing 24–44; Para soccer 7–23;
    para-swimming 163–85; sitting volleyball
    77–97; sustainability 197–8; themes
    187–201; wheelchair basketball 98–112
high performance sport 4, 22, 82, 95
High Performance Sport New Zealand
    (HPSNZ) 62, 67
Hochschild, A.R. 68, 69
Holland, K. 64
Hong Kong 51, 53, 55
hope 38
horses 49, 50, 53–4, 55–8
Howe, P.D. 37, 64, 65, 81, 82, 87, 88, 89,
    90, 113, 114, 116, 117, 118, 119–20,
    121, 166, 179, 181, 193, 201
Humer, Lars 173
Hums, M.A. 29, 190, 193
Hunter, L. 124
hypothermia (cooling) 33

Ibarra, H. 144
identity 196, 200, 202
Inclusive Fitness Initiative (IFI) 179
Inclusive Sport 2
inclusivity 2, 29, 54, 58, 64, 82, 87, 88, 92,
    100, 200
independence 181
infection 65, 69
infrastructure 190, 197
Inglis, S. 75
Innsbruck Paralympic Games 128, 129
Institute of Sport & Exercise Science 2
Institute of Swimming (IoS) 167, 181
intellectual disability 26, 133, 166
International Association of Athletics
    Federations (IAAF) 63, 114
International Blind Sport Association
    (IBSA) 115, 121
international classification systems 25, 33,
    153–4
International Committee of Sports for the
    Deaf 61
International Federation of CP Football 8,
    17, 19, 20
international issues 153–4, 157–8
International Olympic Committee (IOC) 61
International Organisations of Sport for the
    Disabled (IOSD) 113, 121
International Paralympic Committee (IPC):
    Alpine skiing 128, 130, 135; athletics 61,
    113, 114, 115, 119, 121; boccia 154;
    Para-rowing 26; Para soccer 17, 20;
    para-swimming 164, 166
International Silent Games 61
International Ski Federation (FIS) 135
International Sport Organisations for the
    Disabled (ISODs) 78
International Sports Federation for Persons
    with Intellectual Disability (INAS-FID)
    121
International Volleyball Committee 78
International Wheelchair and Amputee
    Sport Association (IWAS) 121
International Year of Disabled Persons 82
interpersonal skills 89
Interski 129
Invictus Games 199
IPC see International Paralympic Committee
Iran 7, 79, 85
Iraq 40, 72, 79

Jacobs, F. 170
Janeiro 6 53
Japanese Handicapped Skiers Association 129

javelin throwing 68, 103
Jesperson, E. 1
Johnston, Jerry 129
Jones, C. 88, 120, 166, 181
Jones, R. 8, 15, 18, 60, 77, 81, 115, 119, 179, 180

Kábele, Josef 99, 105
Kay, T. 164, 179
Kelly, P. 65
Kidman, L. 38, 66, 202
Kimayer, L.J. 116
Kincheloe, J.L. 180
Knapek Trophy 99, 100, 103
knowledge and expertise 117, 118, 192–3, 201, 202
Koh, K.T. 96
Kudláček, M. 105
Kwok, N. 78

Lawless, Jim 151
learning difficulties 119, 174
learning processes 84–6, 160
leaving home 68
Lee, Spencer 85
leg amputations 88, 114
Legg, D. 127
leisure facilities 179
Les Autres classification 78, 128, 153
Levi-Strauss, Claude 173
licences 18
Light, R. 112
Lincoln, Y.S. 173
Lindgren, E-C. 43
living with athletes 68
locomotor dysfunction 145, 146
London 1948 Olympic Games 61
London 2012 Olympic Games 62
London 2012 Paralympic Games: Alpine skiing 132; athletics 61, 62, 68, 70, 113; boccia 147, 150, 158, 159; para-equestrian dressage 45, 46, 47, 53; Para-rowing 26, 30, 35; para-swimming 164, 165, 166, 167, 177
Long-Term Athlete Development (LTAD) 136, 167, 171
lottery funding 42, 164
Loucky, J. 61
love of sport 187–8
LTAD see Long-Term Athlete Development
Lusted, D. 149
Lyle, J. 65, 72, 75, 81, 181
Lyles, Dave 171, 172

MacAloon, J. 113
MacArthur, J. 64
making house 70–1
Mallett, C. 8, 22, 58, 84, 96
managing expectations 37
marginalisation 64, 200
Markula, P. 90
Markula-Denison, P. 87
Marshall, P. 60, 187
Martens, R. 106
Martin, J.J. 4, 35, 201, 204
massage 65, 115,
mathematical ability 195
Matile, Al 134
McCarthy, P.J. 38
McCullagh, P. 138
McGavern, Don 133
McMahon, J. 112, 184
McMaster, S. 18, 60, 65, 86, 139, 187, 188, 195
McNamee, M.J. 1
medal success 173–4, 175
medical knowledge 192–3
medical support 65
mentorship 121, 136–7, 140
Merleau-Ponty, M. 117, 118
Messinger, S.D. 31
Meyer, M. 186
Michalko, R. 91
military personnel 30–1, 40, 43, 77
Milkins, Clive: case study 48–54; editors' summary reflections 57–9; historical context 46, 47–8; recommendations 55
Mills, J. 116, 117, 121
Misener, L. 28, 200
models of disability 200
monoplegia 8, 20
Moon, J. 86
Moore, K. 7
Moorhouse, Adrian 53
Morgan, H.J. 180
Morgan, W. 70, 181
Morrison, C. 64
mothering role 76
motivation 106, 109, 136, 187, 188, 202
multidisciplinary approaches 161
multiple sclerosis 54
Myers, N. 138

Nash, C. 121, 122, 170, 180
National Coaching Certification Program (NCCP) 9, 130, 131, 141
national governing bodies (NGBs): boccia 158; overview 190, 204; Para-rowing

25, 29, 30, 31, 36, 39, 41; para-swimming 170, 173, 180
National Lottery 164
National Paralympic Committees (NPCs) 164–5
National Paralympic Day 159
National Sports Association for the Disabled 129
'natural caring' 70, 71
Nauright, J. 124
NCCP *see* National Coaching Certification Program
Nelson, L. 60, 170, 174, 180, 184
Netherlands 7, 77, 79
Newton, Chris 49
New Zealand 42, 60, 61–2, 68, 70–1, 191
NGBs *see* national governing bodies
Nixon, H.L. 82
Noddings, N. 69, 70–1
North, J. 163
Numerato, D. 111
nutrition 29, 33, 170, 177, 204

Office of Qualifications and Examinations Regulator (Ofqual) 166
Olympic Games: Alpine skiing 132, 135; athletics 61, 62, 113; career pathways 199; para-equestrian dressage 45, 51; Para-rowing 27, 39; para-swimming 164
O'Neill, Nancy Jo 133
Ontario Volleyball Association 93
otherness 82, 92, 96
Own the Podium 8, 11, 20, 135, 137

Para AIM 2 WIN 131
para Alpine skiing *see* Alpine skiing
para-athletics *see* athletics
para-equestrian dressage 45–59; case study of Clive Milkins 48–54; conclusions 54–5; editors' summary reflections 57–9; historical context 45–7; historical context of Clive Milkins 47–8; profile of Sophie Christiansen 47; recommendations 55–6; resources 56
Paralympic Games: athletics 61, 63, 71, 113; boccia 153, 154; overview 2; para-equestrian dressage 45, 47; Paralympic sport identity 29; Para-rowing 24, 26, 29, 37, 39; Para soccer 11, 16, 17, 18; para-swimming 165, 177; resourcing and support 190; sitting volleyball 77, 78, 81, 82, 87, 88; wheelchair basketball 101; *see also* London 2012 Paralympic Games; Rio 2016 Paralympic Games

Paralympic movement 19, 46, 154, 199
'Paralympic paradox' 64
Paralympics New Zealand 62, 70
Paralympic Winter Games 128, 130
ParaPan American Games 11
paraplegic players 61, 105
Para-rowing 24–44; case study of Tom Darling 28–39; definition 25; editors' summary reflections 42–4; funding 28–9; historical context 24–6; historical context of Tom Darling 26–7; overview 24; recommendations 39–40; talent identification 29–31
para snowboard 128
Para soccer 7–23; case study of Drew Ferguson 10–17; conclusions 18–19; editors' summary reflections 22–3; historical context 7–8; historical context of Drew Ferguson 8–10; overview 7; recommendations 17–18; resources 19–20
para-swimming 163–85; case study of Steve Fivash 168–79; editors' summary reflections 183–5; historical context 164–7; historical context of Steve Fivash 167–8; overview 163; recommendations 179–81; resources 181
parental concerns 178, 179
partnership building 43
pedagogy *see* coaching pedagogy
Pennell, K. 68
Penney, D. 66, 112, 202
performance analysis 157, 202, 204
performance directing 32, 44, 184
performance pressure 54, 56, 155, 175
performance teams 19
periodisation 157
personal issues 156, 196
Petry, K.M. 12
Philadelphia Rowing Program for the Disabled (PRPD) 25
physical education 164
physiology 116, 122, 136, 140, 193, 202
physiotherapy 15, 29, 65, 101, 115, 156, 157
Piggott, D. 170, 180, 184
Pistorius, Oscar 113, 114
Pohlman, Rostislav: case study 102–7; editors' summary reflections 96, 110–12; historical context 101–2; overview 98, 188, 191, 202; recommendations 108–10
Pokorný, S. 99
polio 25, 45

Pope, J.P. 75
Portugal 79, 146
positive psychology 38
Potential Programme 116
Potrac, P. 8, 60, 81, 90, 176, 187
practice community 181
pressure 54, 56, 155, 175
Price, M.J. 192
Pringle, J. 87
private sector 40
process goals 174, 175
professionalisation 161
prosthetic running limbs 114
protectionism 65
Prupas, A. 127
psychologists 12, 15, 29, 30, 33, 34, 156
public awareness 14–15
Purdue, D. 37, 64, 65, 114, 201
Purdy, L. 8

qualifications 189, 202, 204
Qualifications and Credits Framework
    (QCF) 166, 181
quality of life 140, 184

Raedeke, T.D. 22
RDA *see* Riding for the Disabled
    Association
Recreation Canada 129
refinement 117
reflective coaching 51, 122, 170
rehabilitation 72, 87, 99, 111
REHA Cup 100, 103
Reid, G. 82, 87, 127
'relatedness of caring' 71
research 4, 132, 163, 202
resilience 65, 196
resourcefulness 65, 66, 198
resources 65, 86, 190–1
respect 89–90, 91, 151
retirements 177–8
Rhodes, Ted 129, 130, 131, 133, 136
Richard, R. 200
Richens, M. 68
Riding for the Disabled Association (RDA)
    46, 48, 56, 57
rights 90, 100
Rimmer, J. 92
Rio 2016 Olympic Games 27, 132
Rio 2016 Paralympic Games: boccia 148,
    150, 155, 159; Para-rowing 28, 32, 34,
    36, 37, 43; para-swimming 164, 165,
    177, 178; sitting volleyball 77;
    wheelchair basketball 106

Robbins, J. 128
Robinson, Eddie 109
Rogers, Matt 79, 93
roles 19, 76, 196, 203
Rome 1960 Paralympic Games 113, 165
rowing 25, 67, 164 *see also* Para-rowing
rural communities 67–8
Russia 7, 79
Ryle, G. 117
Rynne, S.B. 8, 22, 58, 163, 169, 201

safety 56, 120
sailing 56, 164
salaries 39, 136
Salt Lake City 2002 Paralympic Games
    130, 131, 135
The savage mind (Levi-Strauss) 173
Sawicki, Ozzie: case study: 132–8; editors'
    summary reflections 143–4; historical
    context of Alpine skiing 127, 128;
    historical context of Ozzie Sawicki
    130–2; recommendations 138–41
Schinke, R.J. 112, 133
Schreiner, P. 154
science 30, 140, 143, 193
Scottish Disability Sport 146, 158, 159
Scottish Swimming 165
Scott, S. 19
segregation 82
selection of players 17, 195
serendipity 188
service-based paradigm 82
service men and women 25, 30–1, 40, 61,
    128
Shapiro, D.R. 28
Shaw, S. 8
Sherrill, C. 92, 105, 166
Shogan, D. 87
Silk, M.L. 163, 180
Silva, C.F. 78, 87, 89, 90, 90, 91
Silvers, A. 28
Šíp, Jaroslav 104
Šisler, Jan 99
sit-skiing 128
sitting volleyball (SV) 77–97; case study of
    José Antônio Guedes Dantas 81–90;
    editors' summary reflections 95–7;
    historical context 77–80; historical
    context of José Antônio Guedes Dantas
    80–1; overview 77; recommendations
    90–2; resources 92–3
sitzball 77
skiing *see* Alpine skiing
Skills Active 168

Slee, R. 64
Smith, A. 1
Smith, B. 31, 60, 82, 91
Smith, Derald 133, 136
soccer *see* Para soccer
social skills 178
socio-cultural model of disability 200
soldiers 30–1, 33, 43, 72
Spain 78, 146
Sparkes, A. 62
spasticity 8, 20
specialised knowledge and expertise 192–3
Special Olympics movement 61
spina bifida 153
spinal cord injury 33, 61, 114, 129
sponsorship 40
sport as therapy 45–6, 54, 55, 127
Sport Canada 8, 11, 134, 135
Sport England 164, 179, 181
sporting communities of practice 86
sporting interest 187–9
Sport New Zealand 62, 66, 67, 72–3
sports ambassadors 109
Sports Coach UK 146, 181
sport-specific knowledge 88–9
sports psychologists 12, 15, 138
sports science 4, 122, 123, 137, 170,
  175–7, 202, 204
Sproule, J. 170, 180
Stampfl, Franz 120
Statler, T.A. 192
Steadward, Robert 127
stereotyping 96, 200
Stodter, A. 184
Stoke Mandeville Games 61, 113
strength-based approach 65–6
Strohkendl, H. 105, 154
Stryker, S. 19
support 43, 190–1
Supporting & Promoting Inclusive Coach
  Education (SPICE) project 204
sustainability 197–8, 204
SV *see* sitting volleyball
swimming *see* para-swimming
Swim Wales 165
Sydney 2000 Paralympic Games 78, 103, 164

talent identification 29–31, 34–5, 42, 43, 197
'Taming Tigers' 151
Tawse, H. 35, 60, 128, 139, 141, 163, 170,
  180, 193
Taylor, B. 72, 163, 174
Taylor, S. 86
Taylor, W. 72

Team Canada 130
Team GB 37, 40, 41, 45, 46, 54, 56, 165
team management 43, 106, 107, 109, 160
terminologies 199–201
therapy 45–6, 54, 55, 127
Thomas, N. 1
Thompson, Daley 52
Thompson, W. 123
Titscher, S. 186
Toronto 1976 Paralympic Games 78, 127,
  165
track and field athletics *see* athletics
transitional funding 177
travel 69, 191–2
Tromans, Glynn: case study 148–57;
  editors' summary reflections 160–1;
  historical context 147–8; overview 145;
  recommendations 157–9
Trudel, P. 83, 86, 86, 122, 163
trust 19, 34, 89, 151, 176
Turner, Ian 171, 172
Tweedy, S. 16, 20, 82, 113, 119–20, 121,
  193, 194

UK *see* United Kingdom
UK Athletics 116, 148, 149
UKCC *see* United Kingdom Coaching
  Certificate
Ukraine 7, 79
UK Sport: boccia 155; para-equestrian
  dressage 55, 58; Para-rowing 39, 41;
  para-swimming 164, 166, 172, 173, 175,
  177, 181
UK Volleyball Federation 92
United Kingdom Coaching Certificate
  (UKCC) 46, 55, 56, 166, 180, 182
United Kingdom (UK) 38, 39, 42, 79
United Nations 82
United States of America (USA) 24, 25, 26,
  28, 30, 39, 79, 191
United States Olympic Committee
  (USOC) 28, 32, 37
University of Bath 171, 172, 173
University of Worcester 2, 202
unmediated learning 86
USA *see* United States of America
US Department of Veterans Affairs (VA)
  28, 30, 32, 34, 37
USOC *see* United States Olympic
  Committee
US Para-rowing 28–31, 32, 34, 37, 40

VA *see* US Department of Veterans Affairs
Válek, J. 105

Válková, H. 105
Valour Games 30, 40
Van De Vliet, P. 202
Vanlandewijck, Y. 16, 122–3
Van Royen, R. 66
Varontsov, Andre 171, 172
veterans 32, 40, 77, 98, 113, 127
video training 106
Vinson, D. 204
visual impairment 26, 114, 118–19, 128, 165, 174
volleyball 77, 79, 90, 99 *see also* sitting volleyball
VolleySlide 80, 92, 93
volunteering 39, 43, 66
Vute, R. 93

Wagstaff, C. 38
Walker, M. 108, 109
Walton, G.M. 115, 120
Wang, C.K.J. 96
war veterans 32, 40, 77, 98, 113, 127
Wassermann, D. 28
water skiing 129
WB *see* wheelchair basketball
weather conditions 56
Webborn, N. 202
Werthner, P. 83, 86
Whalen, L. 4, 35, 201, 204
wheelchair athletes 61, 69, 70, 101, 114, 128, 200
wheelchair basketball (WB) 98–112; case study of Rostislav Pohlman 102–7; classification systems 88, 194–5; editors' summary reflections 110–12; historical

context 98–101, 127; historical context of Rostislav Pohlman 101–2; overview 98; recommendations 108–10
wheelchair floorball 104
wheelchair rugby 104, 141, 154
Whitbread, Fatima 63, 68
Whitbread, Margaret 63, 68
Williams, A. 68
Williams, T. 195
Winfield, J. 51
Winter Olympic Games 130, 131
Winter Paralympic Games 128, 130
winter sports 56, 128, 130, 131
Wodak, R. 186
Wolff, A. 31
Wolframm, I. 57
women coaches 60, 69–71, 76
work–life interface 60, 68–9, 75, 76, 106, 196
World Class Podium Potential (WCPP) Programme 167
World Class Programme (WCP) 167
World Organisation Volleyball for the Disabled (WOVD) 78, 81, 84
World ParaVolley 78, 79, 80, 92
World Rowing Federation (FISA) 25, 26
World War II 25, 98, 113, 128
World Wheelchair and Amputee Games 61
WOVD *see* World Organisation Volleyball for the Disabled (WOVD)
Wright, T. 54
Wu, S.K. 195

youth clubs 109

 Taylor & Francis eBooks

---

Helping you to choose the right eBooks for your Library

Add Routledge titles to your library's digital collection today. Taylor and Francis ebooks contains over 50,000 titles in the Humanities, Social Sciences, Behavioural Sciences, Built Environment and Law.

Choose from a range of subject packages or create your own!

Benefits for you

>> Free MARC records
>> COUNTER-compliant usage statistics
>> Flexible purchase and pricing options
>> All titles DRM-free.

Benefits for your user

>> Off-site, anytime access via Athens or referring URL
>> Print or copy pages or chapters
>> Full content search
>> Bookmark, highlight and annotate text
>> Access to thousands of pages of quality research at the click of a button.

REQUEST YOUR
FREE
INSTITUTIONAL
TRIAL TODAY

Free Trials Available
We offer free trials to qualifying academic, corporate and government customers.

eCollections – Choose from over 30 subject eCollections, including:

Archaeology	Language Learning
Architecture	Law
Asian Studies	Literature
Business & Management	Media & Communication
Classical Studies	Middle East Studies
Construction	Music
Creative & Media Arts	Philosophy
Criminology & Criminal Justice	Planning
Economics	Politics
Education	Psychology & Mental Health
Energy	Religion
Engineering	Security
English Language & Linguistics	Social Work
Environment & Sustainability	Sociology
Geography	Sport
Health Studies	Theatre & Performance
History	Tourism, Hospitality & Events

For more information, pricing enquiries or to order a free trial, please contact your local sales team: www.tandfebooks.com/page/sales

 Routledge
Taylor & Francis Group

The home of
Routledge books

www.tandfebooks.com

Milton Keynes UK
Ingram Content Group UK Ltd.
UKHW052007190224
437927UK00018B/65